# ULTI
# GHOST TECH

BY
VINCE WILSON



**PUBLISHED BY COSMIC PANTHEON PRESS**

www.cosmicpantheon.com

PROUDLY PRINTED IN THE USA!

# DEDICATION

I would like to dedicate this book to the most special people in my life – Tamma, Harvey and Zaine.

# SPECIAL THANKS

I would like to thank the following people in no particular order:

Russ Noratel, Ron Peacock, Dr. Barry Taff, Dr. Andrew Nichols, Loyd Auerbach, Scotty Rorek, Dale Kaczmarek, Scotty Roberts, Laura Cleveland, Susan Fair, Dale Brechlin, Jane Brechlin, Kathryn Preston, Savannah Brooks, Becky Sewell, Bryan Isaacs, Rie Sadler, Big Jim Jones, Ed Okonowicz, Troy Taylor, Willy Adkins, Christy Necaise, Renée Hamer Colianni.

"We cannot but account it strange that such items of testimony as these men supplied should have been neglected, even by those who were most repelled by the ignorance and fanaticism which infected a large amount of the mesmeric literature."

- Edmund Gurney

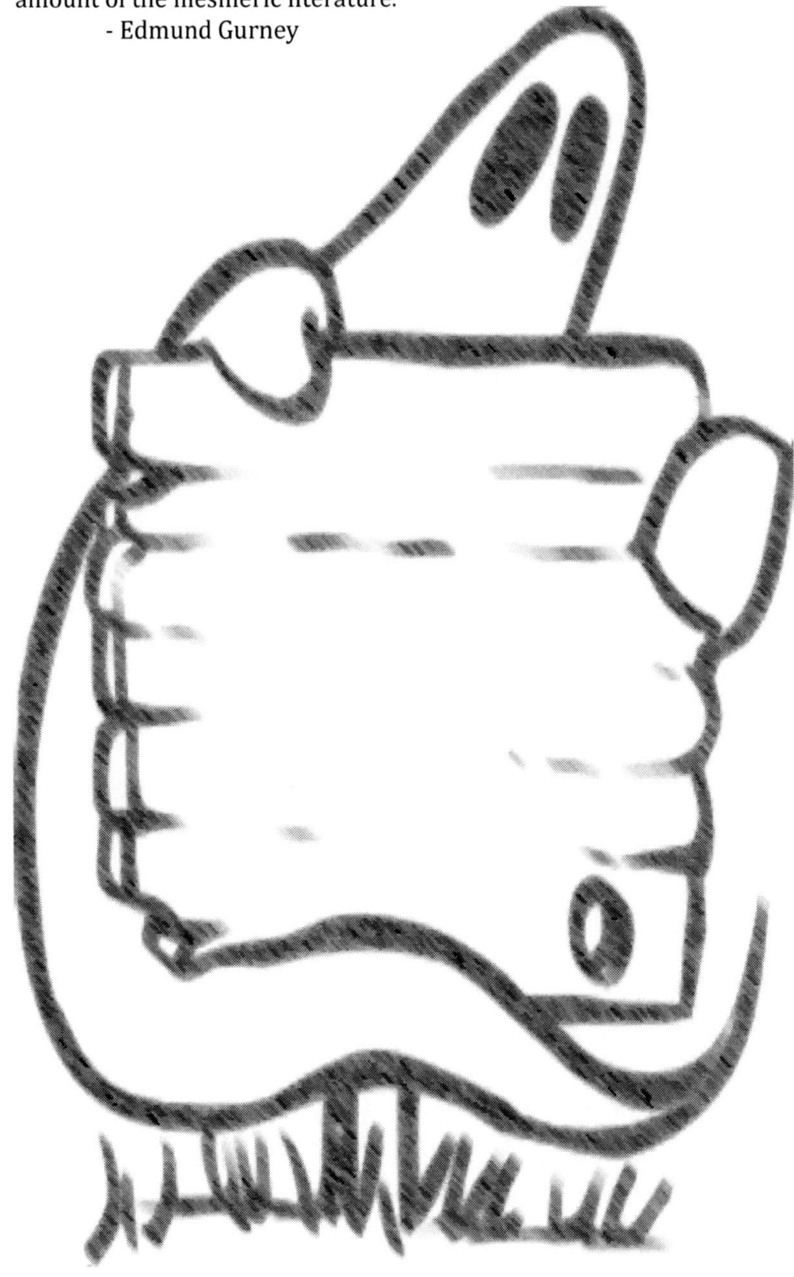

# CONTENTS

# FOREWORD BY DR. ANDREW NICHOLS

An inexplicable noise in the attic, a cold breeze blowing down the hall, a misty human figure appears on the stairs. People have always been equally frightened and fascinated by ghostly manifestations, and human history is filled with accounts of apparitions and poltergeists. An ancient Scottish prayer seeks deliverance from all the shadowy "ghoulies and ghosties and long leggety beasties, and things that go bump in the night...."

For more than a century, the frontier science of Parapsychology has endeavored to explain (and sometimes explain away) these experiences which seem to defy natural explanation. As physicists continue to vigorously demolish a universe once regarded as "machine-like," paranormal researchers are paradoxically demanding better scientific methods to document and explain psi occurrences.

Vince Wilson's new book, Ultimate Ghost Tech provides the aspiring paranormal investigator with exactly that, a comprehensive guide to the "street science" of ghost hunting. I can think of no one better qualified to write such a book, since Vince is a foremost expert in the technological aspects of paranormal investigation. As a parapsychologist, Vince has focused upon the application of the methods of physical science to one of the world's enduring mysteries, ghosts and hauntings.

For the present, the objective existence of ghosts must be regarded from a scientific perspective as a hypothesis. We do not currently have any reliable method to verify their existence apart from the subjective accounts of thousands of witnesses. However, there is certainly no theoretical reason to conclude that ghosts couldn't exist, and it is worth remembering that many scientific discoveries have been made by intrepid individuals on the basis of legend and folklore. It could happen once again.

In another sense, it hardly matters whether there are actually such things as ghosts and poltergeists. They are ample reminders that our knowledge is not complete, and never will be. The final explication of the universe is still very far away indeed, and there are probably plenty of ghosties, and ghoulies, and long-leggety beasties waiting to be discovered.

Andrew Nichols, PhD.
American Institute of Parapsychology
Gainesville, Florida

# FORWORD BY LOYD AUERBACH

The field of Parapsychology has done much investigation of experiences of apparitions, hauntings and poltergeists. Part of the research process has always been to try to find technologies that can provide more data and different data than what we get from human witnesses.

Technology and the Science behind it have a ways to go before anyone can say for sure that this reading or that photo conclusively indicates a ghost. People who offer up their photos as "proof" of the existence of ghosts or who rely purely on technology are ignorant of what constitutes scientific proof (versus evidence). More importantly, they are generally uneducated as to what decades of research and much discussion has led us to understand ghosts and hauntings might be.

First, a couple of definitions to separate the two similar but different types of phenomena.

- **Apparitions** (or ghosts) of the dead -- though there are thousands of reported cases of apparitions of the living -- represent the consciousness or personality (or spirit, soul, mind or whatever you want to call it) surviving the death of the body. Apparitions are capable of interaction with the living (and presumably other apparitions). This interaction happens through mind to mind communication, not through the ordinary senses. When one "sees" a ghost, it is through the perceptual processes (think data processing) rather than through the eyes. Just like a computer can convert digital information into a picture, the human mind can convert received information from the mind of a ghost into images, voices, smells, and even feelings of being touched.
- **Hauntings**, also called "place memory" or "imprints", seem to represent information recorded into the local environment by actual happenings. When one perceives something like a walking-then-disappearing figure in a haunting, one is actually picking up historical information (even recent history) from the location and converting it into an image. Hauntings are much more common than apparition cases, as every place where people have been and emotional events have occurred has the potential to be haunted.

Both have one important factor in common: unless something is perceived and experienced by a witness, there's nothing to indicate a "ghost" or "haunting" is present. We define hauntings and apparitions by the human experience of the phenomena.

The major differences between apparitions and hauntings are around interaction and source. A ghost or apparition is capable of interacting with a living person and vice versa, like two people at either end of a video conference call. In a haunting, you're only perceiving a recording, like watching a video or listening to an audio recording of someone or events in the past.

Haunting phenomena is environmental in nature and often reoccurs in patterns. In haunting cases, investigators using magnetometers have found correlations between unusual magnetic fields and the specific locations people experience the phenomena. The magnetic fields are on different frequencies, including the geomagnetic range, and have no apparent source. Parapsychologists have speculated that some form of magnetic field in the environment "records" events and that humans have the ability to "play back" these events.

Apparition cases -- and whether anything can be experienced or detected -- are dependent on the ghost being present. Since apparitions have free will like us living folks, there's little one can do to experience or detect one if he or she (the ghost) doesn't feel like hanging around. In addition, because an apparition is a form of consciousness, and Science still is undecided as to whether Consciousness actually exists in the body (let alone after death and outside the body), applying technology to such cases cannot prove anything to Science.

However, investigators have found instances when people have experienced an apparition at the same time various detectors have also picked up on something anomalous. The human experience defines the phenomena as an apparition, and the anomalous readings confirm that "something" is present in the local environment that correlates to the experience.

In haunting cases, because it is the environment itself that provides the anomalous information, it makes sense that the readings rarely change. But again, unusual readings, in and of themselves, mean only that something unusual is happening in the environment. It takes a human perception of something to connect that to hauntings.

At present, because we still understand so little about Consciousness and how our own minds really interact with the environment, technology can only confirm that there's something in the environment that may or may not connect to the experience. What technology picks up as unusual or anomalous readings or behavior can only provide evidence that a person's experience has some connection to the real, physical world.

There is no technology today that can be used where we can say with certainty that "it's a ghost" we're detecting.

But let's face it: ghost hunters love their tech – even if they don't know how to use it or to assess the data from it in light of the reported phenomena.

One should always know the limitations of one's equipment and how "false" readings (or photos!) might come up....false in the sense that they are otherwise explainable and NOT paranormally connected when you look closely. You should never rely on technology to tell you a place is haunted or a ghost is present.

Unfortunately, looking at the various paranormal TV shows and what's up on the net shows that people make incorrect assumptions about places and their evidence (or the TV producers have edited the segments that way, at the very least).

Parapsychologists do use technology to try to find any environmental anomalies that can be connected to the models we have of apparitions and hauntings, or help us build new ones. At present, we do have some little evidence, and some leads, that tell us that certain technology, including detectors of magnetic and geomagnetic fields, can help us better understand what's going on when someone sees a ghost and perhaps even communicate with ostensible spirits – or at least demonstrate that the mind of the operator is affecting the devices unconsciously, as we've seen in laboratory studies of psychokinesis.

Ultimately, while it is important to try various environmental sensors and other technologies that develop in investigations of apparitions, hauntings and even poltergeists, two things are clear:

- Investigators must correlate the data from their tech to the experiences of witnesses, psychics, and even the investigators before, during and after each tech session. No experiences, no context or meaning to the readings/results.
- Investigators must know how their equipment works, what it does, what its limitations are, and why it cannot on its own be a "ghost detector" – at least, given our current level of technology and understanding of the paranormal.

Vince Wilson's GHOST TECH, while not able to give you the skinny on which device detects the paranormal – because there's no such equipment as yet – does explain what the devices that are ever-increasingly found in the ghost hunter's "tool kit" are designed to do and what their limits are.

For those who already are out there exploring, reading this book, especially coupled with reading any instructions or technical specs of the equipment you use, can make you a much better investigator – of course, coupled with knowledge of how parapsychologists and psychical researchers have been doing this for 130 years.

For those looking to get out there, this is a good start on a shopping list for tech. But again, learn something about the actual field of Parapsychology (and Psychical Research before it), how real scientists might utilize the tech, and without question spend more time interviewing witnesses than taking readings. A high reading is a lot less exciting than a good ghost story.

Loyd Auerbach, M.S.
Director, The Office of Paranormal Investigations
Professor, Atlantic University
Instructor, HCH Institute, Parapsychological Studies
Adjunct Professor, JFK University
Rhine Research Center Board of Directors

# PREFACE

I wrote this book in the hope that those who read it will use it for paranormal research teams as a sort of training manual or text book. I hope you will find the contents worthy of such an honor.

I had hoped to have this book out in 2010; however, certain events prevented me from doing so, such as moving from my hometown of Baltimore to Harpers Ferry, WV. I also started *The Haunted Cottage Research Center* and *The Anomalous Research Center (ARC)* there as well. I finally gained the status of parapsychologist thanks to the *American Institute of Parapsychology* and also became a licensed hypnotist.

I try to improve myself constantly. Always reading, always discussing new ideas and concepts. I want to expand my horizons to furthest reaches of the imagination. But, most of all though, I want to share this information with all those around me and to discuss their opinions and even hear their criticisms. How else am I going to continue to learn?

Vince Wilson

# CHAPTER ONE: THE HISTORY OF THE PARANORMAL

But psychoanalysis has taught that the dead - a dead parent, for example - can be more alive for us, more powerful, more scary, than the living. It is the question of ghosts.

- Jacques Derrida (1930 - 2004)

Opinions have changed on many things over the centuries.
The shape of the Earth: Not flat
The Earth's composition: Not hollow.
The orbits of the planets: We're not the center after all.

In the past humans used beliefs in spirits and deities to explain things like storms, and demons to explain illness and disasters. When lightning and thunder filled the air, it was Thor with his mighty hammer for the Norse and Zeus with his, well, thunder bolts for the Greeks. If you were sick for no obvious reason, you may be possessed by demons. So you have to ask yourself, if weather and illness have natural explanations, then what about ghosts? When a deceased loved one visits you in the night and tells you goodbye, as is common in many ghost stories of the past, what explanation is there for that? Methinks it cannot be blamed on the weather.

Every culture that has existed in recorded history has some belief in an afterlife. Complex burial techniques and symbolic gestures hint that even prehistoric man believed in life after death. The majority of these cultures also allotted for the existence of a way for the dead to return to the world of the living. You know, those things called ghosts! Egyptian mothers even had nursery songs to sing their children to sleep.

Oh, a vaunt! Ye ghosts of night,
nor do my baby harm;
ye may come with steps so light,
but I'll thwart you with my charm.
For my babe you must not kiss,
nor rock if she should cry--
Oh! If you did aught amiss,
My own, my dear, would die.
O ye dead men, come not near--
Now I have made the charm--
There's lettuce to prick you here,
Garlic with smell to harm;
There 's tow to bind like a spell,
the magic bones are spread;
There's honey the living love well-
-
'Tis poison to the dead.

How sweet!

Belief in ghosts goes back even further still! In the Epic of Gilgamesh, a story from ancient Babylonia around 2500 B.C. (that's over 4,000 years ago!!), there is a bit on ghosts mentioned.

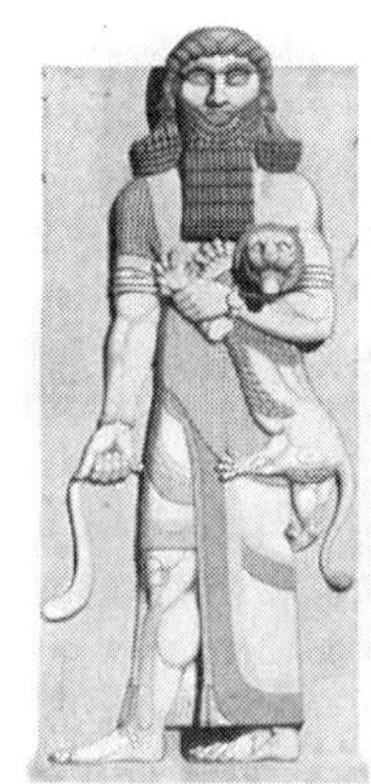

"The desert oasis even when no rain falls."My god," he cried, "when death called for me, my best friend went in my place and he is now no longer living." And Ea, whose waters keep us alive as we journey over desert sands, said this to Nergal, great soldier in arms. "Go now, mighty follower; free Enkidu to speak once to kin and show this Gilgamesh how to descend halfway to Hell through the bowels of earth."

"And Nergal, accustomed to absurd orders, obeyed as soldiers do and he freed Enkidu to speak once to kin and showed Gilgamesh how to descend halfway to Hell through the bowels of earth. Enkidu's shadow rose slowly toward the living and the brothers, tearful and weak, tried to hug, tried to speak, tried and failed to do anything but sob. "Speak to me please, dear brother," whispered Gilgamesh.

"Tell me of death and where you are." "Not willingly do I speak of death," said Enkidu in slow reply. "But if you wish to sit for a brief time, I will describe where I do stay." "Yes," his brother said in early grief. "All my skin and all my bones are dead now. All my skin and all my bones are now dead. "Oh no," cried Gilgamesh without relief. "Oh no," sobbed one enclosed by grief."

Even ancient Mesopotamia (can you say, "5000 B.C!") had some ghost stories that have survived the passage of time. Advancement after advancement in human history has not stayed the belief in life after death and the existence of ghosts. Opinions have changed, empires have arisen and fallen, technologies have advanced and even in the age of this modern age - PEOPLE STILL BELIEVE IN G-H-O-S-T-S! Nay, people still SEE ghosts! A Roman Letter-writer named Pliny the Younger who lived from A.D. 61-115 tells of an eyewitness account of an ancient ghost with a message, one not uncommon even today. William Melmoth translated this version in 1746. I love this story because it may the first to use "rattling chains" and yet it is told as nonfiction.

"There was in Athens a house, spacious and open, but with an infamous reputation, as if filled with pestilence. For in the dead of night, a noise like the clashing of iron could be heard. And if one listened carefully, it sounded like the rattling of chains. At first the noise seemed to be at a distance, but then it would approach, nearer, nearer, nearer. Suddenly a phantom would appear an old man, pale and emaciated, with a long beard, and hair that appeared driven by the wind. The fetters on his feet and hands rattled as he moved them.

"Any dwellers in the house passed sleepless nights under the most dismal terrors imaginable. The nights without rest led them to a kind of madness, and as the horrors in their minds increased, onto a path toward death. Even in the daytime--when the phantom did not appear--the memory of the nightmare was so strong that it still passed before their eyes. The terror remained when the cause of it was gone.

"Damned as uninhabitable, the house was at last deserted, left to the spectral monster. But in hope that some tenant might be found who was unaware of the malevolence within it, the house was posted for rent or sale.

"It happened that a philosopher named Athenodorus came to Athens at that time. Reading the posted bill, he discovered the dwelling's price. The extraordinary cheapness raised his suspicion, yet when he heard the whole story, he was not in the least put off. Indeed, he was eager to take the place. And did so immediately.

"As evening drew near, Athenodorus had a couch prepared for him in the front section of the house. He asked for a light and his writing materials, and then dismissed his retainers. To keep his mind from being distracted by vain terrors of imaginary noises and apparitions, he directed all his energy toward his writing.

"For a time the night was silent. Then came the rattling of fetters. Athenodorus neither lifted up his eyes, nor laid down his pen. Instead he closed his ears by concentrating on his work. But the noise increased and advanced closer till it seemed to be at the door, and at last in the very chamber. Athenodorus looked round and saw the apparition exactly as it had been described to him. It stood before him, beckoning with one finger.

"Athenodorus made a sign with his hand that the visitor should wait a little, and bent over his work. The ghost, however, shook the chains over the philosopher's head, beckoning as before. Athenodorus now took up his lamp and followed. The ghost moved slowly, as if held back by his chains. Once it reached the courtyard, it suddenly vanished.

"Athenodorus, now deserted, carefully marked the spot with a handful of grass and leaves. The next day he asked the magistrate to have the spot dug up. There they found--intertwined with chains--the bones that were all that remained of a body that had long lain in the ground. Carefully, the skeletal relics were collected and given proper burial, at public expense. The tortured ancient was at rest. And the house in Athens was haunted no more."

I am often asked by Christians (I am Christian myself) if ghosts have any place in Christian theology. Some Christians claim that ghosts have no place in their belief system. They must not read the Bible very often! Never mind the Father, Son and Holy Ghost, what about Saul and the witch of Endor?

According to the Old Testament (Samuel: 28:7-16) when David, the slayer of Goliath, took an army up against Saul, king of the Israelites, Saul decided he needed some advice from his predecessor. Too bad Samuel was already dead! So, going against the Law of Moses (which forbids necromancy and sorcery) Saul contacted a "medium". King Saul's servants told the king of a soothsayer, or, witch in the area known as Endor. In disguise, so as not to alarm the witch, Saul sought her out and asked to speak to Samuel. The witch brought forth "from below" the spirit of Samuel. Boy was Samuel peeved! He refused to help Saul since Saul had lost faith in God and never listened to Samuel when he was alive in the first place! The next day David defeated Saul's armies and Saul committed suicide.

It is interesting to note, how could a "witch" summon a soul from heaven? In Judaism, some rabbis teach that your soul hovered around your body for a year after you died. That would explain how the spirit of Samuel was supernaturally summoned by the witch. Some modern theologians believe that the Witch of Endor in fact summoned a demon and not Samuel's soul.

Truth be told, most psi researchers believe that ghosts are copies of what we once were and are, in fact, separate from theology's concept of the soul. A soul after all, is, by its nature, unresearchable.

## GHOSTS AROUND THE WORLD

Ghost, from the Old English gást or spook, from the Dutch spôk. Ghosts have appeared in many cultures and regions around the world. You would be hard pressed to find a culture without ghost stories.

### ISLAM

In Islam, it is believed that your spirit remains in the grave until the day of Judgment. In Islam they do believe in the ifrit, an enormous winged creature of fire, either male or female, who lives underground and frequents ruins.

### JAPAN

Japanese ghosts (called Yūrei 幽霊) have no legs. They also had black hair, limp hands that stretched forward and they always wore white clothing. For the most part, the Japanese believed that your soul went on and only if you were murdered or committed suicide without the proper burial rights, or if you died with powerful emotions in your mind (revenge, jealousy, love, etc) you would become a ghost.

### INDIA

In some parts of India, it is believed that if you are not buried properly, are murdered or commit suicide, you will rise as a blood-sucking ghost. Yes, I know, sounds more like a vampire, but that's what they say in India.

## AFRICA

Whatever you do, don't lose your body after you die. Well, at least don't let your loved ones lose it. In certain African tribes, if your body is not properly preserved before burial, you will become a ghost.

## THE BELL WITCH

A more modern, and local to the author, affair in the US takes place a scant 191 years ago as of this writing. The famous (or infamous) Bell Witch of Adams, Tennessee has captivated the imaginations of historians and ghost enthusiasts alike. Events occurred at the home of John and Lucy Bell that make the Amityville Horror (a probable hoax) look like a story by Dr. Seuss. As a matter of fact, at least three movies have been made on this case in the last three years as of the writing of this book! Opinions vary on what exactly happened at the Bell House but one thing's for sure, something freaky was going on.

An angry ghost that came to be known as "Kate" or, more famously, the Bell Witch, tormented the Bells and their children. There were noises like scratching, gnawing and banging coming from the walls. Later, covers were pulled from the beds of family members. Hands were slapped and hair pulled. In some stories the Bells' 12 year-old daughter, Betsy was even bruised and bled as if stuck with pins. The problems escalated further still when the ghost began to whistle and even talk! When the townspeople got wind of all this craziness they knew it could only be a witch. Eventually, even Andrew Jackson became involved. Jackson, a neighbor of the Bells, showed up with an "exorcist" and his carriage became stuck in the mud. In one version of the tale Jackson was struck to the floor when he said he didn't believe in "ha'nts" (what we call ghosts).

The Bell Witch poltergeist did not stop until finally it caused what is perhaps the only know death of a human being by poltergeist in the United States. On the morning of December 20, 1820, John Bell, Jr. found his father dead in his bed after a prolonged illness seemingly caused by Kate. Suddenly, after discovering a viscous liquid in a strange vial in the Bell's medicine cabinet, the Witch cried out victoriously. Indeed, she claimed to be the one responsible for the death of the tormented John Bell, Sr. Even going so far as to sing vulgar songs at Bell's funeral several days later. The witch exclaimed that it was done with the Bells and that it would return in 100 years time. A prophecy yet unfulfilled.

## THE GREAT AMHERST MYSTERY

Almost five decades after the Bell Witch, in Amherst, Nova Scotia, Canada, nineteen year-old Ester Cox would be terrorized by a poltergeist.

It all started when Ester screamed that there was a mouse in her bed. Although her family could find no mouse, they did see movement from inside the mattress that they could not explain. Attacks on Ester's person in the form of fiery fevers and unusual swelling began and continued for several days fallowed by loud thunderous explosions. Finally, the family witnessed her pillow and bedclothes flung about by invisible hands. One night, scratching was heard above her bed as 12 inch high letters began to appear on the wall. They read, "ESTER COX YOU ARE MINE TO KILL."

Ester continued to be tormented by this unseen force until she left home to save her family from being evicted. The entity or poltergeist wasn't finished until it apparently set fire to the farm Ester found work at. Ester served one month in jail for arson. The phenomenon ceased forever after.

Even in these modern 21st century times people still say they see ghosts and experience hauntings. As a ghost investigator (or psi field researcher) I have been privy to dozens of people who have witnessed paranormal phenomena. Many of these people have careers and family and no history whatsoever of mental illness. Most have everything to lose by fabricating a "ghost story". What if their neighbors or co-workers found out? What if (gasp!) property values went down?

Why would perfectly normal, everyday people make up such things? Often there are other witnesses like friends and relatives who experience these strange occurrences. Centuries of data and yet some people refuse to acknowledge the existence or even the possibility of the existence of ghosts.

## THE SPIRITUALIST MOVEMENT

> Did you hear about the Psychic dwarf wanted by the police for fraud?
> Small medium at large!

As we stated earlier, belief in the possibility of communication with spirits has been around for thousands of years. Many cultures, religions and cults were based on this principle. The Greeks and Romans used oracles to foresee the future by listening to none other than the gods of Olympus themselves. Native American Indians sought spiritual guidance from their shamans. Similar shamanic beliefs exist to this day around the world. In 1921 a Danish explorer named Knud Rasmussen was traveling across the arctic recesses of North America when he came across the Iglulik Inuit tribe. With help from there Shaman, an elder named Anarqâq, Rasmussen learned that the Iglulik's culture was centered around a host of invisible beings or spirits. Some of these spirits were kind and helpful while others were downright evil.

Some people believe that the spirit can leave the body without resulting in death. Known as an out-of-body experience (or OBE), this concept may have been around as long as the belief in ghosts. It has been proposed by many cultures that the astral form, known as the ba in ancient Egypt, could leave the body and return at will. Saint Alphonsus Liguori collapsed during a mass in 1774. When he awoke twenty-four hours later he claimed to have visited Pope Clemet XIV on the pontiff's deathbed. The time of death was confirmed and some at the bedside of the Pope claimed to have seen Alphonsus praying with the other grieving witnesses.

Divination and spirit communications and removal have for a long time been associated with Gypsies. Probable descendents from India, large groups of exotic looking people began moving westward around the 9th century. By the 15th century they were all over Europe and claimed to be from a place they called Little Egypt. The Little Egyptians or gypsies began developing a reputation as thieves and con artists. The gypsies were (and still are) deeply religious. They became known as experts in the occult and supernatural and sold their "powers" to anyone who cared to barter with them. Although palmistry was practiced by the likes of Plato and Aristotle, its origins go back more than 4000 years. The reading of palms was certainly perfected and is best known as being practiced by gypsies who likewise adopted tarot card readings and crystal balls into their repertoire.

Almost exactly four-hundred years after Columbus came across the Americas hysteria swept across an idealistic Christian community in Seventeenth Century New England. As sure as we believe the sun will rise in the morning, the townsfolk of Salem knew that witches and demons were real and very dangerous. Slaves bought in Africa and specifically the West Indies brought with them stories of voodoo and witchcraft. One such slave was Tituba who was owned by the Reverend Samuel Parris. Tituba enthralled the Reverend's daughter Elizabeth, nine and her cousin Abigail, eight with tales of spells and witchery. When the girls began screaming blasphemies and having fits, the Reverend knew exactly who was responsible. Can you say – Satan! So began the Salem witch hunts.

The previous paragraphs are this author's attempt to explain the tidal wave of history that would eventually flood into the 19th and 20th centuries as the so called spiritualist movement. Although many start the beginnings of the movement with the Fox sisters, it clearly has its origins in ancient history. All these sources would fuel the wave that burst the dam of reason and created the deluge of modern day mysticism. It was not helped by the fact that it all began just before the American Civil War, The Spanish American War, World War One and World War Two. Not to mention the outbreaks of influenza, yellow fever, polio and smallpox. Death was on everyone's minds.

Swedish scientist and mystic Emmanuel Swedenborg (February 8, 1688 – March 29, 1772) was probably the person who focused the world's attention on an early form of spiritualism. Around the age of 56, then a very advanced age, Swedenborg claimed to have had a spiritual awakening. He said that God himself had given him the power to visit Heaven or Hell at will and that he could talk to ghosts, angels and even demons. After his death, people who read his works and listened to his teachings (called Swedenborgians) spread across Europe and the Americas. In the early 1840s a man from Poughkeepsie, NY named Andrew Jackson Davis claimed to have received messages from Swedenborg after having been "mesmerized". Although he had no education as the son of poor leather worker, Davis would go onto lecture and write a series of books and papers on his communications with many spirits during his career. In his book Principles of Nature, first published in 1847, Davis made a startling prediction of what was soon to come:

"It is a truth that spirits commune with one another while one is in the body and the other in the higher spheres - and this, too, when the person in the body is unconscious of the influx, and hence cannot be convinced of the fact; and this truth will ere long present itself in the form of a living demonstration. And the world will hail with delight the ushering in of that era when the interiors of men will be opened, and the spiritual communion will be established."

## HAUNTED HOME

Daniel Douglas Home (March 20, 1833 - June 21, 1886) like so many celebrities today, his name was pronounced differently than you would think – it was pronounced 'Hume'. This Scottish psychic could levitate himself over the heads of onlookers; move objects with his mind, change the shape and size of his body and was even fireproof! David Blaine has nothing on this guy! It was believed that Home inherited his "powers" from his mother. Home's family moved to America in 1842 when he was nine to live with his aunt, Mary Cook. She later kicked him out for what she thought were incarnations of the Devil despite protests from clergy who thought he was a "gift from God".

Ten years later Home would accomplish his greatest feat: levitation! At a séance being conducted in wealthy businessman Ward Cheney's Connecticut home the medium known as D.D. Home flew to the ceiling of the room in front of a skeptical reporter and an astonished Ward. The reporter would write:

"Suddenly, without any expectation of the part of the company, Home was taken up into the air. I had hold of his hand at the time and I felt his feet - they were lifted a foot from the floor. He palpitated from head to foot with the contending emotions of joy and fear, which choked his utterances. Again and again, he was taken from the floor, and the third time he was taken to the ceiling of the apartment, with which his hands and feet came into gentle contact."

Home would spend most of his life without a home of his own. He preferred to live in the homes of the rich and upper class. He never charged for his performances though. He would later marry and sire a son and travel in retirement until his death in 1886 from tuberculosis. To this day no one has effectively explained Home's feats of the supernatural. His levitations were done in private homes where he could not have rigged any sort of effective ropes and pulley system. Nor can anyone explain some of his other abilities. Today D.D. Home remains a mystery. But other mediums of the time were not as lucky as Home, to remain to this day a historic enigma...

## ENTER: THE FOX SISTERS

Hydesville, NY will go down in history as the true birthing place of spiritualism. Here is where Margaretta (Maggie) and Catherine (Kate) claimed to have experienced the extraordinary events that would begin their controversial careers.

The Fox family lived in a shanty little cottage in a remote part of New York State. Dimwitted parents gave way to equally dimwitted children (I know it's harsh, but nonetheless true), although Kate was said to be rather pretty. Kate and Maggie had four siblings, but none of them lived nearby. Their parents had the sisters at a very late period in life and were now middle-aged. Maggie and Kate had no friends and were not well schooled. It was 1848 and these girls were just plain bored. They were very, very bored. Did I mention they were bored? Their boredom was thankfully (?) ended in March of that year when the first of a series of mysterious events occurred.

**Kate, Margaretta and Leah Fox**

Shortly after dusk approached on an evening in March 1848, the Fox family staggered to bed for a peaceful night's sleep. Unfortunately for the family they were about to learn that peaceful nights were going to be few and far between. That night noises were heard coming from all over the house. It sounded like furniture being moved around. The house shook from the ferocity of the sounds. When the Foxes tried to investigate the sounds escalated from moving furniture to booming, rapping and cracking. This continued for more than a week. By the 31st of March the family learned that they could communicate with the source of the noises. Kate began by snapping her fingers in which the mysterious source of the noises replied. An ecstatic Mrs. Fox immediately ran to the neighbors to talk about the "miracle".

Soon enough the stories of supernatural occurrences at the Fox home became a local sensation. It might have remained as such if not for Leah Fox Fish. Leah was in fact Maggie and Kate's older sister. She had married and had a daughter by Mr. Fish who turned out to be what we would call a "dead-beat dad" today. Leah, an accomplished music teacher was able to fend for herself.

Leah Fox Fish heard about her sisters' remarkable new foray into the strange and unusual thanks to a pamphlet written by E. E. Lewis of Canandaigua, NY. Lewis had heard about the Fox sisters and, curious, came to see the phenomena first hand. After interviewing several of the eyewitnesses he was able to scribble out the pamphlet that eventually came into the hands of Leah. Lewis more than likely never realized that he would be the first to write anything on the spiritualist movement that was very close over the horizon.

Evidence exists that suggests the sisters were faking the phenomena from the beginning. If Leah Fish Fox knew of any faking, she didn't admit it or seemed to care. She quickly became the girl's, well, for lack of better term, agent. They went public and became national sensations. It has been theorized that by 1852 there were more than 30,000 mediums just in the United States. English mathematician Augustus de Morgan wrote,

"It came upon them like a smallpox and the land was spotted with mediums before the wise and prudent had had time to lodge the first half-dozen in a madhouse."

Leah toured the country with her sisters in tow. They met famous people and visited many famous places. Eventually Leah would remarry a wealthy socialite and would become known as a well respected "medium" herself. She turned her back on Maggie and Kate when they were no longer profitable. By 1888 the two youngest Fox sisters were alcoholics who had, between them, lost their savings, children and husbands. They had renounced spiritualism and admitted they were frauds and then retracted their statements. To this day no one knows if they faked all the events or some of them. Only a few believe they didn't falsify any of it. Margaretta and Catherine both died in 1892 just a few months apart laid to rest in a pauper's graves. Spiritualism was on the move and even the White House wasn't impervious against the invasion! First Lady Mary Todd Lincoln held séances on a regular basis in the president's home. Mediums were popping up on every corner faster than you can say "ectoplasm".

## RESEARCHING THE IMPOSSIBLE

"I said you can go to hell. All you 'psychic researchers' can go to hell!"
"Why don't you guess? You'll all be guessing for the

rest of your lives!"

- The last words of Mina Crandon, otherwise known as Margery the Medium (1941).

It was about 550 B.C. that the first recorded paranormal experiment took place. King Croesus of Lydia, according to Greek historian Herodotus, wanted to know if he should attack Persia. So, he sent seven messengers to the seven top oracles of the day. He told the messengers to wait one hundred days after they left and ask each oracle what the king was doing that day. The king was making a big bronze kettle full of turtle and lamb soup a la Croesus. Well, five oracles got it wrong, one was almost right but only the Oracle of Delphi was dead on.

I count the grains of sand on
the ocean shore
I measure the ocean's depths
I hear the dumb man
I likewise hear the man who
keeps silent.
My senses perceive an odor as
when one cooks
Together the flesh of the
tortoise and the lamb,
Brass is on the sides and
beneath,
Brass also covers the top.

With the Delphi Oracle's clairvoyant accuracy assured the king asked if he should go to war. The Oracle replied, "...An empire will be lost that day." The king went to war, sure of his victory. Too bad it was Croesus' empire that was lost.

Parapsychology (derived from the Greek, ψ psi, twenty-third letter of the Greek alphabet; from the Greek παρά or para which mean "along side", psyche, "mind, soul".) is the scientific study of psychic and/or paranormal phenomena. Psychologist and philosopher Max Dessoir probably coined the term parapsychology sometime in the 1880s. Although many who study the phenomena of ghosts and hauntings call themselves parapsychologists (don't forget Ray, Egon and Peter!) the science was originally meant only to study the psychical such as ESP and telekinesis. Ghosts went in and out and in to the picture a little later. Bigfoot, E.T. and the Loch Ness Monster belong to the fields of crypto-zoology and exobiology.

Clairvoyance (the so-called "sixth-sense"; from 17th century French with clair meaning "clear" and voyance meaning "visibility") appears throughout the ages and even in the bible (the Witch of Endor for example was a practitioner of necromancy or the art of talking to the deceased for profit). Joseph Glanvill studied weird manifestations, which we would call poltergeist phenomena now and wrote about it in 1681. Prospero Lambertini (who would become Pope Benedict XIV) was a Vatican sanctioned miracle investigator in the mid-1700s. University of Vienna student Anton Mesmer developed concepts dealing with, what he called "animal magnetism". His research into the mind led to developments in hypnotism (Mesmer lends his name to "mesmerism"). His animal magnetism concept and belief in the healing powers of "magnetized water" got him trouble with the law while in Paris thanks to Ben Franklin and other scientists of the time who saw to that.

A. MESMER

Easily the vast majority of mediums and clairvoyants of the time were frauds. Many people were conned out of fortunes while mediums became rich. Who were fakes and who were legitimate psychics? Several people and newly founded agencies would answer the call for clarification and, mostly, legitimate research.

London scholars Henry Sidgwick, Sir William F. Barret and Frederic W.H. Myers (who would coin the term "telepathy") would form, with others, the Society for Psychical Research (SPR) in 1882. In 1885 several American scholars would form the American Society for Psychical Research (ASPR) in Boston. These organizations would perform the first controlled experiments into the paranormal. Also on the rise were the first really "hardcore" skeptics.

Smear campaigns, scandal and fraud would tarnish the reputations of the members of SPR and the ASPR for the first few years of their existence. However, the groups would weather the controversies fairly well and establish themselves as leaders in paranormal research, a reputation that remains until this day.

It is interesting to note that the founders of SPR could not have known at the time of their foundation the direction their group would take or the memberships it would acquire, memberships that would include world leaders and clergy as well as leading scientists. Frederick Myers once said,

"The consciousness that the hour at last had come; that the world-old secret was opening to mortal view; that the first carrier pigeon had swooped into the fastness of beleaguered men."

Wow, people just don't talk like that anymore! So, begins modern paranormal investigating.

## SO COMETH THE SKEPTICS

Sir Author Conan Doyle will always be remembered as the creator of Sherlock Holmes. That is what the general public accepts about him. Well, and obviously he was knighted at some point in his life (that would be in 1902), hence the "Sir". What most of the public doesn't know about Doyle was his devout belief in the quasi-religion known as spiritualism. Just before doing a lecture on spiritualism in October 1918 Doyle received a telegram informing him that his dearly beloved son had died from injuries suffered in battle. He went on and did his lecture without showing a sign of grief, secure in knowledge that his son Kingsley was, for all intents and purposes, not truly dead. He completely converted to spiritualism in 1916. At this point it was no longer a point of research (Doyle had joined the SPR in 1893), but an obsession. Doyle was unfortunately easily fooled by his intense need to believe in what he was seeing was real in regard to mediums. Not to mention that he believed that fairies were real too. So great was his support that he was at least partially responsible for the resurgence of the spiritualist movement after decades of faltering. Ironically, it would be the masters of trickery themselves who would serve as foil to fraudulent mediums and Doyle's unflinching dedication. Magicians to the rescue!

It would appear that the problem with some men of science is they have learned too well. They can only believe in what they see with their own eyes. This "problem" would continue even into the 21st century.

Researches, unaccustomed to sleight of hand tricks never believed for an instant that they could be fooled by lower class charlatans. Masters of magic knew better. Anyone who studies prestidigitation knows that. One such person, perhaps the greatest escape artist the world has ever known, made the exposure of mediums as frauds a lifetime duty. His name was Harry Houdini.

Born in Budapest Hungary under the name Ehrich Weisz, Houdini (March 24, 1874 – October 31 1926) modeled his stage name after French magician Jean Eugène Robert-Houdin who he admired. Friends of Houdini called him "Ehrie" before he adopted Houdini and that is where he probably picked up Harry. Houdini started his career as an acrobat in a circus before practicing card tricks and magic. After mastering some very basic magic acts, Houdini billed himself as the "Master of Cards". Not satisfied with the sparse employment available for such magic tricks, Houdini started trying his hand at escape tricks. While performing with brother

"Dash" on Coney Island Houdini met and married Wilhelmina Beatrice (Bess) Rahner. The closest person to Houdini was his mother Cecilia. It was said that on hearing the news of her passing he fainted and did not perform again for several months in a bout of depression. After his mother's death Houdini sought refuge in spiritualism in the hopes of being able to contact her again. He quickly discovered that many mediums were using poorly orchestrated tricks that Houdini easily saw through as one of the world's greatest illusionists. Not only did Houdini's experience as a magician help, but as a poor starving youth he posed as a medium himself and was himself a fraud. His keen skeptical eye saw through hundreds of fakes around the world. This tradition would be passed on to latter generation magicians like James "the Amazing" Randi, Penn & Teller and Criss Angel.

Now, don't get the wrong idea here. Although Houdini is often touted today as one of the past's truly great skeptics, he did want to believe. However, he wasn't about to let charlatans get away with deceiving tens of thousands of people who simply wished to speak to loved ones again. This of course would end up putting him at odds with Sir Author Conan Doyle.

Houdini would often show up at séances disguised in a fake beard and a very concealing hat. Never devoid of ego or showmanship, the "Prince of Prestidigitation" used to announce at the end of a show, "I am Houdini and you are a fraud!" The first time he met Doyle was in 1920 after one of his performances in Portsmouth, England attended by the Doyle family. They became quick friends despite their many differences and beliefs. While Houdini readily admitted his act was nothing more than clever tricks, Sir Author was convinced he was in fact "the fact the greatest physical medium of modern times". Magician's honor prevented Houdini from telling Doyle how the tricks were done. There was always a tension between the two friends due to their individual stubbornness that reached its breaking point in 1922.

On June 17th Houdini was attending a séance conducted by none other than Lady Doyle! Houdini would write later, "I excluded all my earthly thoughts and gave my whole soul to the séance. I was willing to believe, even wanted to believe." Houdini knew that his friends, although perhaps misguided and a bit naïve, at least believed in what they were doing and would never deliberately deceive him. He also knew that Lady Doyle, who claimed to be proficient in automatic writing, was trying to contact his mother. To make a long story short, what Lady Doyle had written was a sprawling series of pages that began with a sketch of the Christian cross that spoke to Houdini as his mother. Houdini knew his Jewish mother would not have introduced herself with a cross. He also knew she could not write and spoke almost no English. When asked how this possible, Madam Doyle replied, "Why Harry, in Heaven, everyone speaks English!" Houdini waited months before writing anything about the incident. A remarkable feat considering his enormous ego. When he did, he made it clear that he did not believe his mother contacted him that evening. Suffice to say, Houdini's friendship with Doyle was at an end.

## MARGERY THE MEDIUM

Ask any psi researcher who truly know the history of paranormal research who the most infamous medium of the Spiritualist Movement ant they will most likely say, "Margery".

Born on a farm in Canada Mina "Margery" Marguerite Stinson (1888-1941) moved to Boston for a better life and more opportunities at a young age. She met grocer and her future husband Earl Rand while working as a secretary at a Boston church. This marriage did not last long. She would fall in love with Dr. Le Roi Goddard Crandon (1873-1939) shortly after meeting him for a medical procedure and then volunteer work during World War I.

Possibly due to his slightly more advanced age (he was 15 years older than 3rd wife Mina), Dr. Crandon became very interested in all things Spiritualist. The couple invited friends over for some table tipping and spirit communication. Dr. Crandon became astonished when wife Mina began exhibiting her never before seen psychic abilities. This happened after another medium told Mina she was in fact a powerful medium herself and that she had the spirit of "a laughing young man" inside her. Soon thereafter Mina claimed to be able to "channel" her deceased brother "Walter. Walter had died in 1911 in a train crash.

Soon after making her claims of mediumship, Mina was tested by Gardner Murphy, William McDougall and a group of Harvard professors and graduate students. They did not believe her. A year later in 1924 Mina gained national celebrity status and infamy when she entered a contest sponsored by Scientific American Magazine. The brainchild of associate editor J. Malcolm Bird, the highly respected magazine offered a prize of $2500 to any psychic medium who could show, under testing, actual psychic ability. Other judges included American psychical researcher Walter Franklin Prince, occult writer Hereward Carrington, Technicolor Film creator Daniel Comstock, Harvard University professor of psychology William McDougall, and master magician and escape artist Harry Houdini.

The Scientific American investigation of Margery (a soon useless pseudonym created by Bird to protect Mina's identity that would become her recognized professional nom de plum) quickly became a farce. Mrs. Crandon's promiscuous (she frequently appeared nude for her seances and produced "ectoplasm" from her vagina) behavior and flirtatious attitude evidently won over the all male judges to the point they were ready to give the $2500 reward to her despite the evidence she was clearly a fraud. Houdini received the news about the decision and raced to Boston from a tour to dispute their findings. As it turned out, although Margery more than likely was a fraud, Houdini himself "cheated" by trying to sabotage some the experiments! Margery would eventually be exposed for the fake she most certainly was. She would begin making claims that fingerprints left in wax were that of Walter. They were, in fact, those of her dentist.

## DON'T GET YOURSELF SLIMED

OK, we all remember the references to ectoplasm in the movie Ghostbusters, right? It is the technical term for the 'slime' substances used throughout the movie and its sequel. Occasionally green or cloudy white, it always looked reminiscent of something more likely to come out of your nose during a sneeze then from a ghost. They actually used methylcellulose (or methyl cellulose).It is a chemical compound derived from cellulose (basically sugar). It is a hydrophilic white powder in pure form and dissolves in cold (but not in hot) water, forming a clear viscous solution or gel. Not only could you eat that slime, it would give you a sugar rush!

Actual ectoplasm is even more disgusting than the methylcellulose variety used in Ghostbusters. No, I don't mean it because it comes from ghosts. Personally, I don't think that there ever was such a thing as ectoplasm. The word was coined by French physiologist Charles Richet to describe the substance a pseudo pod (extra limb) was made out of that was oozing out of medium Eusapia Pallidino in 1849. It means, "Exteriorized substance" and comes from the Greek words ektos and plasma. Soon after Pallidino, a phenomenon that had never been seen before in the history of the world was now practiced by hundreds of mediums in Europe and the US. Eusapia's ectoplasm came out of her ears, mouth, nose and eyes. Such as the case with performance artists trying to top one another, so did the mediums that developed this "skill". The ectoplasm first developed as hands and limbs, then faces and even words. Sometimes a whole living person would appear or miniature version of one. Not content with letting this stuff spring from orifices above the neck, mediums began squishing it out of their armpits, nipples and, um, even their "nether regions". Use your imagination.

Ectoplasm never actually existed. It was usually chewed paper, egg-whites mixed with gauze or boiled animal tissue among other things. So, how could people have believed such a thing? Well, at this time period in history, there was no reference to compare this phenomenon by. Stage magic was evolving almost parallel with the Spiritualist Movement. People simply didn't have a concept of what they were supposed to expect. Mediums were allowed to turn the lights out during their performances since the ectoplasm was "light sensitive". These Spiritualists were also allowed to "perform" behind curtains and in "spirit cabinets" out of view of the audience.

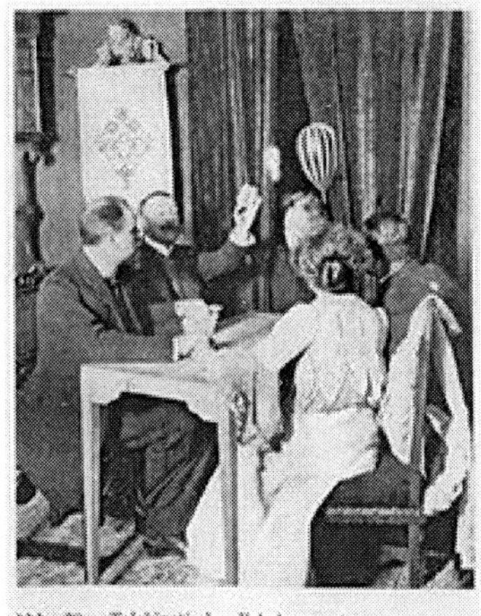

Abb. 20. Telekinetische Erhebung einer Mandoline durch Eusapia Paladino. (Münchner Sitzung am 13. März 1903.)

So, when you are trying to take pictures at a haunted location and a strange glowing mist appears in one of the photos, don't call it ectoplasm. Call any mists in your photos mists. Call them paranormal mists or ghostly fog but do not call the phenomena ectoplasm.

## PSYCHICAL RESEARCH

As mentioned in the story about Croesus of Lydia, paranormal science dates back to ancient times. However, it really wasn't until the 18th and 19th centuries that parapsychology became more than just an amateur's pursuit. Works such as The Secrets of the Invisible World by Daniel Defoe brought a logical and scientific aspect to ghost theory.

There would be a lull in this outlook for some years with the coming of the spiritual movement. Then real research would burst onto the scene with the SPR in the UK and the ASPR in the US. These organizations in return would create directly and indirectly some of the most flamboyant and interesting individuals in the history of paranormal research.

Say what you will about Harry Price (January 17, 1881 – March 29, 1948), he is one of the people who helped bring paranormal research into the modern age. Price was the John Kerry or Ivana Trump of the paranormal world in the 1930's when he married into a lot of money. This made him what we all hope to be in this field – a researcher with unlimited funds at his disposal! Although well financed, his initial equipment list seems a little low tech by today's standards:

- Felt overshoes
- Measuring tape
- Tape, electric bells, lead seals and other items for making motion detection tools
- Dry batteries and switches
- Cameras
- Notebooks and drawing pads
- Ball and string, chalk
- Basic first-aid kit
- Mercury for detecting vibrations

Although the above list may leave the "ghost nerd" in you a bit unsatisfied it was a good start for the early 20th century. A renaissance-man of the weird, Price had his hands in "space-telegraphy", archeology and magic. Price first came onto the scene of paranormal research when he exposed spirit photographer William Hope as a fraud after joining the SPR. Hope used a primitive form of double exposure to create his 'spirit photographs' and when Price secretly switched Hope's photography plates with marked ones, the deception was revealed. When Hope developed the plates, the markings were not there which proved that he had switched the plates for ones that were already partially exposed.

Price would go on to expose many fake mediums and would support at least one as the real deal. Nevertheless, he is best known for his research into ghosts and hauntings. In fact he really is the first actual "ghost hunter". Besides the basic kit mentioned earlier, Price was also a clever inventor with a natural talent for mechanics and electronics. Many of the devices he used for testing psychics and looking for ghosts were invented by him in his laboratory.

Harry Price would eventually become uncomfortable (to say the least) with the SPR's evident bias for mediums. He felt they accepted mediums as genuine far too often with inadequate testing. He became the UK correspondent for the ASPR and submitted material to several other organizations as well. In 1938 Price restarted the Ghost Club (and allowed women in for the first time) and made himself the chairman. The Ghost Club was a semi-secret group of researchers started back in 1862. It was run by Price's successor, Peter Underwood until 1993 when Underwood left to form the Ghost Club Society. Harry Price of course is best known for his investigations of the Borley Rectory, "the most haunted house in England". The Borley Rectory is where he developed many of his experiments and techniques for ghost research, many of which are still used today.

The UK's "number one ghost hunter" has got to be Peter Underwood. Although Underwood and Harry Price never met (a planned meeting never happened due to Price's untimely death in 1948), their correspondences so impressed Price that Underwood was made the Harry Price estate's literary executor upon Price's death. A prolific author, Underwood has written dozens of books including the first real ghost hunter's guidebook naturally called The Ghost Hunter's Guide. Underwood is known for having very strong opinions as opposed to theories on what ghosts are and what the nature of hauntings are and this is reflected in his writings.

So, out with metaphysics and in with PKE and science! We now leap forward in the chronology of psychical research to the 1930s where research into parapsychology really began and took off thanks to Dr. J.B Rhine.

Joseph Banks Rhine was born in a Pennsylvania log cabin in 1895. His father skeptical of all the stories of ghosts and magic that is prevalent in small Pennsylvanian mountain towns. Despite that, Rhine would develop an acute curiosity for the paranormal that would last the rest of his life. Although he felt he had a true religious experience at the age of 12, when he met Louisa Ella Weckesser, a skeptic of religion, he would give up thoughts of a career in ministry for his future wife.

Rhine would also give up a career in forestry for paranormal research after hearing a lecture by none other than Sir Arthur Conan Doyle in 1922 Chicago. Rhine's first Ph. D. was in botany after all.

Rhine joined ASPR in 1924 and began working for ASPR's Journal. It was with the Journal that Rhine began reading stories about the before mentioned Boston medium "Margery". Crandon is mainly to fault for a major upheaval of APSR that resulted in the organization's split, which in turn resulted in the formation of a rival group called the

Boston Society for Psychical Research (which, by the way, shares the same acronym as my own former group, the Baltimore Society for Paranormal Research or BSPR). Although there is much in the way of evidence to suggest that Crandon had some psychic ability, there were also many reasons to suggest part of her séances were fraudulent. After meeting with Crandon and seeing her manipulate objects with her feet and hands in the dark, Rhine resigned from ASPR due to their unwavering support of such an obvious fraud.

Walter Franklin Prince, an Episcopal Minister and psychical researcher, was originally a member of ASPR who also became disillusioned due to ASPR's support of Crandon. He resigned from ASPR as well and moved to Boston to take a position with the Boston Society for Psychical Research. Prince introduced the Rhines to Detroit school administrator John F. Thomas who would later be the first person to receive a Ph. D. in Parapsychology from a school in the US. The Rhines along with Thomas left for Duke University to study under psychologist William McDougall. McDougall, who was originally from Lancashire England, was president of SPR in England and became president of ASPR after accepting a job at Harvard in 1920. After trying to create a better set of standards at APSR, he was later rejected and replaced. It was then that McDougall accepted a position at Duke.

Rhine enthusiastically began as Thomas' and McDougall's research assistant. After Thomas received his Ph. D. in Parapsychology, Rhine became a professor of Psychology at Duke. It was around this time that Rhine began his famous ESP card tests. Rhine's research began taking up so much space that a separate lab called the Parapsychology Laboratory or the Department of Parapsychology had to be created. Just before Rhine retired in 1962 he established the Foundation for Research on the Nature of Man (FRNM). The University's Parapsychology Laboratory moved to FRNM in 1965. J.B Rhine would pass away in 1980, fifteen years before the centennial of his birth when FRNM would be renamed the Rhine Research Center in his memory.

Rhine had divided ESP into three categories. They were:

- Clairvoyance – the ability to acquire information directly from the environment.
- Telepathy – the ability to read minds or communication with others through mind-to-mind contact.
- Precognition – the ability to predict future events and outcomes.

Another, fourth form of ESP was later devised after a visitor to Duke University's Department of Parapsychology bragged that he could make dice land where he wanted. I'd love to take that guy to Atlantic City with me! This fourth type was called psycho-kinesis or PK. A new emphasis on statistical probability would be made that would carry on to this day.

## ZENER CARDS

Are you ready for another Ghostbusters allusion? Remember in the beginning of the movie when Bill Murray's character is testing two college students for psychic abilities? "A couple of wavy lines" appear on one of the cards? Those were Zener cards and they are named after psychologist Karl Zener, who designed them in the 1930s.

There are five different Zener cards:

A hollow circle (one curve)
A Greek cross (two lines)
Three vertical wavy lines (or waves)
A hollow square (four lines)
And a hollow five-pointed star.

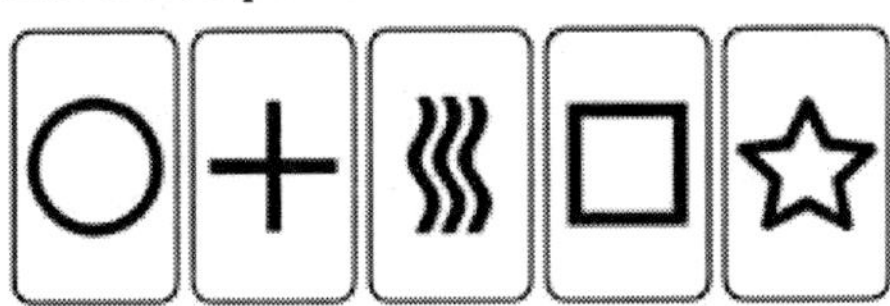

There are twenty-five cards in a set with five of each drawing in that set. Subjects are supposed to guess the next card in a randomly shuffled deck. If the subject is right more often than mere chance will allow (about 20% of the time) then they may be psychic!

## GHOST HUNTING TODAY

By the 1970s serious research in the areas of parapsychology had dwindled significantly. Very few colleges still had any studies programs in the field and the ones that did were not letting many new ideas in and those were horribly underfunded. The paranormal community would get a big boost in popularity from an unlikely source – Hollywood.

In 1974 a troubled drug addled man walked through his family home in upstate New York and systematically murdered his family of six with a rifle. Ronald "Butch" DeFeo would be charged with their murders and was eventually sentenced to 25 years to life.

The house fell into the hands of the Lutz family in 1975. Just little over one year after the DeFeo murders. According to their later accounts their purchase 112 Ocean Avenue would be one of deep and terrible regret. In less than a month, by the Lutz's own accounts, they were forced to flee their dream home due to events right of the realm of nightmares. Pig monsters, glowing red-eyed demon boys, snow with cloven foot prints, walls that dripped slime (or blood by some accounts) were some of the fantastic events that supposedly happened in the Lutz household.

After they seemingly evacuated their house they pursued paranormal investigators to gain insight into what happened to them and their domicile. Eventually the story became public and a national sensation. A book was written and then a movie was released in 1979. Controversy then followed. Many began to suspect the Lutz's made the events up. Later their own attorney would claim that they fabricated the story over glasses of wine. The attorney was also the lawyer for Ronald Defeo and he had hoped to use the stories to help his client. The Lutz's, according to the attorney William Weber, were having trouble with their bills and hoped a book deal would make them enough money to get out of debt.

An amateur paranormal investigator named Dr. Stephen Kaplan was one of the investigators asked by George Lutz to come to the home and look for anything paranormal. Kaplan reported that when he told Lutz he would reveal the truth, as he saw it, regardless of what Lutz said, Lutz changed his mind and contacted the demonologist couple Ed and Lorraine Warren. The Warrens eventually claimed the stories were all true and would later create a smear campaign against Dr. Kaplan (even going as far as saying he wasn't a doctor despite Kaplan having earned a PhD in Sociology from Pacific College). Although some sources claim otherwise, Kaplan never rescinded his claims that much of the Amityville Horror (as the case would become known as) was a hoax and had also never apologized for it. The book he wrote (titled The Amityville Conspiracy) had dozens of examples of anecdotal evidence of fraud that were ignored by supporters of the Warrens and Lutz's. Now many of these inconsistencies can be attributed to author Jay Anson who wrote the book called the Amityville Horror. His hard cover and soft cover editions didn't even match up. So, who was right and who was wrong? Hard to say honestly and sides are much divided on the subject. Writers also seem to take sides on the subject. While researching this section for the book I discovered several sources that actually printed known lies (such as the Kaplan apology myth) as fact. Although no one can prove that nothing paranormal happened there, no one can prove that all the things that the Lutz's claimed happened there were lies either. However, several families have lived there since (the address has been changed and the look of the house as well) and none of them have claimed anything in regards to even a minor haunting.

Oh well, the genie as they say, was now out of the metaphorical bottle. Regardless of the inaccuracies of the books and subsequent movies a paranormal investigating legacy had begun. More movies based, at least partially, on true stories (such as The Entity which will be discussed later) will be made and some fanciful ones as well. Ghostbusters was the movie that changed everything for paranormal researchers forever. With its paranormal lingo ("...free-floating, full-torso, vaporous apparition.") and really cool, if somewhat dangerous gadgets the movie changed the public's perceptions of ghost hunters from background supporting characters to the stars of the show. Now, don't get me wrong, this is my all-time favorite movie. I can quote the film line by line. I am just getting tired of being asked where my proton pack is (Yeesh!). Paranormal Research just became really cool overnight (although nowadays I get compared to X-Files characters more often than Egon) I still cannot be featured in a news article without the Ghostbusters' theme song by Ray Parker Jr. playing in the background or someone saying, "who ya gonna call?" There simply are not any unlicensed nuclear accelerators, PKE meters or "ghost traps" for us to use. Nevertheless, colleges around the country were besieged with requests for information on their parapsychology programs. These requests would go unfulfilled since, by 1984 when Ghostbusters was released, there were no more classes to be had in the US.

Personally, my big introduction into the world of the paranormal came from TV. The show In Search Of... with Leonard Nimoy in the 1970s and That's Incredible in the '80s were big influenced on my young mind. They convinced me there are greater and more amazing things in the world than your eyes alone could perceive. Boy was I a nerd. Still am actually...

Speaking of In Search Of..., one of its producers was none other than Hans Holzer. Dr. Holzer, who had made his home New York City, wrote more than 131 books and countless articles on the paranormal. He also appeared many times on camera as well over the years in countless interviews. He taught parapsychology at the New York Institute of Technology. He received his doctorate from the London College of Applied Science. Holzer can be greatly credited for bringing "true ghost stories" to the public eye arguably more than any other individual. Hans unfortunately died on April 26th, 2009. His daughter Alexandra, seems to be on her way to continuing the Holzer tradition.

Another person influenced by TV and comic books was Loyd Auerbach. Auerbach began his career in television after all, if just behind the scenes. He grew up near New York City and thanks to his interests in sci-fi fiction and tales of the supernatural he began serious research into the paranormal in the 1970s. During his studies in academia (he holds a degree in Cultural Anthropology from Northwestern University and a graduate degree in Parapsychology from JFK University) and the paranormal he would gain membership in the ASPR and the California Society for Psychical Study (where he twice served as president). He would go onto the write the first truly successful ghost hunter's guide – *ESP, Hauntings and Poltergeists* in 1986. This very comprehensive book would go onto influence many successful ghost hunters today including myself, Troy Taylor and Joshua P. Warren. Continuing the tradition started by Harry Houdini, Auerbach is a practicing magician and mentalist. Auerbach has appeared on hundreds of radio shows, and dozens of local and national TV shows, including Larry King Live, Unsolved Mysteries, The Today Show, OPRAH, Sightings, and Popular Mechanics for Kids, Coast to Coast with Art Bell and Late Night with David Letterman. He is constantly haunting occasional new shows and many re-runs on the Discovery Channel, the Travel Channel, Tech-TV, the Travel Channel, A&E, the History Channel and The Learning Channel. He is featured in and was Series Consultant for the Travel Channel mini-series America's Most Haunted Places. In addition, he is co-producer for and appears on camera in the video documentary *The Haunting of the USS Hornet.*

Auerbach's book would inspire a generation of amateur parapsychologists. What once belonged only in psychical foundations and old dark rooms now was a full-fledged "hobby". Now there are thousands of small "ghost hunting groups" all over the country. Some are very large (such as Troy Taylor's American Ghost Society), but many only have a handful of members. Some, like the Paranormal Investigators Coalition are inclusive. All claim to pursue the same thing – *proof.*

This sci-fi/comics theme seemed to continue with Troy Taylor who I know personally as a huge Batman fan. When I 1st started to gather information on proper paranormal research techniques, Troy was one the 1st people I contacted. Troy Taylor is an occultist, supernatural historian and the author of 79 books on ghosts, hauntings, history, crime and the unexplained in America. He began his first book in 1989, which delved into the history and hauntings of Decatur, Illinois, and in 1994, it spawned the Haunted Decatur Tour -- and eventually led to the founding of his Illinois Hauntings Tours (with current tours in Alton, Chicago, Decatur, Lebanon & Jacksonville) and the American Hauntings Tours, which travel all over the country in search of haunted places. In 1996, Taylor organized a group of ghost enthusiasts into an investigation team and the American Ghost Society was launched, gained over 600 members in the years that followed. The organization continues today as one of America's largest and most honored research groups.

In 1997, Taylor launched the Haunted America Conference, regarded as "America's Original Ghost Conference" in Decatur, Illinois. After a number of years in Alton, Illinois, the conference has returned to its original site at the Lincoln Theater in Decatur. The Haunted America Conference remains the most imitated conference in the country and is now preparing for its 15th annual events in Illinois, California and Massachusetts. In addition to the tour companies and Haunted America Conference, Taylor is also the founder of Whitechapel Press, a publishing company for books about the supernatural that he started in 1993, and Dark Haven

Entertainment. Along with writing about the unusual and hosting tours, Taylor is also a public speaker on the subject of ghosts and haunting and has appeared in scores of newspaper and magazine articles about the subject and in hundreds of radio and television broadcasts about the supernatural. Troy has appeared in documentary productions for TLC, The History Channel, A & E, Discovery Channel, PBS, CMT and in various network programs and syndicated news shows. These programs have included America's Ghost Hunters, Ghost Waters, Night Visitors, Beyond Human Senses, Scariest Places on Earth, Children of the Grave, and others. He has also appeared in one feature film about the paranormal. Troy currently resides in an unknown location, somewhere in Illinois. Troy really does bridge the gap between the amateur ghost hunter and the psi field researcher.

Only a few universities in the United States still have parapsychology degrees. One is the Division of Perceptual Studies at the University of Virginia's Department of Psychiatric Medicine. They study the possibility of survival of consciousness after bodily death. Then there is the University of Arizona's Veritas Laboratory. They conduct laboratory investigations of mediums. There are several private institutions, including the Institute of Noetic Sciences and The Haunted Cottage Project in Harpers Ferry, WV that conduct parapsychological research. In 2011 it was announced that new accredited courses would begin thanks to efforts of Loyd Auerbach and Atlantic University in Virginia Beach, VA and another one at The International Metaphysical University.

## GHOST HUNTERS AND CABLE TV

For years there have been the occasional paranormal documentaries and specials. There have even been TV series based on weird phenomenon and unsolved mysteries. There were attempts at having reality show on the paranormal from time to time. There was the short lived British TV series Ghosthunters on the Discovery Channel (1996-1997) and then the very successful British series Most Haunted which lasted from 2002 until 2010. The UK really had begun the paranormal reality show trend. America would finally catch up with the phenomenally successful SyFy Channel series Ghost Hunters. Before this show, if anyone found out I was a paranormal researcher, they thought I was weird. Now, I hear stuff like, "oh, my cousin does that too." Now there are hundreds of ghost hunting teams across the nation.

Want to hear something funny? I have little doubt that some of the "paranormal researchers" on these reality shows know more than they let on. I imagine, since a few them started as investigators before 2005 (around the time the shows first started becoming popular), they may be aware of the influence of the Spiritualist Movement. They might even have been aware of the people who influenced the evolution of paranormal research and had honestly hoped to contribute to its further advancement. However, whatever good they did is overwhelmed by the harm. "Ghost hunting" has devolved into a social networking hobby and is far from a field of study. The desire for TV appearances, book deals and ego stimulation has exceeded individual inclinations toward any sort of professional commitment. There is no peer review, no sharing of information and no true scientific research being done. It wouldn't be so bad truthfully and mostly harmless if not for the fact that these are people with little more training than what they have seen on TV and they are going to people's homes! Can you imagine if this was okay in any field? If your house was being robbed, would you call someone who has seen five seasons of COPS or would you call an actual police officer?

In my updates for the gadget section of the book I will include information on how the tech used by many paranormal investigators differs in their application from how the reality shows often represent them.

# CHAPTER TWO: THE SCIENCE OF GHOST HUNTING

> The most exciting phrase to hear in science, the one that heralds new discoveries, is not 'Eureka!' (I found it!) but 'That's funny ...'
> - Isaac Asimov (1920 - 1992)

Science and the paranormal do not seem to fit well together do they? Most skeptics use that against us (we the paranormal investigators and specifically those that truly believe in ghosts). Those who study the paranormal and supernatural, (i.e. ghosts & hauntings) are often ridiculed by the scientific community in general and more specifically those most influential and infamous skeptics like the flamboyant (and genuinely likeable) James (the Amazing) Randi. Interestingly enough though, and a bit ironic, Randi and those like him seem to believe in nothing at all dealing with the paranormal, supernatural and spiritual to the point it has escalated into a quasi-religion of sorts. They believe in nothing other than what is "scientifically" acceptable, in their opinions, to the point it has become a belief system and a paradox in dogma.

William McDougall (1871-1938), an eminent "mainstream" academic psychologist who was also deeply interested in parapsychology. In his SPR Presidential Address, McDougall complained about the attitude of most "mainstream" scientists toward the paranormal and "occult," which they feared might lead to a renewed popular belief in "witchcraft, necromancy, and the black arts generally:

> "Men of science are afraid lest, if they give an inch in this matter the public will take an ell, and more. They are afraid that the least display of interest or acquiescence on their part may promote a great outburst of superstition on the part of the public, a relapse into a belief in witchcraft, necromancy, and the black arts generally, with all the moral evils which must accompany the prevalence of such beliefs. For they know that it is only through the faithful work of men of science through very recent centuries that these debasing beliefs have been in a larger measure banished from a small part of the world..."

Let's turn the tables for a moment shall we? A super-skeptic would argue that a "hard-core" believer in the Catholic religion could believe, or have faith in, the Virgin Mary to such an extent that they may see Her image in toasted bread (and sell it for a modest sum on eBay!). Ordinary toasted bread with a happenstance likeness to the mother of Christ is a miracle to some. Likewise, they would argue that an extremely biased believer in the phenomena of ghosts and hauntings would see ghosts in pictures with camera straps and dust particles in front of the lens. These two examples do indeed happen and happen quite often. Try as you may to convince the Catholic (we're using an extreme example here! Most Catholics are not that naive) that it is just toast and they won't budge on their opinion; their belief. Likewise, try to convince the would-be ghost hunter that there are just bits of dust in front of his or her lens and he or she will shop it around until someone tells him or her those orbs are indeed ghosts! Equally dogmatic are the skeptics though. Take a picture of an apparition sitting on a grave in broad daylight with plenty of witnesses around and it's either fraud or a trick of the light EVERY SINGE TIME. No amount of data or history will convince them otherwise. Science, they say, is absolute. Well, in their case a very politically correct view of science. Science is absolute, but it is a lot more flexible than Randi would care to admit.

Ask most skeptics if they are at all interested in seeing data that proves the existence of ghosts, hauntings, ESP, etc. and they will probably say yes they would love to see proof – "As long as it is in a controlled environment." Problem is "bias is as bias does". Go into any experiment believing and expecting a certain result and you will probably get that result. Raise your hand if you think that a truly skeptical person will go into any experiment studying the paranormal assuming that nothing at all would happen.

As late as the 1960s scientists were still skeptical that meteorites caused large craters on the moon and on Earth. Many scientists believed the craters were caused by volcanic eruptions here and on the moon. How do we know better now? Someone had a theory, applied the scientific method to that theory, came up with enough proof of that theory that it became established as the most likely explanation. In 1963 Geologist Eugene Shoemaker wrote a landmark paper on the Barringer Meteorite Crater (or Meteor Crater) in Arizona. Using evidence he collected and then compared with the theories and evidence of other scientists Eugene was able to convince the scientific community of the validity of meteorite craters. I suppose a meteorite would have to have hit some guy on the head to do the job otherwise.

Suffice to say what we need to do is apply science to ghosts and hauntings. This is how scientific advancement is done. So convinced are some that ghosts don't exist they can only use science to try and prove why they can't exist. Why don't they try this, use science to explain how ghosts can exist and then see if you can prove it through experimentation? First you will need some theories that are scientifically plausible. Ask the question, "If ghosts exist, how?" Then use applied science to test your hypothesis.

Recently I tried to do an investigation at a location run by the National Park Service. This particular park will remain nameless except for the blatant clues I am about to leave. They said they weren't interested because their only pursuit is that of historic facts. Historic facts? How do we know about history? Yeah, there's evidence like cannon balls and bullets left in the ground. But how do we know someone wasn't trying to plant an iron tree? Well, besides the fact that we hope none of our ancestors could be that dumb and gullible, we learn from eyewitness accounts. We know about the battle at Ft. McHenry during the war of 1812 (it was actually in 1814 that the battle happened) because people like Francis Scott Key were kind enough to tell us about it. The National Park I was trying to investigate was known for eyewitness accounts of ghosts and eerie phenomena. I had to restrain myself from using this example to define the word hypocrite in this book's glossary.

## ENERGY OR FIGMENTS

There are quite a few theories (as discussed briefly in Chapter One) as to what ghosts are. Let us review shall we?

Ghosts are:

1. The souls of the deceased trapped on earth.
2. A remnant of deceased persons or an energy copy of what they were.
3. Psychic projections. So-called “poltergeist agents”.
4. An “astral” projection existing on a higher dimension of reality.
5. A completely magical and ethereal entity outside our ability to comprehend unless you are a shaman of some kind.
6. Demons.
7. Two or more of the above.
8. Other.

Since the dawn of man we have tried to understand what happens to us when we die. Where do we go or do we go? The first seven theories above are probably the most common archetypes, but not the only theories as to what ghosts are. Everyone’s opinions are different. To be honest, I don’t have the answer either. However, this is a book on paranormal science. It is therefore important for us to discuss the kinds of hauntings there are.

In his landmark book *Apparitions*, George N.M. Tyrrell, postulated a classification system to describe different types of ghosts and hauntings.

**Experimental Apparitions** — Cases in which a living person sets out to appear to another person some distance away. Many examples involve astral projection, in which the conscious self leaves the physical body behind-usually in a state of trance-and travels to other places. This class of apparition has little to do with ghosts as such, since the people are still alive.

**Crisis Apparitions** — Cases in which the image of a person who in undergoing a major crisis - an accident, an injury, an emotional trauma, or death - appears to friends or relatives at the time of the crisis.

**Postmortem Apparitions** — Cases in with the image of a dead person appears to the living after the person has died.

**Continuing Apparitions** — Cases in which the image of a dead person is seen by different people over an extended period, usually in a place frequented by the dead person during life. Continuing apparitions are commonly called hauntings.

George Nugent Merle Tyrrell (1879-1952), a student of the Guglielmo Marconi Foundation, was a famous British parapsychologist who became president at the Society for Psychical Research in 1945. Tyrrell joined the SPR in 1908 and completely devoted himself to the subject by 1923. He became very interested in spiritualism and conducted experiments into precognition and telepathy. He seemed skeptical about ghost's and he believed them to be telepathic and only existed in regions of human personality and outside the field of normal consciousness. Tyrrell was also one of the first investigators to introduce topics of a supernatural nature into mainstream psychology. He wrote several books about science and psychical phenomena. The Personality of Man (1946) and Apparitions (1953). Apparitions is often classified as a classic theoretical study of psychical research. Tyrrell believed in telepathically sustained "collective idea-pattern" or thought-form. Tyrrell wrote:

> "It seems as if the more incoherent types of haunting were due to idea-patterns only very loosely connected, or perhaps not connected at all, with any idea in a conscious mind. One wonders whether such subconsciously initiated idea-patterns may in some cases be collective. If they were, they would throw light on many age-old traditions and legends. Popular tradition might supply material out of which such collective idea-patterns could be formed. Take, for example, the idea of the god Pan, half human and half goat-like, haunting certain places in the woods and uplands and playing his pipe. The widely spread idea that this happened might conceivably sink into the mid-levels of the personalities of a whole community, and there form a telepathic idea-pattern, having a multiple agency. Anyone (suitably sensitive) going to the places which, according to the idea-pattern, Pan was especially supposed to inhabit would then see and

hear Pan with exactly the same reality that a person going into a haunted house sees and hears a ghost. And this would account for the firm belief in ancient times in the nature-gods; in Celtic and other countries in fairies, and so on. These people would believe in them because they really did see and hear them as one really does see and hear apparitions. There really would, on his view, be a reason for the universality, vitality, and permanence of these legends, which mere oral tradition scarcely seems enough to account for. This view is surely more convincing than the somewhat lame attempts of anthropologists to explain these things away. Collective and telepathically endowed idea-patterns would also explain epidemic appearances, for example, of the Virgin and the Saints in Catholic countries; the appearances of the Devil in the Middle Ages, and perhaps the sight of witches flying on broom-sticks and the metamorphoses of human beings into animals, etc. It may be that the Flying Dutchman has a similar explanation."

Early parapsychologist Edmund Gurney believed in apparitions as phenomena, relative and unique to the subject, that could be explained only in relation to telepathy. In his opinion, the obvious is not actually present in any sense at the scene of the ghostly encounter. Instead, he contended that the participant receives a telepathic cue from the manifestation, a cue frequently caused by a crisis or near-death experience, which the percipient then employs to project an apparition.

A flaw in Gurney's theory was that it did not adequately account for the occasional occurrence of "collective phenomena," or apparitions seen by more than one person at the same time. Gurney attempted to explain these rare events by introducing the idea of "contagious telepathy," in which an apparition projected by one person might infect the minds of others so that they too see the same figure. The theory, however, was not a very persuasive one, and even Gurney himself did not seem to be entirely happy with it.

Dr. Andrew Nichols is a parapsychologist and investigator of hauntings, poltergeist cases and other paranormal phenomena. He currently resides in North Florida, where he has been a professor of psychology and parapsychology for many years at several colleges. Dr. Nichols has lectured on parapsychology throughout the US, Canada and Europe, and has appeared as a consultant on the paranormal on many television and radio programs. He is the author of numerous scientific papers and popular articles on paranormal topics.

I have known *of* Dr. Nichols for almost as long as I have been involved in paranormal research and first talked to him in 2010. Since then we have become very good friends and regularly discuss some of the most advanced concepts in parapsychological studies. He shares a great deal of commonality in the thought processes and theories of Tyrrell. Here is what Dr. Nichols has to say about ghosts:

After spending more than three decades specializing in the study of apparitions, poltergeists and other ghostly experiences, certain patterns have emerged which lead me to present a hypothesis which, I believe, accounts for all of the reported characteristics of ghostly experiences. This theory might be termed the "Psi Projection Hypothesis". The following is a simplified explanation of this theory.

Since the introduction of quantum physics, science now accepts the unlikely concept that light possesses characteristics of both waves and particles. Human thought also produces waves as neurons within the brain generate electrical impulses of varying frequencies. These brain waves can be traced and recorded by means of an electroencephalograph, or EEG machine. We can speculate that thought, like light, exists in particle form as well as waves. From this perspective, our bodies would be constantly surrounded by a sea of thought-particles, similar in many ways to the shimmering "auras" purportedly seen around living and non-living objects by individuals with a developed ESP faculty. In fact, the existence of such a "Psi Field" has been accepted by many parapsychologists (including myself), for decades.

This Psi Field extends beyond the physical body of the organism, saturating its environment, and capable of interacting with the psi fields of other individuals and objects. Consider the effect of a strong magnet on an electromagnetic field. When a magnet is introduced to such an energy field, it alters the pattern of that field. This is because the molecules of a magnet are not randomly distributed, but are aligned, or focused in a single direction.

According to this hypothesis, a single thought or series of thoughts, strongly charged with emotion, could have a similar effect on a field of thought-particles. This process would be somewhat analogous to the production of video or audio tapes. Recording tape, coated with easily magnetized particles, passes across a device in the recorder which produces magnetic impulses. These impulses cause the random particles on the recording tape to realign into a pattern that matches the magnetic impulses. The result is a recorded image or sound.

Theoretically, a single, powerful thought, or a series of similar recurring thoughts, could cause random thought-particles to realign themselves into patterns that match the original thoughts, and which could be perceived by anyone who had a suitably developed ESP capability. These realigned thought-particle patterns are, in my opinion, the basis for all spectral phenomena, including those described as apparitions, hauntings, or poltergeists.

Psi Projections with little emotional charge would normally disintegrate rapidly, but projections associated with traumatic events, such as a murder, suicide, or military battle, might remain sequestered in a particular environment for decades, or even centuries, depending upon the energetic characteristic of the site. Research conducted by myself and other parapsychologists indicate that locations with unusual electromagnetic or geomagnetic properties are more likely to be regarded as "haunted". I suspect that unusual magnetic fields, artificially induced or created by geological factors such as seismic faults or underground water, create a "containment zone" which can sustain one or more psi projections for some period of time. However, with some notable exceptions, most hauntings do tend to fade away and disappear after a decade or so, and poltergeist disturbances usually dissipate within a few weeks or months.

The hypothetical thought-particle patterns could carry either a telepathic or psychokinetic "charge", or both. A telepathic charge would result in witnesses reporting subjective apparitional phenomena such as visible specters, cold spots, sounds of voices or footsteps, or describe a sense of "presence" or of being watched. A psychokinetic charge would result in objective phenomena such as "knocking" or other percussive sounds, or movement of objects as reported in poltergeist cases. In many haunting cases, the apparition or physical phenomena are repetitive and non-interactive. This suggests that a type of "psychic residue" is present. Residual hauntings would be the result of thought-particle patterns created at some time in the past, which have become detached from the minds of their creator (who may have died, or simply moved away). In cases where the phenomena are more dynamic and interactive, as in poltergeist-type disturbances, the agent is typically a living person within the household. Usually the agent is creating the psi projection unconsciously, and is unaware of their role in the haunting.

Most haunting and poltergeist cases exhibit little evidence of involvement of non-corporeal entities or "spirits". However, in rare cases, these random energy particles may hold the essence of consciousness, at least until the particles are eventually scattered by the process of entropy.

Taking into consideration the impressive amount of evidence to suggest that states of mental intention can have a significant effect on the output of random number generators (RNGs), it seems likely that the human mind is able to organize random subatomic particles, and create a form of phase coherence, similar to that of a laser. This would allow the particles that make up a ghost to combine into a temporarily coherent and semi-stable form. These thought projections reflect the unconscious wishes, fears, and personality characteristics of the living agent, or those of another individual whose psi projection was created at some time in the past and imprinted into the environment, acting independently of the living witnesses.

## INTELLIGENT HAUNTINGS

There are two main kinds of hauntings. What most people are familiar with are what the experts call a "classic haunting", "intelligent haunting" or "traditional haunting". These are actually quite rare. When the general public thinks of hauntings they think of a sentient spirit that can manifest itself into an apparition and communicate with the living. The ghost responds to outside stimuli like questions and statements. It can be friendly or hostile and will let you know the difference. They are capable of opening and closing doors and windows and moving objects like furniture around.

## RESIDUAL OR REPLAY HAUNTINGS

The most common type of haunting is probably the "residual haunting". This is best described as an imprint on the environment. A moment in time, burnt onto the surroundings of a specific location, playing out roles and situations over and over again for centuries at a time. Most researchers compare this to a looped video that repeats itself forever. In these cases you might hear footsteps and other strange noises. However, if you see the event being played out, you will not be able to interfere. The "ghosts" here are not conscious of their surroundings. They may not be sentient, just memories that refuse to be forgotten.

## POLTERGEISTS

There are other kinds of hauntings. The "poltergeist haunting" is probably the least common and hardest to classify (also known as a "PK haunting" or "human agent poltergeist"). You may not even be able to call this a haunting at all. Now, if you have seen the movie Poltergeist and have not read the latest literature on paranormal phenomena then probably you think poltergeists are really pissed-off spirits. They are not. Most researchers agree the poltergeists are not "noisy ghosts" (the German translation from which the word is derived). They believe that poltergeists are in fact psychically powerful troubled young people (usually girls) manifesting their subconscious in the form of psychokinetic activity. In fact, in parapsychology circles, the phenomena is referred to as Recurring Spontaneous Psychokinesis or RSPK. I know... Sounds like a bad science fiction movie to me too. But there is strong data to support this theory.

In cases of P.A.'s (Poltergeist Agents or PK agents as I prefer to call them) the phenomena usually surrounds a young child, usually a girl. The P.A. (the child) is almost always around when the poltergeist activity occurs. This usually involves objects being thrown around when there is no one around, unexplainable tapping and scratching noises and objects disappearing and reappearing hours, days or weeks later. In worst-case scenarios there can be injuries to human beings from thrown objects and scratches appearing on the flesh of the P.A. Fires are also known to occur in the worst cases - sometimes with catastrophic results.

The poltergeist agent is usually a pre-teen (sometimes older) girl (in rare occasions a boy). No one knows why this is. In some of the less common cases the P.A. is actually able to manifest a conscious separate entity. Perhaps this entity is an incarnation of the P.A.'s own subconscious. Like the "id monster" from the movie Forbidden Planet, this manifestation is rarely benevolent. Some researchers including myself believe this is what may have happened in the famous real-life "entity case".

## PORTAL HAUNTING

A recent controversial theory is that of "portal hauntings". This theory suggests that there are locations where a nexus between our world and the next exist. In these locations spirits can cross over from the other side in great numbers. Portal hauntings are supposed to be prevalent in cemeteries but can also account for some haunted houses. In these cases the hauntings might have nothing to do with the past events of a location. In fact they may allow stranger things than ghosts through. A few "portal" spots are said to harbor entities of varying size and less than human shapes. The problem with portal hauntings is that they would require huge amounts of energy to exist. Ripping open the fabric of space-time is no easy task. If you weren't incinerated by the release of energy, you would probably get several types of cancer from the radiation being released. There are other kinds of hauntings that are significantly less common, like crisis apparitions and ghost lights. However, their nature makes them difficult to detect with scientific equipment since they tend to be completely unpredictable and/or one time only events.

## CRISIS APPARITIONS

If you remember your Shakespeare, then you should know what a crisis apparition is. Crisis apparitions appear to people when the person reflected as the apparition is near or at the moment of death. Some have given warnings to living relatives or appear simply to say goodbye. Many say nothing and leave their visit to the interpretation of the witness. Still others will gesture to their wounds as if to say, "Solve my murder".

## GHOST LIGHTS

Ghost lights tend to only appear in remote areas. They come in various oval shapes and differing colors. They tend to be elusive and react to noises and are sometimes accompanied by buzzing or humming sounds.

Ghost lights are more associated with local folklore and are virtually impossible to research.

## PHANTOM PHONE CALLS

Sometimes a person will receive a phone call from a loved one – after that loved one had already passed away! Usually dying in a tragic and random accident the deceased will call a loved one – wife, daughter, son or husband – then leave a brief and sometimes cryptic message. Mostly the message will be simply an "I love you" message. Calls vary in message content.

Some paranormal researchers have speculated that the participant in the act of receiving the call does not actually physically answer the phone at all. Instead, since in modern society, the telephone is the most common type of communication reception tool, your brain creates the illusion of receiving the call. This is due in part since your mind is probably unaccustomed to processing complex psychic messages. Perhaps, soon, we will be hearing more and more about "phantom texting", IM'ing and "Skyping".

## SPECTRAL SHIPS, TRAINS, PLANES AND AUTOMOBILES

This subject may be more folklore perhaps, but interesting to note nonetheless.

On dark mysterious roads around the world people have encountered phantom vehicles. A bus in England will drive into oncoming cars and then disappear at the last possible moment. Likewise in Somerset, England a phantom motorcyclist from World War II appears from time to time and has even been photographed.

Coastlines across the globe have reported spotting ships from centuries long past sailing in with mist and moonlight. The most famous of which are the Flying Dutchman and the Mary Celeste.

In Pearl Harbor, Hawaii and over the fields of Britain and France witnesses have claimed to have seen planes from the great wars. Triplanes from World War I and dog-fighters still battling enemy forces in an eternal flying dance of the damned.

In Baltimore, MD residents used to tell tales of Lincoln's funeral train passing in front of Camden Station (now part of Camden Yards, home of the Baltimore Orioles) on its trip across the country. As it passed a flag draped coffin would be visible in the funeral car!

## PHANTOM ANIMALS

Almost always these are domesticated animals or pets. There are tales of a cat that haunts the White House in Washington, DC. In parts of the US and Europe there are stories of huge black dogs as big as calves that haunt and protect cemeteries and/or openings to other realms.

## DEMONS AND SHADOW PEOPLE

In all the years I have been investigating the paranormal I have only encountered what might be considered demonic once. I was asked to attend a church service in Baltimore by a friend of mine from El Salvador. He told me that there was a woman in the congressional who was experiencing demonic possession. I of course was very intrigued by this. The first time I went something happened. When I got there my friend introduced me to the pastor and he asked that I please not take notes or pictures. They just wanted my opinion. I was supposed to appear as just another one of the worshipers at the church. I sat and the back and waited. About 45 minutes into service a women up front and to the right of me began getting strange stares and reactions from those around her. There were about 20 people attending service that day. She was mumbling in what I discerned as Latin. "Nos es hic! Nos es hic," she cried over and over again. It roughly translates to "we are here".

Next I knew she was on the floor up front writhing in contortions I didn't think possible for a human being. She hissed and spat profanities in Spanish and English and laughed with a voice way to deep for someone, I guess, around 5' tall and only 115 lbs tops. The pastor and many of the congressional formed a circle around her. They placed one hand on each other's shoulders and one hand on the head of the seemingly possessed woman. They prayed loudly in Spanish. After a few minutes, she seemed confused as to where she was. Later all I could say was that I didn't know what to think.

Was she really possessed? I can't say for sure. Are demons real? Well, I can only speculate that in some cases a house may be haunted by, who was in life, a very, very bad person. Demons from hell? Ask John Zaffis. I am not experienced enough yet.

Now shadow people? I think they are just ghosts – sometimes anyway. I do not think they are demonic, as some people do. The rest of the time it is probably your peripheral vision playing tricks on you. In your eyes (assuming you have both) are cone cells and rod cells. The cone cells focus light very well and are responsible for details and color. The rod cells, which surround the cone cells, are far less detailed oriented. Rod cells pick up dark colors and motion well, but little else. Suffice to say, in a dimly lit room a coat rack may be the actual cause of your "shadow-man".

I saw some shadowy figures once at the Waverly Hills Sanatorium in Kentucky (see the end of this book for more on that story) but I think the general darkness kept us from seeing details.

## THE UN-MATERIAL: WHAT ARE GHOSTS?

Previously mentioned were several theories as to what ghosts are and a theory titled "Other". Most people agree that if ghosts are real, they must be some form of energy. Some form of energy would certainly account for why ghosts are apparently able to be recorded using modern technology like video cameras and EMF detectors. But what kind of energy and where does it come from? To answer this more thoroughly, we must first ask some more obvious questions:

Why is it that you can read a ghost sometimes with an EMF detector and other times cannot (Even when enough data of its presence exists)?

How can our instruments detect a ghost's presence even when a reliable "sensitive" (a person who can "feel" paranormal phenomena more than the average person) cannot?

Vice Versa – How can a reliable sensitive detect a ghostly presence when our instruments cannot?

How can any of this be possible without breaking the laws that govern reality?

Higher dimensions of our own reality come to mind.

We live in a four dimensional universe – height, width, length and time. You have height, width and length and travel forward through time. But, mathematics proves that there are other dimensions. There are levels of reality beyond our perception. Places with five, six even more than a dozen different dimensions! The problem is we cannot see these higher dimensions because our brains are hardwired for just four dimensions. However, there could be exceptions to the rule.

## A STUDY OF HIGHER DIMENSIONS

In 1854 a mathematician named Edwin A. Abbott wrote a book called Flatland: A Romance of Many Dimensions. In it he describes what would happen if a two-dimensional character named A. Square met a three dimensional being named Lord Sphere. A commentary on Victorian society it made some interesting observations on dimensional perceptions. In the story Mr. Square meets a 3D sphere that tries to convince Mr. Square of the reality of fourth dimensional space. You see, Mr. A. Square lives on Flatland, a two dimensional world where only length and width exist, but no height. When the 3D Lord Sphere puts himself through Flatland to demonstrate his higher dimensions, Mr. Square sees Lord Sphere start as a point then become a series of small then large and small again circles that returns to a point and then disappear. Of course Mr. Square is horrified at this monster. By the end of story Mr. Square is convinced of the reality of three dimensions but still cannot visualize it.

We, similarly, cannot visualize dimensions outside of our four because our brains are hardwired for four dimensions. If we unfold a cube into two dimensions it becomes a cross. If we put the cross on Flatland, Mr. Square would perceive it as a twelve sided shape. As we fold the cross "up" into a three-dimensional cube Mr. Square would see the cross disappear a section at a time until there was nothing but a square left in its place. A tesseract (or octachoron) is essentially a three-dimensional cross. If we were to encounter a fifth dimensional being, they could fold the three-dimensional tesseract into a five-dimensional hypercube (or n-cube or measure polytope). We cannot visualize a hypercube with our limited 3D brains. However, with computer modeling we can see what light passed through a hypercube would look like and that is the shadow of a hypercube!

When we look down on Flatland we see everything at once - all the people, houses, towns and roads are viewable to our 3D minds. We even see inside the houses and inside the people! A fifth-dimensional person would be able to see inside us too. They would see our front and back at the same time. A 5D man could see through and walk through walls just like a ghost! Fifth-dimensional people can also go anywhere they want instantly. Just like we can poke our finger through anyplace in Flatland, a 5D man could walk from New York to Tokyo instantly. To us they would be virtually omnipotent.

Higher dimensions are inaccessible to those of us who are limited to just three dimensions of space. This fact can be demonstrated by an analogy proposed by mathematician and bigamist Charles Howard Hinton. English mathematician Charles Hinton was fascinated with the concept of higher dimensions. After being fired from Uppingham School in 1885 after having been arrested for bigamy, he packed up his stuff and one of his two wives and went to live in the land of the free. Too bad bigamy is bad here too. After a brief pause in his research into higher dimensions, when he invented the baseball-pitching machine, Hinton was able to return to his passion. When asked if we could ever access the realm of higher dimension Hinton said that higher dimensions are too small for us to see. Imagine a room full of smokers. After a brief coughing fit imagine the smoke curling off into the four corners of the room. The smoke will eventually travel to every inch of the room. When measuring this experiment in lung cancer we can determine that the smoke has not exited into higher dimensions. Most researchers believe that in the case of residual hauntings, a ghost walks through walls because the wall wasn't there when the spirit was alive. Since the ghost isn't conscious of its

surroundings it does its decade's old routine regardless of environmental changes. Higher dimensions may explain why interactive spirits can walk through walls.

Hinton suggested (as most scientists believe somewhat today) that higher dimensions exist at too small a level to be measured. Smaller even than an atom. The energy requirement needed to access this incredibly small size is about a quadrillion times greater (Yes, that's a real number, represented as a one followed by 24 zeros) then today's most powerful atom smasher. We literally have to bend time and space to do it. However, for anything already in a higher dimension, accessing lower dimensions is child's play.

Now, if you read just this chapter and were previously not versed in the theory of higher dimensions, then you may come away thinking that I was the first one to make the connection. You would be wrong.

The concepts behind our perspective of the universe in regard to dimensional perspective go back to about 370 B.C. Socrates talked about some weird stuff sometimes. No wonder he never wrote anything down! Luckily Plato knew how to use a pen, or chisel, or whatever they used back then. Anyway, imagine some guys living in a cave underground. Now imagine those guys have been chained and restrained (see what I mean about weird!) since birth. Restrained in such a way that they cannot move any part of their bodies and they were forced to look straight ahead at a wall. Behind them is a wall that is slightly inclined. Behind the wall is a light source that reflects the shadow of anything on the inclined wall onto the cave wall in front of the men a la Puppet Theater. If there were an echo that bounced off the cave wall then any voice spoken to them from behind them would appear to come from the shadows. If they were also able to converse with each other (but not see each other) then they would come to believe they were shadows themselves. Since these poor saps entire lives were spent in front of 2D shadows they would believe they were also 2D! What a deep, twisted philosopher Socrates was!

What if we were prisoners as well? What if our consciousness exists in a higher dimension but is restrained by the bonds of our physical 3D bodies? Since even before we were born we have been chained to a three dimensional reality, never knowing anything else besides three dimensions until we are released from bondage through death. Take that Socrates! I can philosophize too! Yes, I know that some theologies have hinted at concepts like these for centuries. In all myths and legends there is always some degree of truth, some higher truth in many cases. Perhaps this is another case in which earlier man could not quite comprehend this concept and developed a mystical explanation to accommodate ingrained and fundamental facts. Like I said, these are just theories.

Charles Hinton had names for the extra dimensions found beyond length, width and height. He called them "ana" and "kata". Just like a Flatlander cannot move "up" out of Flatland, you and I cannot move ana or kata. There could be a ghost just two feet ana and three feet kata from you right now! Although Plato and Socrates hinted at one's perspective in regards to higher dimensions it was a fellow philosopher named Henry More who associated higher dimensions with ghosts a little over 400 years ago.

More (coincidentally a Platonist) believed that ghosts had more (pun intended) to them then just metaphysical conjectures. He believed that ghosts, and consequently your soul, occupy space like normal matter. G=M or GHOSTS equal MASS. But two pieces of matter cannot occupy the same place at the same time! That is, unless the extra mass rests in hyperspace (higher dimensional space). Then it is not an issue at all. This suggests that your hyper-self (your soul/spirit/ghost/etc.) exists in hyperspace but is tethered in three-dimensional space by your body and mind. Like Socrates' cavemen, although you're part of a larger dimensional picture, you have no concepts outside of what your eyes perceive. When your 3D body dies your hyper-self would become un-tethered in this theory and "move on" so to speak.

It was German astronomy professor Johann Carl Friederich Zöllner from the University of Liepzig who really deserves credit for the introduction of ghosts into modern concepts of higher dimensions.

In 1875 Zöllner visited England to see cathode-ray tube inventor Sir William Crookes (actually Crookes wasn't knighted until 1897). Crookes was a bit of a conundrum in that he was a very serious, and probably boring, man of science and yet was really into spiritualism. He supported Henry Slade, an infamous medium from the US. Slade was a self proclaimed psychic who claimed to be able to contact ghosts from higher dimensions. In fact Slade was a clever magician who used sleight of hand tricks to fool the gullible. Would you believe that the some of the people he fooled included some of the most prominent scientists who ever lived? Not just Crookes and Zöllner either but some who would go on to win the Nobel Prize. This included the famous classical physicist Lord Raleigh.

Zöllner was convinced that Slade was in fact the "real deal". Using what many modern magicians would recognize as clever "magic tricks" Slade convinced Zöllner and many others that his "ghosts" could tie knots in rope that was sealed with wax at both ends, connect solid wooden rings together and affect objects in sealed jars. When in 1877 Slade was arrested on fraud charges, Zöllner shocked London society when he, and many other prominent scientists, came to Slade's defense.

Slade was convicted anyway. Many were not surprised when Slade's friends from the fourth dimension didn't bust him out of jail.

## NOT WORMHOLES!

In Stephen Spielberg's paranormal film Poltergeist, journeys into higher dimensions are hinted at throughout the movie. In the movie the little girl Carol Ann is apparently sucked (or pulled) out of our universe and into the "other side" (a ball thrown in the bedroom lands in the living room). Would these be portals, as we know them today?

Many ghost hunters believe in a phenomenon called a portal haunting. Portal hauntings are places where there seems to be a nexus between our world and a mysterious "ghost zone" where the dead exist and other supernatural beings. These portals are used to explain hauntings at places where there is an unusual amount of ghostly happenings. Could ghosts be coming in through these in great numbers? Are these places a crossroads between worlds? Maybe... But they are not wormholes!

It would appear that too many ghost hunters are also Star Trek fans (not necessarily a bad thing until you start applying Star Trek science fiction to ghost hunting). Wormholes are theoretical astronomical objects. When a star many times larger than our Sun dies it may explode and then collapse in on its self. There is only so much matter that can be in one place at one time and still have a stable gravitational pull. This is not one of those times. The matter present will collapse into an infinite density; a point in space where not even light can escape its gravitational pull. This is called a black hole. We know they exist because they have been observed by modern radio telescopes. Some scientists think they may exit into another universe or connect places in this universe or even places in other times. They call these theoretical objects wormholes.

Recently I came across a website that hinted that portals are wormholes. I guess that is logical conclusion. I mean they are both supposed to be entrances to other places, right? Well, yes, except for two blaring differences: radiation and extreme pressure. If you were a ghost hunting at a cemetery and a wormhole opened up you and your team would be bombarded with radiation in the form high energy x-rays. Then if you lived long enough to get a little closer you would be burned up from the heat and then torn to pieces from the intense forces present. Maybe that's not a problem for Jean-Luc Picard, but I think it may be for you and your team.

## UN-DEAD CATS!

> "Those who are not shocked when they first come across quantum theory cannot possibly have understood it."
> - Niels Bohr on Quantum Physics
>
> "God does not play dice with the universe."
> - Albert Einstein on Quantum Physics
>
> "Einstein, don't tell God what to do."
> Niels Bohr in response to Einstein

"If you want to exist in this universe, you have to obey its rules." I cannot count how many times I have said that in conversation, at lectures and in my books. I try to stress how fundamental a rule this is. It is very important to the structure of the universe and reality that this rule never be broken. Whatever ghosts are doesn't matter. For them (ghosts) to exist they must and will affect the environment in some way. "But how do know this is true Vince," you might ask. Well, that's what this chapter is about. If you bought this book (good call!) then you are probably already sure that ghosts have a place in scientific research. At least you have a pretty good idea. Some of those who believe in ghosts might argue that ghosts are "ethereal" and "supernatural" and have no place in science. They would say that I am wasting my time with trying to collect theories of their existence since they can neither be proven nor disproved. Ghosts are magic some people argue. If they don't want you too, you will never detect them.

If ghosts are magic and they don't want you to detect them then that would mean when you die you develop "ghost powers"! Upon your demise as a living being you suddenly become aware of magical ghost powers. You can levitate objects with your ghostly mind. You can pass through walls since you are a ghost and you know it! You are *Casper* and *Slimer* rolled into one. You also have a mission! Now, as a ghost, your job is to scare people out of your house. Kind of like the poor couple in the movie *Beetlejuice.* Maybe you'll even have an instruction book on how to act like a proper spook. You'll have detailed instructions on the correct way to rattle chains and techniques for getting just the right BOO!

Modern day paranormal investigators use scientific instrumentation to try and detect the presence of ghosts. They use EMF meters, digital thermometers and the like to try to see if ghosts are in the room with them or maybe out in a field or cemetery. Not to sound like a broken record, but they do not use them to detect ghosts directly. Once again – we are not the Ghostbusters! We do not have devices that work like PKE meters like Egon and Ray had. I wish we did, it would make our job so much easier.

Now, the title of this section is Undead Cats, which makes it seem like something written by Stephen King. But no, this chapter is not about zombie, vampires or were-cats. The section title is derived from a thought experiment dreamed up by one Erwin Schrödinger who was trying to debunk the Heisenberg Uncertainty Principle. He ended up contributing to it instead. Whoa! I'm getting ahead of myself now. There's some splainin' to do here Lucy! When I am done explaining I hope you will understand a little better why everything that exists must obey the laws of the universe! Now, pay attention. What we are about to go into befuddled Einstein all the way until his death in 1955 at the age of 76.

## SCIENCE'S UNCERTAIN PRINCIPLES

As I mentioned earlier this is a very complicated subject. However, do not let that daunt you from reading on. I will not be going into too much of the history of subject of quantum mechanics. That information could easily fit into its own book and in fact already has (read the excellent *In Search of Schrodinger's Cat: Quantum Physics and Reality by John Gribbin* for more on that). I really think you're smart enough anyway since you bought this book in the first place.

Earlier in this book we mentioned how we take it for granted that meteorites exist and have created some really big craters here on Earth. It's funny now thinking about how only a few decades ago many scientists weren't sure if meteorite craters were caused by rocks from space or extinct volcanoes. Many things that we take for granted as simply existing were not so easily accepted not too long ago. The concept of atoms, for example, existed as early as ancient Greece. We now accept atoms as a fact of life and take them for granted, although it wasn't until the early twentieth century that the scientific community started taking the theory of atoms seriously. As early as 370 B.C. Democritus of Abdera suggested that all things could be broken down into smaller pieces until eventually you got to an unchangeable object called an atom. "The only existing things are atoms and empty space; all else is opinion," he said. However, the more romantic concept of four "elements" of air, earth, fire and water proposed by good ole Aristotle remained the more popular theory for centuries.

Seventeenth century English chemist Robert Boyle liked the idea of atoms and so did Sir Isaac Newton.

## NEWTON ON ATOMS AND THEIR HISTORY:

> "Atomism arose as an explanatory scheme with the ancient Greeks (around 400BC), Leucippus and Democritus, and Epicurus, and the Roman poet, Lucretius. At the most fundamental level atomism is the belief that all phenomena are explicable in terms of the properties and behaviour of ultimate, elementary, localized entities (or 'fundamental particles'). Thus it prescribes a strategy for the construction of scientific theories in which the behaviour of complex bodies is to be explained in terms of their component parts. That strategy has led to many of the successes of modern physical science, though these do not prove that there actually are 'ultimate entities' of the type postulated by atomism.
>
> "Their (the atomists) analysis goes 'behind' the appearance of minute, unchangeable and indestructible 'atoms' separated by the emptiness of 'the void'. It is the void which is said to make change and movement possible. All apparent change is simply the result of rearrangements of the atoms as a consequence of collisions between them. This seems to lead to mechanical determinism, though, in an attempt to leave room for freewill, Epicurus and Lucretius postulated that atoms might 'deviate' in their courses.
>
> "However if 'what exists' is 'atoms', what of the 'void'? In different ways both Aristotle and Descartes denied that there could be such a thing as literally 'empty space'. Physically therefore they saw the world as a plenum. Atomism was also associated with atheism, since as Lucretius put it, 'Nothing can ever be created out of nothing, even by divine power.' Conversely no thing can ever become nothing - so the atomists proposed a strict principle of conservation of matter.
>
> "The attempt of the ancient atomists to solve a

metaphysical problem about the nature of change resulted in a brilliantly fruitful strategy for the construction of theories in the physical sciences. However there are unanswered philosophical objections to atomism and the very successes it has stimulated suggest that 'the stuff of the world' cannot ultimately be understood in terms of atomism. A thoroughgoing positivism will continue to hold that 'atomic theories' are simply devices for talking about observable phenomena."

(The Concise Encyclopedia of Western Philosophy and Philosophers, 1991)

It wasn't until the early nineteenth century that a color-blind fellow named Charles Dalton put atoms on the map. It was Dalton, a British chemist and physicist, who gave atoms many of the characteristics that high school kids learn and quickly forget today. One thing he got wrong though was that atoms are indivisible. Can you say atomic bomb? I knew you could...

It was a relatively (pun intended) short time later that Albert Einstein proved the existence of atoms once and for all in 1905. His paper on the photoelectric effect demonstrated the emission of electrons from a material as a result of light striking its surface, something that could only be proven with atoms. Einstein would later win the Nobel Prize in 1921 for this work.

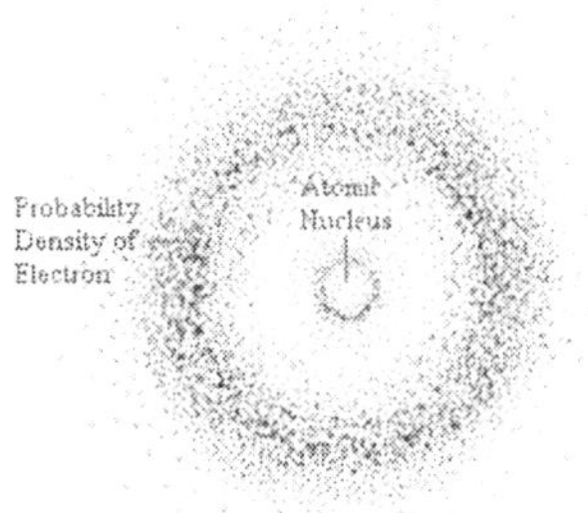


New Zealand born Ernest Rutherford developed a theory in regards to the structure of atoms in 1911. Unlike the image of a nucleus surrounded by spinning electrons, akin to moons rapidly orbiting a weird planet, like we were taught in school, the atomic structure is a bit different in reality. Rutherford (who invented the first EMF detector in 1897!) showed that the atom is more like a nucleus surrounded by an electron "cloud". Although most of the atom is empty space (Imagine the period at the end of this sentence is a nucleus of an atom. If you placed the nucleus on the torch of the Statue of Liberty, the circling cloud of electrons would be no closer than the bottom of the base 306' 8" below. The nucleus by the way is 100,000 times smaller than the atom itself) an electric charge, protons and neutrons keep the electrons from falling into the nucleus and also keeps other atoms from (under normal conditions) interacting.

Just too round things out, it was British physicist (there are a lot of British and German scientists in this book aren't there?) Sir Joseph John Thomson who discovered that cathode rays are composed of negatively charged particles called electrons. Ernest Rutherford would discover the proton in 1919 and predict the existence of the neutron. Rutherford's colleague James Chadwick (also a Limey) would discover the neutron in 1932.

"So what's the point Vince?" The point is I think some of the readers possibly need a little set up to refresh their memories in regard to the nature of atoms and the subatomic world in general. Now we're getting into the really weird stuff!

The most amazing principle, one that has stayed experiment after experiment, of quantum theory is the Heisenberg Uncertainty Principle. It is the genie in the bottle. It is Pandora's Box. It is... Some other metaphor I can't think of right now. The Heisenberg Uncertainty Principle clearly states that you cannot measure the position and velocity of a subatomic particle at the same time. If you measure its speed, you change its position. Measure its position and you change its velocity. Amazing, huh? Ok, let me elaborate since the implications may not be obvious at first.

The Global Positioning System, or GPS, is an amazing bit of technology. Using multiple government satellites orbiting the Earth, pocket-sized devices can calculate the latitude, longitude and even altitude of a moving object within a few feet. Astronomers can calculate the position of planets and other heavenly bodies so precisely we can land a robot on Mars millions of miles away or send a probe to a comet while it's moving at thousands of miles an hour through our solar system. But no scientist anywhere can predict the speed and position of a little ole electron with absolute certainty. This is the part that made Einstein say, "God does not play dice with the Universe." Why can we not measure a subatomic particles speed and position? Well, because electrons, protons and the rest of the subatomic particles are really, really small of course.

So, how does one even try to measure the speed or position of, let's say, an electron? Unfortunately you will need to shoot another electron or photon or some other subatomic particle at it. There are things smaller than electrons but nothing smaller can be measured. And even then we will have to shoot something at it that will no doubt alter its direction and/or speed. Since rulers and gauges are made of atoms and

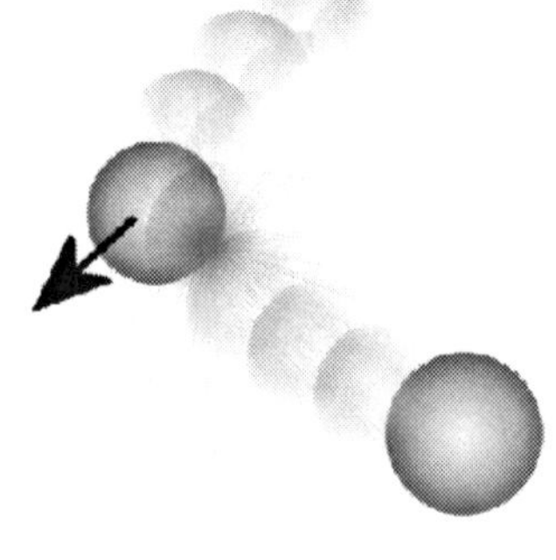

we cannot make a measuring device small enough to measure an electron so we look at the reactions that are created by shooting other particles at it.

German born Werner Heisenberg will always be associated with the theory of quantum mechanics due to his famous principle of uncertainty. The Uncertainty Principle is an elaboration on the fact that attempting to measure a subatomic particles velocity and position is impossible. The concept was, and is, extremely controversial. Many scientists had some major issues with this concept. People of science like to believe that everything and anything is measurable. Scientists once thought that is you could measure the speed and position of every particle in the universe you could know everything that was and could be. It was believed that one-day building sized computers would predict the weather. So much for that! Some scientists thought that Heisenberg's theory was a challenge to the scientific community. Papers were regularly being published that contained "thought experiments" trying to prove Heisenberg wrong. Even Einstein got into the fray. However, the most famous thought experiment proposed to discredit the uncertainty principle in fact only proved how weird the reality of it really was.

## DEAD... OR ALIVE?

Austrian scientist Erwin Schrödinger tried to show how silly a concept quantum mechanics was. No one thought to tell him how silly a first name Erwin is.

In case you haven't picked it up yet, nothing is real, according to quantum mechanics, which is not observed. Besides the inability to measure the momentum and position of subatomic particles, the other revelation of the uncertainty principle was the effect of consciousness on reality. See... I told you it would get weird!

The effect of human consciousness on reality becomes evident when you use a quantum event (subatomic-sized interactions) to determine the outcome of acroscopic events (people-sized interactions). This is where Schrödinger's "cat in a box" experiment comes into play.

> Imagine - if you will, a cat in a box,
> Secure on all sides with four silver locks.
> Every side of the box is completely opaque.
> Nor could you hear what's inside for the experiment's sake.

Whoa! The ghost of Dr. Seuss momentarily possessed me! Um, so anyway... Also inside the box is a vial of poison placed beneath a delicately balanced hammer. The hammer is connected to mechanism that is connected to a Geiger counter. The Geiger counter is right above a radioactive element with a 50/50 percent chance of decaying within a certain time period. If the Geiger counter detects the decay it will activate the mechanism that will drop the hammer and smash the vial of poison. If it doesn't detect the decay, Morris will live to father more kittens. Also, PETA might be more lenient on your lawsuit. Nah.

**"Quantum theory shows that every object exists in all possible states until the object is measured or simply observed."**

Now, it gets really weird. In order to find out what happened to poor Morris we have to open the box. But before we open the box we can speculate. All the apparatus was internal. We cannot see the hammer, vial or cat. It was sound proofed too so we couldn't hear the vial breaking or Morris' last "meow" or sigh of relief. However, Morris was able to breathe thanks to a previously unmentioned oxygen supply so we cannot suppose he asphyxiated. So what do we speculate about our unfortunate (either way, he's part of an awfully nasty lab experiment) feline friend - Dead or Alive? How about – both! Until we open that box Morris exists in a flux of existence. He is both dead and alive at the same time! No, I do not mean "the kitty that walks at midnight". He exists in two realities simultaneously until someone opens the box or what is known as a "*super positioned state*". In one reality he will once again know the joy of toy mice and kitty litter and in the other reality, well - he is litter. Only by opening the box can you force one reality to take president over the other – through conscious observation! Schrödinger himself thought this was ridiculous, but repeated experiments over the years have shown the theory to be quite solid. Quantum theory shows that every object exists in all possible states until the object is measured or simply observed. The moon has Jackie Gleason's face on it until you look up and prove it does not - so far, so good on that one.

Another implication of these facts is that you cannot measure or observe anything without changing it. Not just sub-atomic particles – anything! When a duck hunter peeks over the brush to view his prey, he has, through his observation, changed the conditions of the environment.

Photons enter your eye and are reflected off the retina back into the environment, which influence other photons and other particles that would not have otherwise been influenced by your presence! Your warm breath will excite the molecules in the air and increase the air temperature. Your will also draw mosquitoes to the carbon dioxide you exhale if you are outside in the warmer months of the year. Oh, and of course you will be consciously forcing the outcome of different states of reality by your mere presence. Theoretically, such small changes can cause large-scale changes to occur. This is the nature of Chaos Theory. It has been speculated that a butterfly in China can flap its wings and cause a hurricane in the Gulf of Mexico (that's why you should always buy American – even butterflies in other countries don't like us). This is called the Butterfly Effect (no, I didn't just make that up and it is not just the name of a really bad time travel movie). In one of science's more holistic aspects it states, for the most part, everything influences everything else.

So you see – if you want to exist in the universe you have to obey its rules. No matter what a ghost is – if it influences physical reality, it will influence the environment in some way. Now, remember what you have learned in the past few paragraphs. It will be important later when we talk about psychics, poltergeists and sensitives.

## MEMORY POSSESSION

Have you ever heard of ghost story where a guy walks down a flight of stairs and suddenly feels an icy hand give him a shove? How about when someone feels the sensation of a cold breath down the back of his or her neck? Did you ever walk into a room and have a feeling of dread, sadness and/or some other emotional response? Many haunted locations have areas in them that have brought about human experiences like these. Are these ghosts or the effects of ghosts? Is that a specter touching your arm? Is that the ghost of the living past giving you a shove or breathing on your neck? On the other hand, maybe you're being possessed!

Now I am not saying there is a Linda Blair thing going on here. There are no demons in this theory or even ghosts necessarily. What I am proposing is something I like to call memory possession. Is a ghost pushing you down the stairs or are you reliving the sensation of someone else being pushed down the stairs? Ah! Now that's an interesting spin isn't it?

Many experienced ghost investigators agree that there exists a phenomenon called a residual or replay haunting (as we mentioned earlier in case you're just "flipping in"). As defined in the Glossary:

**Residual Haunting**: probably the most common type of haunting; this is best described as an imprint on the environment; a moment in time, burnt onto the surroundings of a specific location; playing out roles and situations over and over again for centuries at a time; most researchers compare this to a looped video that repeats itself forever; in these cases you might hear footsteps and other strange noises; however, if you see the event being played out, you will not be able to interfere; the "ghosts" here are not conscious of their surroundings; they may not be sentient.

In a residual haunting the ghosts are not necessarily conscious beings, merely an imprint that has somehow managed to make an impression on the environment so that events of the past repeat themselves over and over again. What if those imprints were so strong that, not only could you see these events and actions played out, but you could also experience the events as a participant? You are literally possessed by the events of the past. Most of the time this is manifested as a sensation like that of an icy hand on the arm or powerful emotions that emanate to the very core of your being. Some who have experienced the strong emotions of a haunting will weep uncontrollably or become angry and confrontational. In extreme circumstances they will even, over time, change in character. Others have claimed they were a person in the past for a few moments and could even see a battle take place as a soldier on the field. That's silly though. Memory possession? Nothing like that exists in the scientific or medical fields after all. Bah! ...Oh, wait a minute!

It is a fact in the field of medicine that some recipients of organ or limb transplants have acquired the memories of the previous owner without knowing any data on the previous organ/limb owner! Evidence exists of there being atomic systemic memory, molecular systemic memory and cellular systemic memory. It is called: *electromagnetic resonance in regard to systemic cellular memory*. In these cases donor recipients will acquire new tastes and personality traits as well as unfamiliar memories and/or nightmares. The 1997 book titled A Change of Heart: A memoir of Claire Sylvia by Claire Sylvia and William Novak documents such a case. The true-life story tells the tale of a woman who's appetites and fashions change after receiving a new heart and lung. A health nut, Sylvia suddenly found herself craving KFC. The donor was found with the Colonel's special recipe nuggets in his pockets. In another incident a young black violinist dies in a drive-by shooting. His heart goes to a 47 year-old white construction worker who suddenly finds he loves listening to classical music. Some people who receive transplants from those of the opposite sex will actually change sexual preferences!

One of the most famous instances of this phenomenon is that of a young boy who kept experiencing nightmares involving a man who would chase him and then try to kill him. It turns out that the previous owner of his "new" heart was murdered by the man in his dreams. Later, a description given by the boy helped find the murderer!

Some medical researchers believe that information can be sent electromagnetically between the brain and the nerve endings at the heart. Through electromagnetic resonance information from the donor is sent to the recipient's brain.

Could this explain what happens in residual hauntings? Could an electromagnetic signature be imprinted on the environment? In some cases, maybe, the room is the tape and we are the tape players.

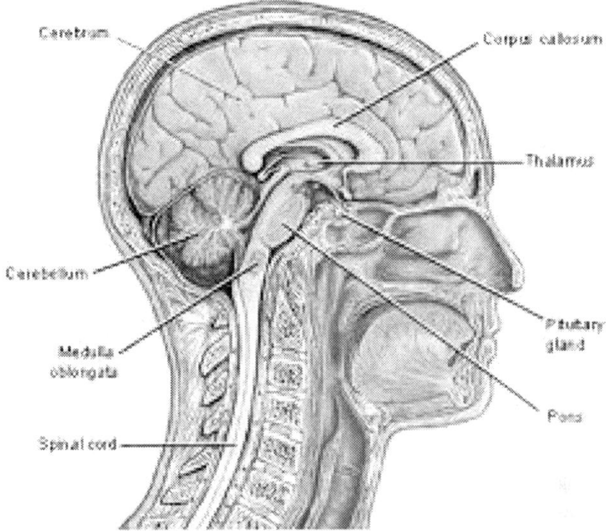


*Systems Theory* is a field of study that covers several scientific fields on the abstract organization of phenomena, regardless of their substance, type, or when or where they exist. It investigates both the principles common to all complex entities, and the models that can be used to describe them. Researchers in the 1940s were the first to seriously suggest that all systems based in reality are open and, interact with, their environments causing changes in both. Dynamical energy systems theory suggests that all dynamical systems store information and energy to various degrees. All I can think of is a bunch of nerds in tie dyed lab coats sitting around existentially describing Karma. "Dude, Dr. McKenzie looks like Buddha!"

Anyway, an area (any area, albeit a room, house, battlefield, etc.) can acquire an electromagnetic resonance (EMR). If this EMR is on the same, or close to the same, wavelength and frequency as that of the human brain, then perhaps they can influence the electrically stimulated proteins of the human brain that store memory. (Okay, now read that over three more times so you got it, all right?) Under the right circumstances the EMR of an area can overlap memories stored in the brain's synapses. If this were true than that would certainly explain my memory possession theory. I wonder though, could it explain other haunting phenomena as well?

## EMF FIELDS AND THE DEAD

Gravity - most people think it's pretty strong. "Do you understand the gravity of the situation?" That is supposed to imply the seriousness of a given situation as if what could be more serious.

Gravity can kill after all. Fall out of an airplane and you are in big trouble without a parachute buddy. How strong is it really though? What would you say if I told you that it's the weakest of the four forces? Think about it. The Earth weighs about 5.972 sextillion (5,972,000,000,000,000,000,000) metric tons. All that mass and all you have to do is put a refrigerator magnet over a paper clip and ta-da: gravity is defied.

Now electromagnetism, there's a powerful force. It's everywhere. It's around you and inside of you. You even emit it. Your cell phone, your car, your TV and your CD player all put out electromagnetic waves. The computer I am typing this on and the coffee maker keeping me awake both put out electromagnetic waves. They are even coming from outer space! It's everywhere! Don't worry though, you're use to it. The earth puts off more electromagnetism than those power lines over your house. You're not going to get a tumor from your cell phone either. Oh, and those bracelets that claim to heal you because they use electromagnetism? Uh-uh, isn't going to happen. Electromagnetism is the bond that keeps your soda carbonated and your molecules together. Appreciate it for what it is.

So, do ghosts give off electromagnetic fields (EMF)? Maybe...

I am still not sure if ghosts actually emit electromagnetic waves. However the theory I, and many other ghost researchers, are working on is that they may be electromagnetic waves. Actually, I am suggesting that they are some sort of electromagnetic resonance or EMR. Now, this theory may possibly explain memory possession and residual hauntings to some degree, but what about classic hauntings?

From the Glossary:

**Classic Haunting:** also called an "Intelligent Haunting" or "Traditional Haunting"; rare, a sentient spirit that can manifest itself into an apparition and communicate with the living; the ghost responds to outside stimuli like questions and statements; it can be friendly or hostile and will let you know the difference; they are sometimes capable of opening and closing doors and windows and moving objects like furniture around.

Here is where the theory gets really complicated! Wait! Don't close the book yet! You're smart you can keep up.

Perhaps in the right environment, when someone passes on (you know, drops dead), they can leave an imprint on the area in question in the form of an EMR. Our brains mostly pick up this imprint as a repeating pattern. We may feel strong emotions, experience flashbacks, and feel the memory of someone being pushed or shoved. We may even see events from the past being played out in front of us. If the sensation is strong enough, we can actually experience the events of the past as if we were eyewitnesses. Smells, sights and sounds are all clear to us as if it were happening now. However, like Turner Classic Movies, it's the same thing over and over. In the case of an intelligent haunting, perhaps more than an imprint is left behind. How about an entire copy?

Inside a tape recorder are two electromagnets that receive a signal from a microphone and translate the signal into a magnetic flux (a measure of the strength of a magnetic field over a given area) that is "remembered" on one half of the tape as a stereo audio signal when it spools by at 4.76 cm per second. When you make a copy of a tape for a friend (You pirate! I'm calling the FCC!), you are repeating the magnetic flux from one tape onto another. Maybe when the conditions are right not only can the events of the past be saved into an area via EMR, but a copy of a person's mind! Like copying a computer hard-drive, the memories that make up the human consciousness can survive after death! However, this would be very rare indeed. Also, the ability to gain additional memories for an EMR ghost would be impaired. They may be capable enough to answer questions in an EVP experiment, but unable to remember it later. Once dead, your ghost would be a copy of you as you were at the moment of death, never changing or evolving or learning. As a ghost you can interact with your environment but never remember any new experiences. You would be PLAY ONLY, never RECORD. This would explain why a civil war era ghost never asks what rap music is. I guess it's not so bad after all.

But what about cases in which objects are physically moved? Now, I imagine that in most cases when someone says that the ghost keeps hiding their keys, the resident homeowner is actually losing the keys and blaming it on the poor ghost in the house. However, reports of floating objects and the like are too numerous to dismiss. An electromagnetic field is the field of force associated with electric charge in motion. It has both electric and magnetic components and contains a definite amount of electromagnetic energy. If acted upon by a, currently unknown, form of EMR reactions, perhaps some of the energy can be converted into kinetic energy (energy possessed by a body in motion) and be released in the form of an object being tossed or moved about. Since we are only speculating here, perhaps the ghost can "manifest" a reproduction of the electromagnetic field that all solid matter uses to be, well - Solid. This could be how some ghosts are capable of being photographed and seem to lift objects on their own, possessing only a "shell" that looks like the ghost as it did in life, but containing no organs or muscles. This would explain why some ghosts appear transparent or "mist-like". A "residual self image" of the ghost in question that may or may not be self (i.e. the ghost) generated. Now, imagine yourself for a moment. Picture yourself as someone else might see you. Are you picturing your whole self? If you didn't, maybe some ghosts can't or won't either. Hence, the ghosts who appear to have no legs!

## CONSCIOUSNESS SURVIVAL

The concept that consciousness can survive bodily death is a controversial subject of course. The term used by many parapsychologists, as you might have guessed, is "*consciousness survival*" as apposed to ghosts. Personally, I believe in a combination of factors contribute to hauntings. That, at the moment of death, the consciousness of a human being can be imprinted on the geography of the location they die in or, through psychic projection, imprint themselves onto another location. I am sure there would be lots of mitigating factors. The subject themselves, the physical make-up of the location being projected upon and atmospheric conditions may all be factors. If this theory is correct then sometimes, there would be conditions that are not quite right. You would only get parts of the whole consciousness sometimes. This theory could explain both replay hauntings and intelligent hauntings.

I created graphs to illustrate this concept. Like an interrupted download from the internet, you might only get a level of residual information and only some aspects of the personality. Level One characterizes an *emotional residual haunting* or *imprint*. When a person walks into a room that has an emotional residual haunting they may be overwhelmed by an emotion. Usually the emotion is negative (such as anger, melancholy and fear). Turns out, most people, not happy about dying!

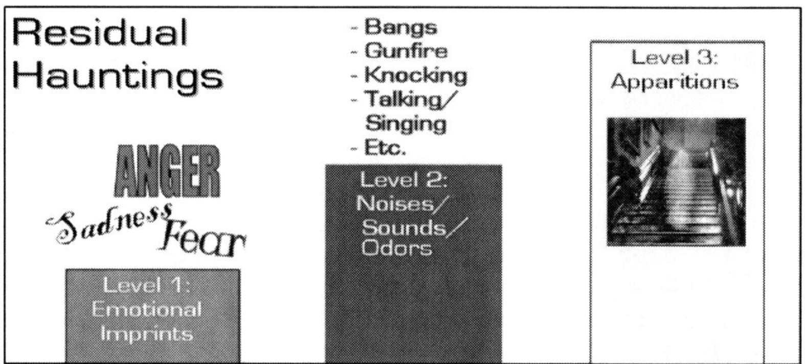


Level two involves noises, sounds and odors. Level Two on the Residual Scale is a combination of information combined with stored energy. Imagine you are in the battlefields of Antietam, you catch the scent of gunpowder in the air, you might hear rifle fire and the ground tremble beneath you, and finally, you might feel the tremble of cannon fire beneath your feet.

Level Three on the Residual Scale is a combination of more information combined with even more stored energy. Here you would have actual visual confirmation of the ghost. Whether they are actually appearing physically in front of you or just in your mind, I cannot say. The appearance of an apparition is extremely rare due to so many variables being play. Every aspect of the environment would have to be just right. Level Three is also the ghost many people think walk through walls. The "ghost", not being aware anything, much less construction practices, would appear to walk through the wall.

In the cases of possible intelligent hauntings, you would have to have an almost perfect set of conditions. Perfect environmental conditions, the perfect human subject and other unknown factors. The difference between the residual and intelligent hauntings is that intelligent hauntings would have some level of communicative abilities. I genuinely believe that this level would be limited. Although I do believe in the reality of ghosts, hauntings and psychic phenomena, I am forced to acknowledge their limitations as far as experimentally reproducing and therefore scientifically establishing their existence. To establish an intelligent haunting, you would have to record signs of two communication with the the intelligence you are trying to contact. That is, the "ghost" would have to view and acknowledge changes in their environment. For example, if you recorded a disembodied voice commenting on your hat's symbolism (in my case, a big white "O" on an orange background for the Baltimore Orioles), then that would show true intelligence. There is the possibility that you may instead be dealing with a *stimulation activated residual imprint*. EVP recordings such as "get out" does not mean you are dealing with a disagreeable entity. Nor does a response like "yes" to the question, "is there anyone here". Stored imprints can be misdiagnosed as intelligence very easily. Triggered responses are much more common than true intelligent answers. What do you need to play a VHS tape? A VCR! What do you need to watch a DVD? A DVD player. What do you need to play back stored human memories and/or personality traits? How about – our

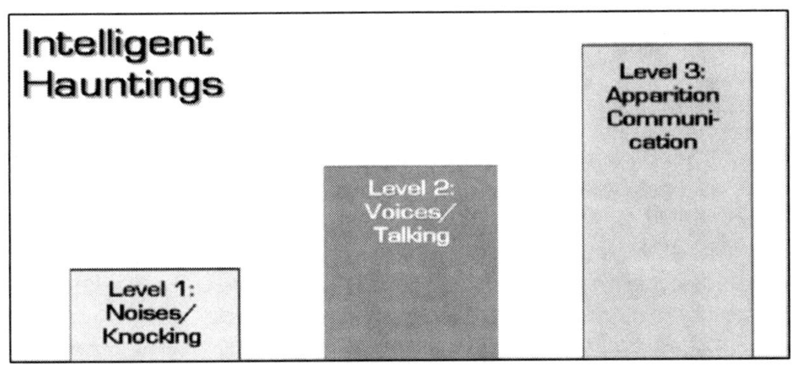

minds!

The three levels of an intelligent haunting include Level One, where the noises and knocking may indicate communication. For example, the investigator might ask, "tap once if you are content with us being here, twice if you are not". Level Two includes voices in which a disembodied voice would answer instead of knocking. Level Three, and this is beyond rare, would include an apparitional appearance. You are more likely to get his by lightning and then eaten by a shark to have this happen to you.

Personally, I think that too many would-be paranormal researchers are taking the more romanticized approach to ghosts and psi phenomenon. They want to believe that ghosts are souls trapped on Earth with unfinished business. Besides the obvious, that ghosts would have to be pretty stupid to haunt a house for nine-hundred hundred years and never figure out their unfinished business, there are other holes in this theory. One, you will have to accept that there are supernatural "rules" that govern the departed, like the *Handbook for the Recently Deceased* in the film *Beetlejuice*.

Ghost haunt houses because that's what ghosts do. They are not allowed to reveal themselves as ghosts of course. Nor are they allowed to reveal the existence of ghosts to the world. To accept this theory, you must accept the existence of magic and that spells and incantations can affect ghosts.

Truth be told, if ghosts acted like many mediums and psychics on TV said they do, we probably would have better proof that they exist. When a ghost "manifests" in any way, I highly doubt they do it with any thought toward making themselves appear. I do not think they play tricks or have messages for people (at least not in cases of hauntings). However, if you think a loved one is there with you or watching over you after a recent death, I do believe you. I just think that you are not dealing, in that case what is generally thought of as ghosts. Maybe they are stopping by one last time before moving on. I am not denying the existence of the soul, but I do truly believe the soul is not what a ghost and/or haunting is.

## CLEARING GHOSTS

Ever seen someone clear a house of ghosts before? On TV perhaps, or, if you are a ghost hunter or paranormal investigator, you may have seen such a clearing in person. It doesn't matter how it was done. Smudging, incantations, prayers, electromagnetic broadcasting, etc. A medium, shaman, priest or ghost hunter performs the clearing through some procedural mechanisms and, supposedly, the house is "cleared". No more ghosts. Is this true?

I am curious, have you ever heard of house being cleared in

which someone had returned to the house to confirm said clearing? Probably not. Not even a month later? Definitely not a year, five years or ten years later. Are these people sure they did anything? Did they "pause" the hauntings or actually stop it? I will discuss possible clearing techniques later in this book, but I am not going to guarantee any of them will in fact work.

# CHAPTER THREE: PSI STUDIES - UNDERSTANDING PSYCHIC PHENOMENA

> Here's something to think about: How come you never see a headline like 'Psychic Wins Lottery'?
> - Jay Leno

Before I begin talking about psychics I want to talk about "oogey-boogey" terminology. I define oogey-boogey terminology thusly: terms that are meant to describe a phenomenon but have no meaning or further definition themselves. Ghost is an oogey-boogey term. We do not know what ghosts are so it is a paranormal study as opposed to a scientific study. Thunder was something to be awed at by our ancient ancestors and was once an oogey-boogey term until we learned that thunder is side-effect of lightning. It is very important to not use oogey-boogey terms to define oogey-boogey things. However, sometimes oogey-boogey terms are the best thing to describe soemthing when we have no choice. For example, some people think that ghosts are psycho-kinetic in origin. Since we do not know what psycho-kinesis is, we are using an oogey-boogey term to describe an oogey-boogey thing.

## WHAT IS PSI?

As I have mentioned before, we have used sensitives in investigations in the past. These are people that I have learned to trust and believe in and some of whom I call friends. I couldn't tell you their names though. Not because I don't remember them (some friend!) but because they chose to remain anonymous. Most true sensitives do. It's the flamboyant "I feel the soul of U.S. Grant" psychics that I have trouble believing. Not that all public "out of the closet" psychics aren't genuine; it's just that I have seen too many people taken advantage of by charlatans. Most of the sensitives I have come in contact with that seem to exhibit real paranormal abilities are not that open to discussing them. So, assuming that the sensitives I believe are actually gifted with something akin to ESP are real, how is that possible?

It is well known in the medical community that some people evidently exhibit an over-sensitivity to electricity and electromagnetic fields (EMF). This is sometimes called *electric hypersensitivity*. Due to the risk of creating paranormal hypochondriacs (or *para*chondriacs), I am going to tell the readers that no doctor will diagnose you with electric hypersensitivity since there is not nearly enough information available on it and certainly not enough funding. Why some people are electrically hypersensitive is still unknown.

Those who apparently have electric hypersensitivity will get sick when in close proximity to cell phone towers, power lines, fuse and circuit breaker power boxes, CRT monitors, etc. Victims may have dermatological problems such as dry and itchy skin. Other problems include dizziness, fatigue, headache, difficulties in concentration, memory problems, anxiety, depression, etc., respiratory problems (difficult breathing), gastrointestinal symptoms, eye and vision symptoms, palpitations, and so on. As someone who is around electronics all the time I couldn't imagine having an illness that would make me sick to be near my wonderful gadgets! Gasp!

A few of the sensitives I have met have exhibited symptoms of electric hypersensitivity. They do indeed get sick and/or uncomfortable around strong electrical and electromagnetic fields. At a location the Baltimore Society for Paranormal Research investigated in the summer of 2004 the sensitive on the team had headaches and dizzy spells every time we walked through a certain area between the kitchen and the living room. Now there was no way this person could have known this, but there was a large number of power lines and boxes on the wall outside supplying the apartment complex we were at. We didn't find out until we started using our EMF meters and picked up the unusual fields present in that area. Also, the power lines were in the back of complex and we came in the front. None of the investigative team had been there before that night. Is it possible that some people may be more susceptible to ghosts and hauntings in the same way that some people are susceptible to EMF and electrical fields? Perhaps sensitives are like antennas for memory possessions. Due to their hypersensitivity they can pick up the electromagnetic resonance of events from the past. This is of course, just another theory.

Psi doesn't just involve the ability to see and feel ghosts of course. Many parapsychologists don't even study or acknowledge this aspect of ESP. What they do study is thepreviously mentioned: clairvoyance – the ability to acquire information directly from the environment, telepathy – the ability to read minds or communication with others through mind-to-mind contact and precognition – the ability to predict future events and outcomes. If we are really going to try to understand how some people are able to communicate with ghosts to the degree that they can reveal unknown (at least to the sensitive in question) information about the past (or retrocognition without the help of ghosts) and/or location being investigated then we should really look into these other aspects of Extra-Sensory Perception.

So, forget about the movie Scanners. Super-powerful psychics in real life have exploded no heads, at least as far as I know. However, clairvoyance has been studied and researched enough to suggest that at least that much is possible. The word clairvoyance comes from the French "clear seeing". It is sometimes called the "second sight". It is the ability to see things as they happen from a distance and without Superman's telescopic and x-ray vision. Remember the Time-Life Books commercials in the '80's for Mysteries of the Unknown? There was one where the narrator describes a woman who feels a sharp pain in her hand and hundreds of miles away her daughter burns her hand. Coincidence? I think not.

Was the mother of the burn victim feeling the sensation of her daughter's burn or was she reading her mind. Some parapsychologists do not differentiate between what is clairvoyance and telepathy (the ability to read minds). They prefer the term General ESP or GESP. So how can either be possible anyway? Perhaps they are subconsciously really good at chess? Well, chess as metaphor anyway. To know the rules of chess is not enough to be good at it. You have to be able to predict your opponent's next move. Some excellent chess players can predict an opponent's next few moves. Sometimes as many as ten moves in advance or more! Is it possible that that some people are subconsciously putting together the outcome of events? Sometimes they get the information at the same time as an event happens and sometimes before. For every possible outcome that occurs in their lives they are able to predict the outcome of every 50/50 chance. But there are other possibilities.

Now we come to precognition. Many have heard the report of the parapsychologist who was always on time for his appointments. He always rushed to get to the airport and always made sure everything was ready in advance. Then one day he took his time. He didn't know why this time he decided to take it easy. He was late getting to the airport that one day and missed the airplane. Later, the plane crashed and some of his colleagues were killed with all the other passengers onboard. Was he just lucky?

A few scientists believe that the only reason we go forward in time is because our brains are hardwired for "forward only". What if, sometimes, memory possession works both ways? What if information can travel from the future or a possible future in the form of magnetic resonance that can register in the minds of certain individuals? But, what if certain individuals create their own futures? There is also Quantum Entanglement.

## SPOOKY ACTION AT A DISTANCE

Einstein called it "spooky action at a distance". Two subatomic particles are created simultaneously during radioactive decay. One particle is created in an "up spin" direction and the other in a "down spin" direction (as the name suggests, *spin* was originally conceived as the rotation of a particle around some axis). Let's say that Barry takes the up particle to San Francisco and Russ takes the down particle to Alpha Centauri, a binary star system that is 4.24 light years from our Sun. If Barry reverses the spin of his particle to down, Russ' particle would instantaneously spin up despite the significant cosmic distance. Even though it would normally take more than 4 years to get there, the information would defy the speed of light.

The question I want to know, as well as many other parapsychologists, is – can people become entangled? Is that what telepathy is?

Remember in a previous chapter we discussed how according to the Heisenberg Uncertainty Principle we influence reality through observation? I don't know, but what if some people can pick and choose, on a subconscious level certain outcomes? What if they could influence probability? They didn't predict the outcome of a dice roll - they made it happen! There exists a great deal of evidence (hundreds of Parapsychological experiments) to suggest that human beings can influence probability. It is possible that a human can consciously force a random state of reality into a state that favors a specific desire and/or chosen outcome.

Finally, we come to hyperspace. No, we're not jumping in the Millennium Falcon for a trip to the Death Star. We're going to discuss the possibility of higher dimensions again. Perhaps some people are more open to higher dimensions than others. These persons would have a more open mind than most people and wouldn't be quite so hardwired for three or four dimensional thought. Time itself is thought to be the fourth dimension. Can some people see beyond three dimensions? Can they "remember" the future like we remember the past? Perhaps, perhaps, perhaps. More research is definitely needed.

# POLTERGEISTS, THE REAL-LIFE "ENTITY" AND A GHOST NAMED "PHILLIP"

Poltergeist Agent (PA): Phenomena usually surrounding a young child, which is usually a girl; the P.A. (the child) is almost always around when the poltergeist activity occurs; this usually involves objects being thrown around when there is no one around, unexplainable tapping and scratching noises and objects disappearing and reappearing hours, days or weeks later; in worst-case scenarios there can be injuries to human beings from thrown objects and scratches appearing on the flesh of the P.A.; fires are also known to occur in the worst cases - sometimes with catastrophic results.

Many parapsychologists today do not use the term poltergeist or poltergeist agent. They prefer recurrent spontaneous psychokinesis or RSPK. Why can't they just keep it simple? A poltergeist phenomenon is not ghost related at all. Unlike cases of hauntings (which can last for decades if not centuries) poltergeist phenomena doesn't last for very long. As of 1991 in half of all the hundreds of cases recorded half lasted less than two months with most of those lasting only a few weeks. In most of these cases the activity surrounds an adolescent who seems to be under psychological stress.

In 1967 Germany an 18-year-old secretary named Annemarie Schneider seemed to be the focus of a major poltergeist outbreak at the offices of the lawyer she worked for. The local electrical company was at a loss to explain major electrical disturbances throughout the building. Loud bangs and power outages wreaked havoc around the office. Ceiling lamps would sway back and forth, sometimes violently. Light bulbs exploded and electrical fuses blew for no apparent reason. Later when poltergeist investigator Professor Hans Bender of the University of Freiburg visited the phenomena increased! He noted filing cabinets weighing more than 400 lbs moved from the wall and drawers would open by themselves. Only when Annemarie started at another job did the disturbances cease.

In California there is the case of Renee Waters who her friends called "the fuse blower". Often after being irritated or following the experience of a crowded train journey Renee would experience extreme electric disturbances. She could not even replace a light-bulb without causing it to blow. Many times she could not operate devices like the television or radio unless she asked one of her roommates for assistance. In one very extreme circumstance at her place of employment she became very annoyed by a co-worker. The lights in the space they were standing shut off and when they tried the switch it was hot to the touch. Suffice to say the maintenance worker on duty was befuddled as to the cause.

More recently in 1984 there was a case of a poltergeist agent in Columbus, Ohio. John and Joan Resch were two remarkable people. By 1983 they had helped over 250 disturbed and homeless foster children! On any given day the house would have in it: John and Joan Resch, their son Craig, their adopted daughter Tina (pictured) and maybe four or more foster kids.

The strange things that started happening in the Resch household began with all the lights in the household turning themselves off. All of them, all at once! An electrician was called in and he couldn't find anything wrong at all. It would get weirder.

Objects like clocks, candlesticks and pictures would leave their spots and fly through the air. Knives would fling themselves from their drawers and wine glasses would shatter. The shower would start running on its own and eggs would pop out of their carton and shoot up at the ceiling. Witnesses saw objects from other rooms fly into a room Tina was sitting in and smack into her. It quickly became obvious that Tina was the "focus" of this particular poltergeist phenomenon.

Tina was a very troubled young lady. She was abandoned shortly after her birth in 1969. She was often misunderstood by classmates and teachers due to what might have been attention deficit disorder. After she was beaten badly by school bullies and tied up and left in the school yard on one occasion Joan Resch decided that perhaps home schooling was best for her.

After a botched exorcism didn't work the Resch's were at their wits end. They started referring to the strange phenomena as "The Force". The house was a disaster zone from all the activity. Not just poltergeist activity either! By this time the place was full of reporters, policemen and firemen. One of these reporters would take a photo that would bring this story into national attention.

The picture appeared to show a phone fly on its own across Tina's lap. All the media attention piqued the interest of parapsychologist William Roll. Roll would become absolutely certain that this was a case of recurrent spontaneous psychokinesis or RSPK.

Later however Tina would be caught by a video camera that was left on by accident tugging a lamp cord to make the lamp appear to fly at her. Despite dozens of eyewitness accounts by many people who had nothing to gain by lying, skeptics would use the video data as a "smoking gun" to prove the whole thing was a hoax. Tina said she only started faking things to get the reporters out of the house. However, the damage was done.

The stress that seemed to have created the poltergeist focus in the first place never seemed to leave Tina's frail psyche even though the activity did. In 1994, at the age of 23, she was sentenced to life plus twenty for murdering her three-year-old daughter.

In the now famous "entity case" that took place in 1974 a poor downtrodden woman named Doris Bither and her four children experienced horrendous events at the hands of what appear to be Asian-looking phantoms. Events that included the violent rapes of Doris Bither herself! This well documented case involved several paranormal investigators including Dr. Barry Taff and colleague Kerry Gaynor from UCLA. While having lunch and discussing paranormal phenomena at a bookstore they were approached by a woman who overheard their conversation. Her name was Doris Bither.

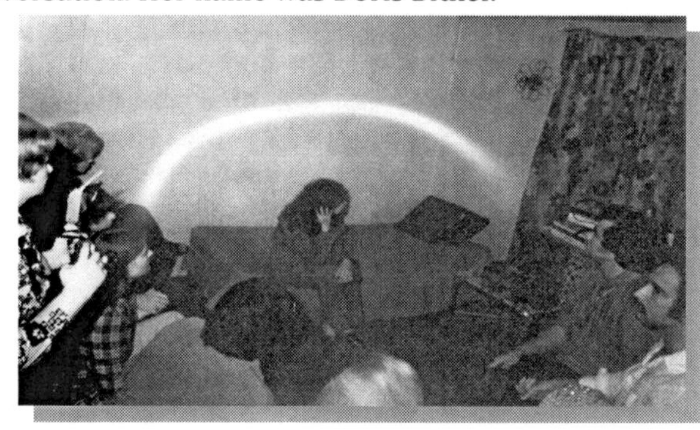

During the subsequent investigation over 30 researchers crowded themselves into Doris Bither's small squalid home as she tried to incite the "spirits" into action. Soon afterward a swirling green mist appeared and began surrounding the room and eventually formed a male figure that caused one of the investigators to faint away. They actually took pictures of the swirling lights that appeared. Arcs of light appeared to hover in the room.

Could Doris and/or her children cause all this? Could the entities witnessed in fact be subconscious manifestations of Doris' own fears of rape and xenophobia?

Now you have to wonder how far you can take the concept of artificially created ghosts or "entities", subconscious or otherwise. Well, in 1972 members of the Toronto Society for Psychical Research and parapsychologists A.R.G. Owen and Iris M. Owen set out to create their own ghost! It would seem they accomplished this task without any of the members having any obvious paranormal sensitivity or psychic ability.

To begin this imaginative new experiment they needed to create a history for their ghostly Frankenstein's Monster. They named him "Philip", that is "Philip Aylesford". Philip had an elaborate history too:

- Born Philip Aylesford in 1624
- Joined the military at 15.
- Fought in the English Civil War between 1639 and 1640.
- Was knighted in 1640.
- Philip became friends with Prince Charles the first.
- He then worked as a secret agent for Charles the second.
- He knew Oliver Cromwell, the infamous English politician and soldier.

He was married but had an affair with a gypsy. When his wife found out about the affair she accused the gypsy of witchcraft and had her burned at the stake. Philip could have intervened, but didn't. He killed himself out of guilt in 1654 at the age of 30. What a life, huh?

They began having "séances" and tried to manifest an apparition through vivid concentration. Although some of the members claimed to feel a presence, nothing happened for months. They began table tipping experiments bases on research done by British psychologist Kenneth J. Batcheldor. Batcheldor believed that table tipping was a form of telekinesis manifested from the belief of those present in séances and was not in fact "ghosts".

After three or four tries they began to feel vibrations on the table. After awhile the vibrations became taps and knocks and the table moved beneath their hands. A member of the team asked out loud if Philip had done the knocking and there was a loud rap that answered. Using "one tap" for yes and "two taps" for no the team was able to converse with their creation. It is interesting to note that the "spirit" could not answer questions outside of the history that was created for him.

The "haunting" escalated when Philip began greeting latecomers to the séances by moving the table toward them and sometime he'd even trap a team member in the corner with the table. He even tapped to the beat of music from time to time.

Communication with Philip continued for several years. Attempts were made to record Philip using EVP that were somewhat successful. They thought they heard a lot of whispering with some clear responses. Interest in Philip finally waned in 1977 when no further progress was made in understanding the mechanics of the phenomena.

So, what is Psi? What is PK? Is it previously unknown form of energy or are the persons involved in these events manipulating reality and/or existing energy fields? There are more questions than answers right now and it might be a long time before we see any real answers.

Much more research and study is need by newer and fresher investigators.

## PSI TEST

I created a test not too long ago based on testing done by parapsychologists. It is an HTML based test on the Baltimore Society for Paranormal Research website and can be found at http://www.ghostscience.net. On the site is a random number generator composed of a single integer. According to the laws of averages when you refresh your browser you have a 50/50 chance of getting a 1 or a 0. Theoretically, if you refreshed your browser 100 times you should get approximately 50 zeros and 50 ones. Give or take only a few. 1000 refreshes should get you 500 zeros and 500 ones with a slightly larger margin of error.

It is an experiment in micro-PK to see if you can affect the outcome of the integer. Take a piece of paper, preferably a large one, put it to the side. Now what you need to do is focus on 1 or 0. Focus as hard as you can. Then start refreshing your browser. Every time you refresh the browser, score your paper. If you score your paper 10 times it should look like this:

So, one score for every refresh. Got it? Above each group of scores write the number of times your chosen number came up. For example: If your chosen number was 0 and 0 came up five times out of ten as odds are they will, it may look like this:

Suffice to say, if you are truly psychic, then you should beat the 50/50 odds with a high margin. For example: If you chose 0 and 0 came up 60% of the time, you may be powerfully psychic or at least unusually lucky. Or you can simply flip a coin a bunch of times.

## DO YOU SEE DEAD PEOPLE?

So you have a team of ghost hunters or you are on a team of ghost hunters. If you do not already have someone who claims to be a sensitive on your team, someone will come along. Trust me. As Agent Smith told Neo “it is inevitability”. But how do you tell a real sensitive from a fraud or someone who exaggerates his or her talents? Well, it depends on whether you want to be taken seriously or not.

I have come across three disturbing situations when it comes to team sensitives:

- The team has on it a sensitive that is a fraud or exaggerates his/her abilities and doesn't care to do anything about it.
- The team has on it a sensitive that is a fraud or exaggerates his/her abilities and exploits their flamboyant personality for personal gain (i.e. media coverage, etc.).
- The team has on it a sensitive that is a fraud or exaggerates his/her abilities and the team relies completely on this person since they do not know any better.

So how do you know any better? How do you decide if the person who says they are a sensitive is a sensitive? Well, it's not easy, but I'll give you some hints.

- Are they very flamboyant? Look for the clichés! Do they wonder around saying they feel the presence of famous historical figures or celebrities. "I smell peanut butter and bananas! The King is here!" Do they hyperventilate when a powerful "energy/entity" is present? You have to determine if they are really sick from their over-sensitivity or are they "I want to go home from school early to play video games" sick (i.e. faking it).
- Can they determine real history from a location without previous knowledge? Take them to a place where they don't or couldn't have known the area's history, but you do. See if they can figure out details about names and events by themselves.
- Are they uncreative in their "made-up" histories? I have been on several investigations with other teams that have, possibly, a bad sensitive. With one team their seemed to be an abundance of "Sarahs" around. "I feel the presence of someone named Sarah," she said at one Civil War era location. "Someone is calling to me… Her name is Sarah," she said at a colonial era location. Also, with some there seems to be an abundance of slave ghosts in Civil War era locations. Even in places that history says there were no slaves!

So, how do you spot a real sensitive?

- They are not flamboyant. Most sensitives are nervous about talking about their "gift". You may have to quiz someone who starts acting a little strangely in a haunted location. Sometimes they will not volunteer information unless asked.
- They can reveal details about a location's history in advance of actually knowing. This is almost always a sure sign. If you take someone into an obscure location (i.e. somewhere not mentioned often on the History Channel) how can they know its historical information in advance?
- They have an annoying tendency to wonder off by themselves. Those that I believe are truly sensitive seem to do this all the time. I think it may be because other people sometimes distract and that they don't want people staring at them. They have to be reminded of safety though.

At the *Paranormal Investigators Coalition* we do use sensitives on investigations of ghosts and hauntings. However, we keep their identities private. We do not go around saying, "This is [CENSORED], our team psychic." There are several reasons for this anonymity:

- The media has a tendency to ridicule people who claim to be "psychic". No matter how much you try to claim to the press your group uses the latest in scientific theories to examine the phenomena of ghosts, you will be surprised how much focus will made on your group's sensitive. Then you will be surprised about how much
- Sarcasm makes its way into the final report.
- Ego. There is a risk that the person in question may become too big for his/her britches. Anonymity will help prevent a need to exaggerate to please an audience.
- Discomfort from residential owners or property managers. You are being invited into the homes and property of people who may be scared already. They are probably uncomfortable having a team of paranormal investigators in their house and are possibly hoping you will find a "natural" "non-paranormal" explanation for what's going on. They may be uncomfortable with the idea of their being a psychic on the team. It is best to not even mention it.

There seems to be an increase in the amount of people claiming to be sensitives in the field of ghost research these days. Are we headed into a resurgence of the spiritualist movement? Probably not. It is possible that there are many people out there who have had these "feelings" but have not been aware of what they are until they caught those "ghost shows" on cable. Also, I have little doubt there are persons out there with low self-esteem that are taking advantage of naive new groups of ghost investigators. Just use caution.

## HOAXES

Unless you had been living on another planet during the summer of 2008 then there's no way you can be interested in the paranormal and not know about the Sasquatch excitement that went on. Just in case you were doing the old Klaatu-barada-nikto two-step with ET, I will recount the events for you. Two Georgian men looking for Bigfoot in the woods actually found one. Actually they found the wilderness primate version of road kill. Yes my friends, the legendary ape-man is dead. Well, one of them anyway. According to Matthew Whitton and Rick Dyer there were several Bigfoot (Bigfoots? Bigfeet? Sasquatches?) in the immediate area. They, the rare North American primates, watched as the two men dragged their kin away evidently for fame and fortune. They then proceeded to take their hirsute embellished cadaver to the nearest scientist and forever justified the claims of crypto-zoologists everywhere! Okay, actually they "claimed" they took the poor creature to an undisclosed location and tried, unsuccessfully, to freeze it in ice. You see they used a frost free refrigerator.

So, they tried to freeze the carcass until they figured out what to do. So the story goes and they contact renowned Bigfoot hunter Tom Biscardi. Actually, I am not sure if renown is the right word, perhaps infamous would be better. Biscardi has been involved in a number of Sasquatch hoaxes in the past. His questionable reputation began in the 80s with fake Bigfoot video he tried to market for Ivan Marx, a notorious hoaxer. In 2005 his reputation was further tarnished when he was involved in another Bigfoot scam involving the George Noory Show. On the Noory Show Coast to Coast AM, he claimed he would have a live ape-man that he would reveal via pay-per-view internet streaming video. When the day arrived he claimed that he himself was scammed by those detaining the specimen. So, now he is representing Whitton and Dyer and has created yet another media circus. So, it turned out to be another scam. It is unlikely Biscardi's reputation will survive this time, such as is already.

So, how is this relevant to ghost investigating? This story is very significant in that hoaxes happen all the time in ghost hunting. They probably happen just about every day actually and mostly by nice enough people that would normally never do any harm at all. Some of these people even believe they are not perpetrating a hoax. Many ghost hunting groups claiming to be "scientifically minded" teams have tried to pull the wool over the eyes of the ghost hunting community. They do this using fake EVPs and altered photographs and fabricated videos. Be wary of any group that regularly produces "evidence" that is too good to believe. It probably is! Often times there are logical explanations for evidence they claim is genuinely paranormal that the team leader will ignore. However, the vast majority of hoaxes and fraud in the ghost hunting community is from those claiming supernatural abilities themselves – psychics.

I get criticized a lot for my skeptical approach to psychics, but I can assure you it is justified. Fake mediums have been around since before the Oracle of Delphi. Their heyday however was during that marvelous time in World History known as the Spiritualist Movement. Ah, the good old days, when mediums had to really work for their dishonestly earned money. A psychic usually needed a staff of people to help with her scam, er, show. They had props like trick chairs that helped with rope escapes. They had to make tambourines and trumpets float through the air and play a tune too! This was a lot of work! Today's fake psychics are getting pretty lazy. All they have to do now is point at empty space and say, "I feel the presence of restless spirit". Some of the more dramatic ones will feign illness or act as if possessed. But they never produce ectoplasm out of their orifices anymore.

About a year before this writing I was invited to investigate the home of a popular local celebrity near Baltimore. This individual insisted we come to his/her residence as soon as possible. Evidently the haunting was quite intense. It was also a late Tuesday night and most of my investigators had to work the next day. Suffice to say, I told them the earliest we could make it, unfortunately, was Friday and it was unlikely, due to the history of hauntings, that there was any real threat to the family. Regrettably, my assurances were ignored. The impatient person in question used their considerable media contacts to call upon the services of a nationally known medium. What did the medium say? Well, without even visiting the home, from hundreds of miles away, the medium completely terrified the family by telling them there was a "portal allowing dark forces into the house" and that "they should leave as soon as possible". Wow, I am doing this all wrong! Who needs lugging all this equipment around when I can just "call in" and diagnose a haunting regardless of where it is!

Now don't get me wrong, I believe in psychic ability. I have worked with people I truly believe may be psychic. However, they are few and far between what I normally experience when it comes to "ghost whisperers". Just this past weekend someone told me, "the level of fraud a medium propagates is directly proportional to how much money they charge for their services." There are exceptions to this rule of course. Some ghost hunting "sensitives" fake it for free. These generally consist of very sad individuals indeed. For the most part they are not out to hurt anyone, they just want attention. Some probably are dissatisfied with how their lives turned out. Perhaps they expected to have done bigger and better things by the time they reached "this point" in their lives. Others perhaps have low self esteem and are enthralled with the attention and occasional adoration that they receive when they demonstrate their abilities. I believe that these are majority of the fake psychics out there. Depending on how long the reader has been ghost hunting, you may have met some of these people yourself. Even though, for the most part, they do not intend to cause any harm, they do. They hurt all of us. I usually refrain from criticizing these people out of pity. I feel sorry for them. On the other hand there are people out there that don't deserve pity, but condemnation!

I know a very popular writer in the ghost hunting world, who, a few years ago, never claimed to have any psychic ability at all. Now this person claims to not be able to see ghosts but is able to clear buildings of spirits as well. Nearly pushing sixty this person suddenly gained psychic powers? Perhaps it was a radioactive meteorite or something. This person attacked me as well for wanting to work with a sensitive before assuming their authenticity. Hey, I'm not asking for a background check and urine samples, just a little reassurance. I am supposed to assume that anyone who claims to be psychic is the "real deal". I don't do that for techies!

I know some people are going to read this book and take what they want from it. They are going to skip over the fact that I said I do believe in, and in fact work with, sensitives. I will be admonished for having any doubts whatsoever about anyone. Nevertheless, someone has to say something. The Bigfoot community took a major kick in the butt in the credibility department when the summer 2007 story turned out to be a fraud, which is very unfair of course. Most Sasquatch researchers are very dedicated to the belief that the creature is real. They would never do anything to harm their credibility. Unfortunately, every time someone "pretends" to be a psychic for the cameras, the ghost hunting community takes a hit. People in the crypto crowd like Biscardi only get this kind of press once every few years. We get press like that several times a year and it's really bad at Halloween. Reporters absolutely love making the group sensitive look like a nut-job. The answer to this problem comes in a simple metaphor – "Don't feed the lions!"

Regardless of whatever reason (money, self-esteem, etc.) they are doing what they are doing; those who would fake psychic ability require attention. This is always the case with frauds. Don't give it to them! Establish a policy in your group – there is only one team leader and we are all equal otherwise. Don't give your team members titles like Tech Expert, Lead Photographer or Psychic Investigator for example. Stick with co-captain, administrator, etc. Do not categorize your team members like that since it will single out some members as more "special" than others. If the press asks if you have a psychic on your team, tell them that if you did you would not reveal who they were to avoid them being persecuted by, oh, I don't know, people like the press! If, instead of admiring your decision to promote equality and fairness among your team members, your resident psychic expresses discontent for not highlighting his/her unique gifts, you might have an ego too big for your group of ghost hunters. Here's the point: you are trying to prove that paranormal phenomenon exist, right? If you did that you would be world famous and there is no need to try to become celebrities in the meantime. As more and more teams go "scientific" I see fewer psychics sticking around. Perhaps the ones that do are the real deal. I certainly hope so. As far as the frauds, well, they'll be OK. Many of them are forming psychic exclusive teams and forgoing any science at all.

Ghosts will be proven to exist one day and so will psychics. Perhaps both will be proven at the same time. Perhaps one will be proven before the other. Either way, they both will be proven with science.

# CHAPTER THREE: GHOST TECH AND GHOST HUNTING EQUIPMENT

For a successful technology, reality must take precedence over public relations, for Nature cannot be fooled.
- Richard Feynman (1918 - 1988)

For a list of all the ways technology has failed to improve the quality of life, please press three.
- Alice Kahn

How many times have you seen ghost hunters on cable use EMF meters like they were Egon's PKE meter from Ghostbusters? I'm sure it's way too many times to count on one hand. They wave the meter around like a once cocaine addled Robin Williams (remember when he was funny?) and claim every beep or click is a spirit. Devices like the tri-field meter and Gauss meter do not detect ghosts. They detect variations in electromagnetic fields. The tri-field meter is so sensitive (particularly the Natural EM Tri-field Meter) that it can detect the geomagnetic field of the Earth! That means every time someone waves one of these things around like their swatting flies with it, they're actually detecting the variance between east and west. But they'll say it's a ghost for the listening audience. Actually, it's more because they didn't read the instructions or maybe didn't understand them.

As I stated earlier, if you exist in the universe you must obey its rules! No matter what ghosts are or what laws there are which allow them to exist, they must obey the same laws that govern reality in our part of the universe. If they didn't obey those laws then they would be a monkey wrench into the sophisticated mechanisms that govern time and space and reality itself.

When a ghost enters a room or any area, it has to influence that area in some way. In the case of EMF meters we are speculating that they influence electromagnetic fields. When we, as ghost hunters, enter a room with any type of EMF meter we are seeing if any naturally occurring electromagnetic (EM) fields are being disturbed by the presence of ghosts.

Truth be told, what are most of all of gadgetry that ghost hunters use? Meteorological equipment of course! We are looking for environmental changes caused by ghosts remember? Any device that can detect any changes in the environment would be helpful in this pursuit.

## PART ONE: MAGNETIC ATTRACTION AND YOU

EMF only exists where current flows. No electrons moving around, no EMF. This brings us to the most popular must-have paranormal investigative equipment around – the EMF Detector! This is a got to have tool for any ghost tech nerd out there. Your paranormal organization just can't be without one. When the media does a story on your group they'll probably say something like, "they go in with their video cameras, night vision goggles and EMF detectors." But what kind of detector should you buy?

We are going to discuss the most popular EMF detectors out there:

The Dr. Gauss EMF Meter
The Cell Sensor Meter
The ELF Meter
The Tri-Field Meter
The K2 Meter
The Mel Meter

One of the strangest things that has ever happened to me occurred in Harper's Ferry West Virginia. We were doing a tour/investigation of the entire town. Near the beginning of the evening, as darkness approached, we ascended the hill that leads to St. Peter's Catholic Church. In the 1700s Thomas Jefferson supposedly surveyed the Potomac River from a rock formation along the path up the hill toward where the church stands now. The formation is now known as Jefferson's Rock. We were videotaping the path and taking pictures. Our flashlights were on because it was getting dark fast and we had the Gauss Meter running. As we passed Jefferson's Rock all our electrical equipment went completely dead! Our flashlights, video camera, EMF detector and cameras had just stopped working. Here we were, in the dark on a hill and six feet from a sheer drop with no light! It was what you might call a little scary. Well, we managed to feel our way along until we left this "dead zone". Once we were out of it everything just sprung to life. Even the video camera that normally needs to be switched back on after a reset just came back on! Was it a powerful magnetic field? I am not sure we can say ghosts emit EMF, although that is certainly possible. It could be that ghosts alter the environment in such a way that EMF are increased or created. Perhaps whatever method ghosts use to manifest is a catalyst for the creation of electromagnetic fields. Certainly enough cases exist that suggest that EMF fluxuations do not need to be present in order for there to be paranormal activity. There are many theories out there. So do not take it for granted that ghosts give off EMF. I have heard of too many stories of groups out there that will point there EMF meter directly at a circuit breaker box and say, "there's a ghost!" As I hinted in the beginning of this book, an EMF detector is not a "ghost detector". This is not Ghostbusters okay?

The next, and equally difficult question, is how does an EMF detector/meter work? Follow closely; it gets a little more technical here...

First of all whether they are EMF meters, EMF detectors, magnetic field meters, Tesla meters, Gauss meters, milliGauss meters, EMR meters or magnetic flux meters they all do the same thing: Detect magnetic fields. Most EMF detectors read 30 to 500 Hz. An Alternating Current (AC) like what comes out of your wall outlet (in the US anyway) has a fluctuating magnetic field that expands and contracts 120 times per second at 60 cycles per second. Hence you have a standard 120 outlet at 60 Hz. At 60 Hz you have an extremely low frequency (ELF). Electric field strength is measured in volts per meter (V/m). Magnetic field strength uses a measurement called amperes per meter (A/m). A/m is used to measure the magnetic field in relation to electric current. What the average ghost hunter is going to be worried about though is magnetic field exposure. Magnetic field exposure tells us how dense the environment is with magnetic fields. This is measured in Gauss. EMF meters use milliGauss (mG or one thousandth of a Gauss), well, in the US they do. In Europe they use the microtesla (μT; 0.1 μT is equal to1 mG) as the standard unit. We made it through all that but we still haven't covered the differences between some of the meters.

Most meters like the Gauss meter, cell sensor, ELF meter and basically any other meter under $150 are single axis meters. This means that they can only read what they are pointed at. They use a magnetic coil (or probe) that is sensitive to fields in mG. A triple-axis meter or tri-field meter uses three coils and three metal plates on an x, y, and z-axis. That way you can read fields from all directions at the same time. The metal plates detect AC (or in some cases DC) electric fields. Each setting has a different calibration that lets you detect different wavelengths of the electromagnetic spectrum. They are, on most models, magnetic, electric and radio or microwave. On most models you can switch between each setting or, using a computer circuit that does the math for you, read the sum of all three. A tri-field meter usually runs about $150 to $300. They generally have a needle type mechanical read-out, but some have digital displays.

## THE DR. GAUSS EMF METER

I keep hearing people say; "This EMF meter is great for the beginner ghost hunter, just starting out." This EMF meter is great for the pros too!

On April 30th 1777 a man, whose name just about every paranormal investigator would learn to mispronounce, was born - Carl Friedrich Gauss. Gauss was already a mathematical prodigy in his Braunschweig elementary school. Although he would go and prove the fundamental theorem of algebra and provide the trajectory of an asteroid, his most notable accomplishment (at least for us) was his work on the theory of magnetism. I wonder what he would think if he were alive today if he knew what we used the Gauss meter for? Maybe we should put an EMF meter on his grave to see if he's rolling in it.

The Gauss meter is named after Dr. Gauss but it wasn't invented until a few hundred years later. As mentioned earlier, the Gauss meter is a single axis meter. It's also simple to use and inexpensive at around $40 to $100 depending on whether you get a needle meter or a digital display. We use the needle model and that's just fine. It makes a rapid clicking noise when it detects EMF and increases in volume and intensity when the field is stronger. It has an "on" button but no "off" button. Instead it automatically turns off after about three minutes if it doesn't detect any EMF readings. The button is located on the side and when depressed and released will cause a brief diagnostic in which it will "bury the needle" and make a loud squelch. After that it's good to go and will measure EMF between 0 and 10 mG. Hold the button down and, on most models, it will increase its sensitivity to detect 0.1 to 1 mG as long as you hold down the button.

When you are using the Gauss Meter it is best to use a grid pattern (a how-to will be coming up later in the book) to map out your location in reference to electromagnetic fields that are present in said location. After drawing a rough sketch of the area on graph paper, walk along the room using the grid technique and mark on your map locations where there are obvious artificial EMFs. You will be looking for wiring in the walls, power lines outside, wall outlets, entertainment electronics, circuit breaker boxes, etc. Mark all these down on your map with a little lightning bolt. After you have begun your actual investigating walk around again in the grid and look for anomalous EMF. Have someone with a camera nearby. When you detect any EMF not on your map, nod your head to your photographer to signal a picture should be taken. Mark on your map a blue lightning bolt for the anomalous EMF. Be careful using the button on the side to increase the detection strength. It can pick up artificial EMF from other rooms and outside better too, which is bad. So, just use the standard setting and don't hold the button down. The lack of sensitivity can be beneficial, as you will learn when reading about some other models.

## THE CELL SENSOR METER

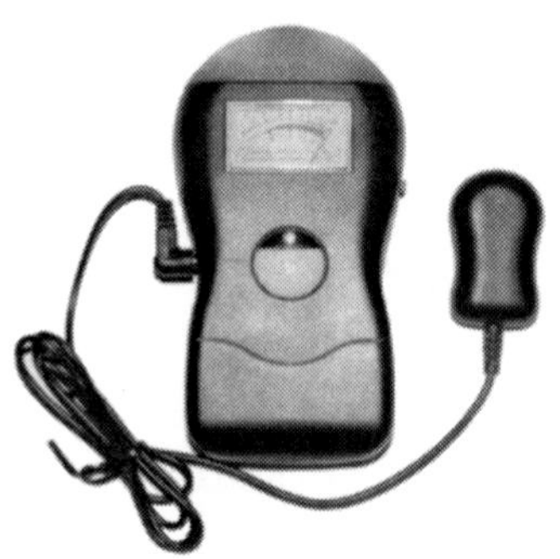

This is the EMF detector mentioned in the introduction at the beginning of this book. Yes, the $29 meter from the Discovery Channel Store. I often wonder if the reason this product was dropped was because the packaging encouraged kids to go near high voltage towers. Anyway, it was our first such device and I have a bit of nostalgic fondness for it. We do not use it now only because we have a Gauss meter and tri-field meter and the cell sensor just falls in between the two. Also, I think I lost it.

This little guy is definitely your low-budget visual impact tool of choice when it comes to EMF detectors. Yeah, the tri-field meters look really scientific, but this has a flashing red light on top and goes bleep-bleepbleep (the higher the EMF reading, the faster it bleeps) when it detects EMF.

They call it a "cell" sensor because it was designed to detect cell phone signals. In fact, without an attachment (a little black probe with a wire) that plugs into the side of most models, it's useless as a piece of paranormal equipment. Well, unless it's the ghost of a recently deceased Verizon salesman. "Can you hear me now? Good."

The Cell Sensor does have a fairly decent EMF range at 0 to 5 mG on one setting and 0 to 50 mG on another setting. Now, like the Gauss meter, it isn't very powerful when it comes to detecting magnetic fields at a distance. However, that's sort of good thing. Some of the more sensitive meters will pick up too much. With these, you would practically have to be standing 'in' the phenomena. To operate the device you simply press and release the button on the front. Many models have a light on the front that indicates the power is on. I have read that some researchers have a problem with you needing two hands to operate this meter since you have to extend the wired probe. I always recommend that you never let anyone go anywhere without another person on an investigation. This increases the reliability level of any witnessed activity and you have someone else there in case there's an accident. Another person can also take any pictures when you detect something. Nevertheless, if you have to have one hand free, you can clip the probe to an extendible wand/pointer like the ones used for presentations. A 1½' wooden stick would be better since it's none conductive. These days a cell sensor runs from \$39 to \$59. Should have picked up another one from the Discovery Channel store...

## THE ELF ZONE METER

Inside each ELF meter is a 2" being commonly referred to in cracker commercials and around Christmas time (just kidding of course).

"ELF meter" is a generic term for your more economy minded EMF meters. These devices do not get any simpler. In fact, at around \$13 to \$20, they have recently started showing up on haunted tours! In Gettysburg recently I saw an ad with one of these pictured in it. It said that you could hold one of these "ghost detectors" and see if you can find a ghost just like the pros do. Obviously they bought a bunch of these meters at a low cost and figured them into their tour. Clever.

Although shape varies, common characteristics of these budget EMF detectors are LEDs (Light Emitting Diodes) that indicate field strength as opposed to a needle or digital display indicator. Some of these can be pretty powerful though and can measure mG from 1.3 to

30mG! Most will pick up about 8mG though. Still, not bad for the price.

Speaking of price... If you really want to save money there is an ELF meter that sells for less than $15 sometimes! Called an "ELF Zone Meter" it only has three LEDs on it. They read green for 0 to 2.5 mG, yellow for 2.5 to 7 mG and red for 8 mG. I recommend not getting this one due to the fact you cannot get accurate readings with it. What if 5mG (I jut picked that off the top of my head) is discovered to be important to discovering ghosts one day? You could have discovered that fact except your group's using an "El Cheapo" Zone Meter. As of this writing I read they were discontinued. However you may still be able to get one on eBay if you're so inclined.

## THE TRI-FIELD METER

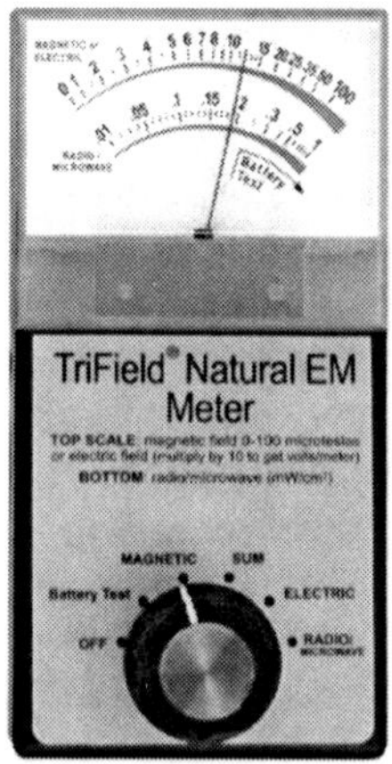


The Tri-field meter is the most coveted of all EMF detectors. If two separate paranormal investigative groups show up at the same historically haunted location, the one with the tri-field meter will garner the most leeway. It would be like an episode of National Geographic, where t As you have read already, the tri-field meter is a triple-axis meter and therefore utilizes three coils instead of one. They are designed to cover the entire non-ionizing electromagnetic spectrum that exists between the ultraviolet and microwave levels. These specially calibrated coils allow you to view all the fields around you instead of having to point it straight at something. Along the same x, y and z-axis are three metal plates that detect electric fields. Generally these devices can detect magnetic fields in the 0 to100 mG range, electric fields in the 0.5 to 100 kilovolts per meter (KV/m) range and the radio and microwave spectrum from 0 to 1 milliwatts per square meter (mW/m$^2$) at 60Hz. Most US homes use a frequency of 60Hz in the electrical systems of the house. Hertz (Hz) is the international unit for frequency. For an alternating current (AC), the frequency is the number of times that the current goes through a complete cycle per second. The standard Tri-field meter runs about $139 to $239. They are extremely useful for mapping out artificial sources of EMF and as handheld EMF detectors.

A more advanced tri-field meter is the tri-field natural EMF meter (what a mouth full). The tri-field natural EMF meter is the preferred EMF detector for paranormal investigators because it detects DC generated EMF. All AC (alternating current) generated fields are artificial. DC (direct current) fields can be artificial or natural. A flashlight gives off DC fields but then so does a lightning bolt. It was, after all, designed to detect geomagnetic storms and solar flares. So, never use this device, inside or outside during a storm or during solar flare activity.

There is another issue with this device. It is very, very sensitive. The 'Electric' setting on the tri-field natural EMF meter is so sensitive that it can pick up the field surrounding a human being (even through walls!)! They are often used as motion detectors in advanced security systems. There are exceptions to the rule but, for the most part, it is simply not a good idea to use the 'Electric' setting while holding this device because of the risk of detecting yourself. That goes for the 'Sum' setting too since it uses the 'Electric' option in the equation. I am not saying this cannot be used completely though. The tri-field natural EMF meter's 'Electric' and 'Sum' settings are best used for remote viewing. Situate a video camera on a flat surface and place the tri-field natural EMF meter in front of it with the auto-focus option of the video camera turned off (auto-focus will focus on the EMF detector too much and ignore the rest of the room). Adjust the focus manually so you can clearly make out the tri-field natural EMF meter's display and the rest of the room. Some models even have bells that go off when they detect EMF so you can leave them unattended. The standard model has a squelch control knob on the side that can be used to adjust the volume and frequency of the tone the tri-field meter makes when it detects a sufficient amount of EMF.

The 'Magnetic' settings can be used with the grid technique as a handheld. However caution must be exercised! Although this sounds complicated, to use the grid technique you must walk in straight lines parallel to the Earth's magnetic field. That means walking only from north to south and south to north. The Earth's magnetic field gives off about 500 milliGauss. Switching back and forth between north and south (east and west) too rapidly will cause a reading of about 100. So, use a compass with this device or point the front of the meter toward the approximate location of magnetic north. I like to put masking tape on the floor in a straight line from north to south. I walk parallel to the tape. From that direction rotate the meter until you find the direction that has the least amount of reorientation. Your best bet is to stand still every few feet while the needle settles and then take a reading.

The tri-field natural EMF meter can be a real asset to your team if you use it right. It can be a real hindrance if used wrong. Do not go around pointing it at everything and automatically assuming that every time it picks up a reading there's a ghost present. That's bad ghost hunting and not the kind of behavior that is acceptable to the professional paranormal investigator.

## THE K2 METER

This EMF meter was made famous by its liberal use on the Sci-FI Channel TV series Ghost Hunters. Ever hear of that show?

The meter is constructed from a flat gray plastic. It has four LED lights on it that claim to detect EMF from 1.5 milliGauss to 20+. Its packaging says it detects the ELF range (50 to 1,000Hz) and VLF range (1,000 to 20,000Hz). Below the lights is a tab that must be depressed at all times in order for the device to work. By placing a coin into the slot half-way you can keep it open without numbing your thumb for hours (that would certainly depress me).

Here is my favorite online quote about this meter – "Preferred by the ghosts as well! Seriously!!!!! This meter gets readings that other meters don't pick up!" Wow! So, not only is it preferred by the ghost hunting community it is preferred by the ghost community as well. Why no self-respecting spirit would ever allow itself to be investigated by a drab Mr. Gauss meter! This device will set you back between $70 and $200+ depending on where you buy it at. But that's not all!

## WHY DO GHOST HUNTERS USE EMF METERS AGAIN?

First of all, EMF meters do not detect ghosts. Well, they probably don't. Researchers who have been doing this for decades will tell you that using equipment like EMF meters is for the purpose of detecting the effects ghosts have on the environment. Since we still don't know what ghosts are, it is the only way. We take base readings and then we compare those reading against supposed paranormally active situations and then we look for differences. Even many of the investigators on TV will tell you this. How the TV producers spin this information is usually very different. It is often easier to say EMF meters detect ghosts as opposed to explaining the science behind the technology. The big mistake many researchers do is take the shows for granted as a source of real science and hard work.

## THE ELF-ZONE METER REDUX

The previously mentioned ELF-Zone Meter is a product of paranoia. It was created for those fearful of getting cancer or brain damage from CRT computer monitors, microwave ovens and other high energy devices. Laboratory tested and calibrated, the ELF-Zone Meter is a model of simplicity. It has only three colored indicator lights for different levels of electro-magnetic field levels. These levels are Green: 0-2.5 mG ("Safe"), Yellow: 2.5-7 mG ("Caution") and Red: 8 or more mG ("Danger"). It will measure ELF/VLF (Extremely Low Frequency and Very Low Frequency) magnetic fields in the frequency range of 20-10,000 Hz, with a minimum sensitivity of 0.25 mG. Very Low Frequency is the spectrum extending from 10 to 30 KHz, as designated by the Federal Communications Commission and Extremely Low Frequency is the band of radio frequencies from 3 to 3000 Hz. ELF was at one time used by the US Navy and Soviet/Russian Navy to communicate with submerged submarines.

The ELF-Zone Meter is a very simple to use single-axis meter. Single-axis means the meter is directional and must be pointed in the direction you want it to detect. We have often used it to detect artificial sources of EMF when mapping a location for non-paranormal magnetic sources. Alarm clock radios, stereo speakers, ceiling fans and CRT monitor have been known to set it off. It has even gone off in what can only be described as high-energy paranormal environments. These are situations in which case no artificial or natural sources can be accounted for. Natural sources would include the area between the Earth and Earth's ionosphere where electrons are made to oscillate from lightning strikes. The oscillation gives off a resonance frequency of 7.8 Hz. Sudden ionospheric disturbance (SID) in the atmosphere caused by solar flares can also cause a natural spike on these meters in the right situations.

## TRUTH OF THE K-II EMF METER

Contrary to popular belief, the K-II Meter is not a second generation EMF meter. There never was a K-I version. Actually the K-II comes from K-II Enterprises, the manufacturer and creator of the K-II EMF Meter. They also produce sonic dog trainers and deterrents. The K-II meter is usually priced from $50 to $100. The previously mentioned ELF-Zone meter is usually priced around $13. The K-II meter is tch. Without the alteration of an installed toggle switch, the K-II requires you to hold down a top mounted thumb switch. Releasing the switch turns it off. When you first touch down on the switch, does a quick battery check and will light up for about a second. Some paranormal investigators will place a coin into the switch to keep it on.

The K-II Meter also detects ELF/VLF. Its range in ELF is 50 to 1,000 Hz and in the VLF range 1,000 to 20,000 Hz. This, as Ron and I discovered later, opens a whole can of worms when it comes to using the K-II anywhere near civilization. As far as EMF is concerned, the K-II

Meter (or simple the K-II in paranormal circles) has five colored indicator lights versus the ELF-Zone Meter's three. The levels as indicated by the lights are two Greens: 0-2.5 mG and , one Yellow: 2.5-10 mG and two Red: 10-20+ mG. Almost exactly like the range of the ELF-Zone Meter, huh? Not exactly when you consider that extra sensitive VLF range going all the way to 20,000 Hz (or 20 kHz).

## TOO SENSITIVE?

Hertz or Hz is named after Dr. Heinrich Hertz, the physicist who developed the theory of radio waves. It is the unit of measurement of one cycle per second when one radio wave passes one point in one second of time. So, if I am at point A and you are at point B and I send you 20 radio waves to you at point B from point A in exactly one second, that is 20 Hz. Electromagnetic radiation is a phenomenon that takes the form of self-propagating waves. It consists of electric and magnetic fields which oscillate (frequency) in phase perpendicular to each other and perpendicular to the direction of energy production. EMF carries energy and momentum that interacts with matter it comes in

As many paranormal researchers know, the K-II Meter cannot be used anywhere near someone with a cell phone in which the cell phone's power is on. It does not matter if it is on vibrate or not. Just being on and capable of receiving calls generates enough of an RF (radio frequency) to register on the K-II. This will vary depending on brand and how often the cell phone will check for incoming calls, text and SMS messages. There are two common frequency bands that all cell phone carriers use. The cellular band referred to as 1900 uses the frequencies 1850-1990 MHz. The other band is PCS which is the 800 MHz band which uses frequencies in the 824-894 MHz range. Most of our cellular phone signal products work on one or the other. Cell phones give off varying degrees of ELF and VLF depending on what "mode" it is in, the model and manufacturer, etc. 2 Hz: to avoid uncomfortable modulation for the ears from the surrounding noise, when speech is absent. 8.34 Hz: emission frequency of the signal related to reception conditions. 30/40 Hz: emissions of various electronic elements and internal oscillators within the cellphone. 217 Hz: modulation of the carrier-frequency namely the microwaves used by GSM/DCS cellular systems. All of these fall within the detection range of the K-II. Cordless phones, WIFI stations, pagers, RFS radios, walkie-talkies, microwave ovens, radar detectors, cable boxes, ceiling fans, traffic lights, cb radios, ham radio towers, cell phone towers, power stations and thousands of other examples of modern technology also give off RF signals within the range of the K-II Meter that would would not really be considered EMF sources.

## A LITTLE HELP FROM E. A. POE

When friend and colleague Ron and I drove through Baltimore City we left the the K-II Meter on and running. Ron has the model that has an added toggle switch. We would switch back from simply holding the front mounted switch to using the toggle. Low and behold, we occasionally received different readings depending on which option we used! It would appear that the toggle switch acted like some sort of powered antennae when used instead of the push-button and increased the signal. A colleague of mine with both versions confirmed this. When we drove by a WIFI coffee bar, the K-II peaked. When we were within 40 feet of a radar equipped intersection, it peaked. When we drove by someone in another car who was using a cell phone it, peaked. Many times we simply coundn't tell what was setting it off. When we reached the Westminster Burying Grounds in downtown Baltimore we began to search around using different EMF and RF detectors along with the K-II. This included the Alpha Labs Natural Trifield EMF Meter, a MagTemp, a Cell Sensor EMF Meter, a Ghost Meter EMF Meter, a Gauss Master and an E.Smog Scout Lux. When we found artificial sources of EMF, the Cell Sensor EMF Meter, Ghost Meter EMF Meter, Gauss Master and E.Smog Scout Lux all detected the same sources equally. They were also unaffected by RF signals. The Natural Trifield Meter did not detect artificial sources unless it was set for RF. Then it detected some things even beyond the range of the K-II. We were not, unfortunately, privy to any paranormal activity that day. We also did some readings at my own house that confirmed some of the earlier sources of RF.

## HOW SOME GHOST HUNTERS USE THE K-II

How I have often seen this device used since 2008 is thusly: A K-II Meter is placed somewhere (on the ground, floor, table, etc.) and someone talks to it. The impression is given that the investigator(s) is talking to the spirits present and encouraging them (the ghosts) to interact with the K-II Meter. I have been given two theories behind this technique. One: That the ghost or ghosts get close enough to the K-II Meter that they (the ghosts) affect the readings. Two: The ghost or ghosts actually enter the electronics of the K-II Meter and manipulate it for communication. Honestly, the second reason is not only far-fetched, but downright ridiculous. There is no evidence anywhere in the annals of paranormal research to suggest that people become electronic engineers when they enter the state of ghost-hood. The first possibility is far more likely and believable. Nevertheless, we cannot prove scientifically that what is being witnessed is by ghostly interaction.

How do we know it isn't psychic influence by the investigators? You want results and therefore project results.

## IN CONCLUSION OF THE K-II...

The K-II Meter is built like a McDonald's Happy Meal toy. It may be used for paranormal research in places like the Amazon or Congo and maybe even the Arctic Circle. Any place too close to other pieces of technology and it will give the user false positives. When I first began seriously researching the paranormal in 1999, I thought all orbs were ghosts and misty pictures taken in the wintertime were as well. I learned otherwise. The best known users of the K-II Meter, Jason Hawes and Grant Wilson of TAPS and TV's Ghost Hunters fame recently renounced the K-II Meter in an online article. Some sources have come forward to me and have said that they have seen certain K-II endorsers using the push button (original unaltered) to "fake" a reading. What they do is hold the button down, release it, and then press again so that the battery-check function looks like a ghost detection. Some, more clever con-artists have used their cell phones and other RF sources in order to hussle would-be investigators and clients. If you are looking for an inexpensive EMF Meter, I recommend the Cell Sensor EMF Meter, Ghost Meter EMF Meter or Gauss Master. Even a compass is better than the K-II Meter.

## THE MEL-METER

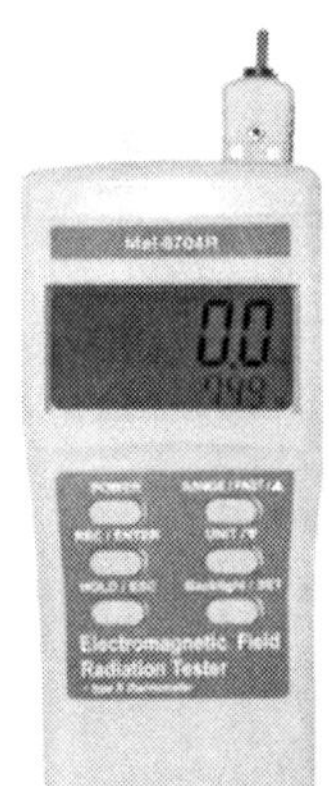


I am very skeptical of many aspects of the paranormal, especially when it comes to new "pseudo-scientific" concepts and untested technology. A few years ago, a fellow from Great Brittan brought, from across the ocean a marvelous sounding contraption called the Paranormal PC. Here is what the manufacturer claimed this miraculous devise could do for paranormal researchers:

The most valued outcome of a paranormal investigation is data, not only that but data from credible sources. That is why we at Paranormal Investigation are proud to bring you the Biggest Innovation in Paranormal Research in the last 25 years; we have combined the power of modern computing with the sensitivity of the latest scientific monitoring equipment. Not only can you detect potential paranormal anomalies you can also record them straight onto your PC or Laptop.

The 'Influence Triggering' based system will monitor and

record all of the following parameters:

- Temperature
- Motion
- Sound
- Luminance
- Infra Red Night Vision Video
- Electro Magnetic Field (EMF) Meter Readings
- Negative Ion Levels / Static Interference
- Natural Magnetic Fields / Geomagnetic Fields

Anomalies in these fields are often associated with paranormal activity. Not only can you use the ParanormalPC to monitor haunting investigations, it can also be utilized in other paranormal investigations such as crop circles, UFO landing sites, alien abduction, séances, Ouija board, etc.

Astounding, right? The only problem was it was difficult for the average person to set-up, required many separate programs running at the same time and the attachments tended to detect one another! I am also not sure of the claims that it can be useful for crop circles, UFO landing sites, alien abduction, séances, Ouija board, etc. I suppose if you happen to be abducted by aliens while holding a ParanormalPC that might work. Otherwise, not so much.

Despite these issues and others, the ParanormalPC was a big seller for a few months. Many would-be ghost hunters worldwide dished out more than $800 for one of these untested high-tech paper weights. However, unlike many other devices currently available, it eventually fell off the radar for the most part. It may have had something to with price and the difficulty in using it. If paranormal researchers are going to ever be taken seriously, they are going to need to learn that sometimes they are wrong about the technological bandwagons they are so quick to jump on. Now, I could go on about how paranormal investigators are misusing K-II meters, "spirit boxes" and the Ovilus, but I'm not. This article is focused on the Mag-Temp or MEL Meter.

## THE AMAZING STORY OF MELISA'S METER

When this device was first brought to my attention, I was asked to field test it by my friends over at www.LessEMF.com. When I received my new EMF/thermocouple thermometer in the mail, I was very, very impressed. It was of rugged, solid construction. It had a back-light and many other useful features. It even had a record mode to help you keep track of Max & Min temperature and EMF changes! and it was very accurate too. This device easily matched or surpassed some of the old standards like the Alpha Labs trifield meter and the classic analog Gauss meter. I couldn't help but include it into my latest book Ultimate Ghost Hunter in 2009.

I didn't even do my usual background checking into the device since all my self-testing passed with flying colors. After my book went to print, I started hearing numerous stories about the "Mel Meter" device. People were telling me it was designed just for ghost hunting! I found that hard to believe. Why? Up until this point, any "made just for paranormal research" devices were shoddy at best. The Mel-8704 Meter simply looked too well made! Also, devices like this are designed by teams, not by one inventor. I refused to believe it. Then, I heard even more! That the Model number, Mel-8704, was assigned to represent the birth and death of the inventor's daughter. Great, I thought, more out of control gossip and rumors! More misunderstanding about how technology works. The girl's name was Melody or Melanie. The "8704" was the year the young lady was born (1987) and the year she died (2004). I didn't believe it for a single second! I had to research further to get to the bottom of this.

So, I got out my note pad and called Mr. Gary Galka, the actual inventor of the Mel-Meter. So, I introduced myself and explained to Mr. Galka that I am going to set the record straight on the misinformation out there on his invention. Sure enough, there never was a Melody or Melanie. Her name was Melissa.

Wow, so I was wrong big time! I did not expect to find any truth in any aspect of that part of the story. Gary was retired as of 5½ years ago. His daughter Melissa, or Mel as he called her since she was very young, was on her way home one evening around midnight. For some unknown reason, she swerved off of the road and struck a tree in a terrible car accident. "I jumped out of bed that night," Gary told me, "I knew something had happened to her." The accident happened on September 24, 2004. Mel was born in 1987. She was on life-support until September 28th before being allowed to pass on. It was soon afterward that Gary's new obsession with the paranormal would begin.

"Most of the proceeds from the product go to charities such as Compassionate Friends and other known charity organization," Gary told me with some pride.

"From the moment my wife and I and two daughter's got home," Gary explained, "Mel began to let us know that she was still around." Gary explained how Mel began playing around with electronics in the house. The TV, radio and lights would come on and turn off and switch channels by themselves. "We could smell her perfume," he added, "Over a period of time we could feel her hugs and kisses." These experiences didn't just happen to him either. His wife, Cindy and daughters Heather and Jennifer also had these wonderful After Death Communications (ADC's) as well. They all believe that Mel reached out to them in order to help them to heal and move forward with their lives. Within six months of her passing, Gary and his wife began to reach out and help other bereaved parents in their homes and through the formation of grief counseling groups. He began researching the paranormal and related topics to better understand what was going on in this field. After reading several books, and watching a few of the paranormal shows on television it became apparent that most paranormal enthusiasts had to resort to using mainstream gadgets and devices that were typically intended for a totally different purpose. Many were modified or adapted to suit the application of paranormal research. Gary, with over 30 years of test and measurement experience sat down and began to design the Mel-Meter. Not only to help give the paranormal community a push forward, but the biggest accomplishment, as Gary explained with pride is that, "Most of the proceeds from the Mel product series goes directly to grief support charities such as Compassionate Friends and other known charity organizations".

So, in conclusion, it's been five and a half years since Mel passed. Gary is still getting signs and visits from her, though not as frequently. He is still highly motivated and working on even newer technology designs that will be introduced to the paranormal field in the near future, including the new RT-EVP device, P-SB7 spirit box and numerous additions to the popular Mel meter series. He will continue the trend of those who saw that there was a connection between EMF and the paranormal going back to UCLA parapsychologists in the 1970s, Loyd Auerbach in the 1990s and Chris Flemming, Troy Taylor and Dale Kaczmarek in the 21 Century.

## THE LEAST EXPENSIVE EMF DETECTOR IN THE WORLD

Those generic ELF meters were pre cheap, huh? What if I told you there are EMF detectors that are so sensitive they can detect the Earth's magnetic field from here all the way to the arctic (this is unimpressive of course if you are reading this from the arctic)? What if I told you that EMF detector was so cheap you could get one for under $5? Well, by now you have looked over the rest of this page and seen tł compass picture so I'll stop there.

Yes, a magnetically charged needle placed horizontally on top of a cork or Styrofoam and allowed to float in a glass of water will work as a primitive EMF meter. A magnetized compass' needle is really just that: a simple EMF meter. When suspended on a nearly frictionless pivot, the needle will point toward magnetic north. Since it is a magnet it is sensitive to magnetic fields. Strong magnetic fields in its proximity will cause the magnet to spin away from magnetic north. It has been reported that in some cases a paranormally active area will cause a magnet to spin uncontrollably. The compass is best placed flat and parallel to the floor or ground. Compasses usually run about .50¢ (or less) to over $50 for a fancy outdoor model.

## PART TWO: METEOROLOGY = GHOST DETECTION

You're walking through your room in a colonial era bed and breakfast when suddenly, although it was 75 degrees a moment ago, you feel chilled to the bone. The hairs prick up on the back of your neck. You shiver slightly and when you turn around you see a man in a red British infantry uniform from 200 years. You take a gulp and as he raises his rifle he vanishes into nothingness. You take a step back toward the door and as you do you re-enter warmth. You have stepped out of a cold spot.

What are cold spots? Well, to be honest, some of them are just natural air currents in badly insulated areas. However, they can also be the side effect of paranormal activity. It has been recorded many, many times over the centuries in reports of ghosts and hauntings. Cold is often a forbearer or omen in many myths, legends and fictions. From Shakespeare and Dickens to Poe and even Stephen King, countless times we have read about sudden drops in temperature and people who see their breath in a well heated home. These cold spots can move around the room or remain completely stationary. They can be only slightly lower in temperature or downright freezing. They are perplexing to say the least.

What causes ghostly cold spots anyway? Here are some of the more common theories:

A. Ghosts need energy to become more tangible and draw that energy from the air.
B. By entering this dimension ghosts draw the necessary energy from the air.
C. Dead people are cold.
D. Other.

Okay, I think we can agree number three doesn't make any sense. So, let us look at numbers one, two and four.

The most common belief is that a ghost needs more energy to become tangible. This doesn't mean that it consciously pulls the energy from the air though. Do you think about the calories you burned when you flipped that last page? (I'm guessing, unless you're the world's most serious health nut, probably not) Cold spots are created at an atomic and molecular level as opposed to a sub-atomic level. This is obvious from the fact that your wall outlet doesn't become cold from the lamp drawing electrons from it. Some sub-atomic reactions probably do take place, but are not measurable with current technology. Heat is energy. According to the "zero law" of thermodynamics no heat can flow from any two bodies that are the same temperature. The second law states that heat will always flow into a colder area or body unless worked to do otherwise. This can be demonstrated with some canned air, the kind you use to clean a keyboard or computer parts. When you release the air from the can by pressing the top, you release the energy from the can. The can subsequently becomes cold and will occasionally frost over. Shake the can while spraying and it will become colder still only faster.

Another possibility involves higher dimensions. If ghosts do indeed come from a higher dimension, it is possible that cold spots are created from the act of moving between dimensions. The energy escapes into a higher dimension like the air released from the can mentioned above. The release of energy from this (our 3D) dimension causes a drop in temperature.

The above theories are only theories. We have no idea which if any are true right now. What we do know is that ghosts and cold spots are linked in some way. Although you may not always feel them, they are probably there somewhere. That is why one of the most essential pieces of ghost tech to bring with you is a thermometer.

## A BRIEF HISTORY OF THERMAL DETECTION DEVICES

Although the Greeks knew about the expansion of air when heated over 2000 years ago, it was Galileo Galilei who invented the thermometer in 1593. It was an air thermometer (that also functioned as a barometer) made from a glass bulb attached to a tube. The tube was dipped in water and the bulb put over fire. Some of the air escaped as it expanded from the heat. When Galileo took away the heat, the water would run up the tube as the air returned to room temperature. Not a perfect set up.

Alcohol was used for a while until 1714 when mercury finally came into play. We owe that to some guy named Fahrenheit. Then another guy in 1742, this time going by the name Celsius, added the measurements where thermometers were calibrated to the freezing and boiling points of water. Interestingly enough, he had 100 degrees as freezing and 0 degrees as boiling! It was a biologist named Linneaus who had enough common sense to switch it around. Finally in the nineteenth century a scientist proved that scientists are never content with enough ways of measuring things. A man named Kelvin named yet another scale of temperature measurement and did so after himself.

Thermometers, for the most part, have some sort of element in them that expands and contracts in relation to the temperature. Depending on the degree of expansion or contraction the thermometer can tell to what degree (greater or lesser) a substance such as air, water, chocolate, etc. is. An infrared thermometer does not measure temperature thru expansion or contraction. Passive IR thermometers send out an invisible cone of infrared light. When the cone contacts another object it is reflected back and read by a sensor on the IR thermometer. Non-passive IR thermometers use lenses to detect radiated IR from objects the device is pointed at. The microprocessor inside IR thermometers covert the information gathered from the infrared radiation given off by the object into a temperature reading. Digital thermometers use electric resistance to measure temperature. A thermo-resistor reads the electric resistance of a substance such as air or water and sends that information to a computer or circuit to translate the information into a discernable temperature reading.

## IR THERMOMETERS... DID YOU WASTE YOUR MONEY ON ONE?

The infrared thermometer is a pretty good example of the devices used by most paranormal investigators today. These devices can detect the temperature of an object instantly. They are used for everything from food service to detecting the temperature of jet engines. They are lightweight and small. They are also really cool gadgets. This last bit of information is very important. A cool gadget does not a great ghost detector make. Let's learn what makes these things work, shall we?

When you pull the trigger on a passive IR thermometer an area of a surface in front of the thermometer is scanned for reflected IR light. The further away the device is the larger the area it detects (the light cone) and the more inaccurate it becomes. A chipset inside the device computes the amount of reflected infrared light and figures out the temperature from that information.

The basic IR thermometer (also known as a non-contact

thermometer because it doesn't physically touch the object it's measuring) is composed of four visible parts – the display screen for showing the readings, the infrared emitter for sending out the infrared beam, the sensor that receives the reflected infrared beam and the trigger that activates the beam. It's usually housed in a durable plastic casing in the better models or what resembles a McDonald's toy in others. There is a lens on the front where the IR light is detected. The trigger is usually spring loaded and recoils back when released. Some models have a fourth part – a visible laser beam pointer. On some models the laser pointer is activated by a separate switch, on others it goes off the same time the IR beam is fired. It is placed parallel to the IR detector in the housing and the better-calibrated models will point dead center to where the IR sensor is pointing. However, the visible laser and light cone will veer off from one another the further the distance the IR thermometer is from the object is pointed at. IR thermometers range in quality in most cases parallel to their price tag. They range in price from $40 to over $800.

So, how does an IR thermometer pick up temperatures anyway? Well, to know that we have to have a basic understanding of light; specifically infrared light. Infrared light is part of the electromagnetic spectrum and falls just between visible light and radio waves. Light is measured in microns. Infrared's spectrum is between 0.7 and 1000 microns. There are several factors that IR thermometers take into account in order to get a reading. These are - emissivity, distance to spot ratio, and field- of-view.

Every object reflects, transmits and emits energy. Only emitted energy indicates the temperature of an object. When infrared thermometers measure an object's surface temperature they detect all three kinds of energy, therefore IR thermometers are adjusted to read only emitted energy. An IR thermometer will detect the temperature of fire. That is only because of the intense infrared heat. Errors can be caused by reflected light sources. Uh oh. We scientifically minded paranormal investigators no like errors. But, I digress, we will return to this later.

Distance to spot ratio refers to the distance from an object the IR thermometer is in relation to the size of the IR beam's cone. The spot is at the end of the cone. The resolution of the "spot" determines the accuracy of the device and the smaller the spot, the better the accuracy. Also, this means the further you are away from the object the less accurate the measurement. Another side effect is the further you are away from an object, the more likely you are to pick up the temperature of the area around the object. Particularly if the object being measured is relatively small. Boy, this is becoming an increasingly inaccurate piece of equipment!

The field-of-view refers to what was just mentioned. The

closer you are the better. If the light cone is larger than the object being measured, you will get an inaccurate reading.

So, to summarize, infrared thermometers detect the reflected light given off objects and determines the temperature of that object. IR thermometers have a high margin of error due to a number of factors. Reflections from light sources can create inaccurate readings. The distance from an object can adversely affect accuracy. The size of the object is also an important factor.

Well, it's starting to look like there are a few things going against these handy little devices. I think the most important factor to take into consideration is whether they can detect ghosts in the first place. As mentioned, the IR device only measures the IR light given off by solid objects. It cannot, by design, detect air temperature. In fact, some are specifically designed to block out air temperature interference. When you aim your IR thermometer at a window, you are reading the temperature of the window, not the ambient air temperature between you and the window. Now, you have to ask yourself, do ghosts reflect infrared beams aimed at them? Most people will agree that ghosts are intangible, less tangible than air perhaps. In that case, I would say no, the IR sensor will not detect a ghost.

So, does this mean that the IR thermometer you already purchased is not good for ghost investigations? No, there are still a number of uses for your purchase on your investigations. In some cases objects can be haunted or have paranormal activity around them. In these cases it would be important to monitor the surface temperature of the object in question. In these situations it is best to have a person with a camera nearby to take a picture when a noticeable difference in temperature is recorded. In fact, on any paranormal investigation, it is important to have an extra hand with a camera nearby with any piece of ghost tech.

Do not fret if you were really looking forward to having a really cool IR thermometer as part of your gear bag. There are other options after all, some of them even cooler (oh, and more reliable) than IR thermometers.

## PROBES THAT HAVE NOTHING TO DO WITH ALIENS

First of all, when someone asks you, "What is it that you have there?" don't say, "This is just a thermometer." Say, "This is our thermal scanner" or "this is our thermal-differential monitor. We use it to detect atmospheric temperature fluctuations." Not only will it keep nosey non-investigators off your back (most people are to embarrassed to say, "Uh, what does that mean?"), but also it will make you sound more professional and cool. Okay, maybe a little nerdy too. This is ghost tech though and you wouldn't have bought this book if you weren't a little nerdy.

So what could be cooler than going into someone's home and shooting a laser beam at everything (careful there Freud students)? How about a probe on a stick!

A digital thermometer (or thermo-coupler) uses a thermal probe attached to the unit via a cord (usually between 3 and 5 feet) to measure outdoor temperature and an internal thermal sensor to monitor indoor temperature in the home. You would hang the device near a door or window and run the external probe outside. As in most models, the display's top shows the outdoor temperature while the lower half shows the indoor temperature. These devices are available everywhere including hardware stores, drug store chains and of course Wal-Mart. They are also relatively inexpensive at prices ranging from $12 to $50.

Digital Thermometers use electric resistance to measure temperature. A thermo-resistor reads the electric resistance (called the Seebek Effect) of a substance such as air or water and sends that information to a computer or circuit to translate the information into a discernable temperature reading. Nearly every thermo-resistor has a negative temperature coefficient which means their resistance decreases as the temperature increases. A multimeter from Radio Shack (or the electronics supplier of your choice) can demonstrate this effect. Boiling water has a high resistance and reads 4000 at 100 degrees Celsius. A circuit in the digital thermometer does the math for you. Thermo-resistors take several seconds to get their info. The smaller the thermo-resistor, the faster the input will be. The smaller the thermo-resistor the more expensive it will be too. So, you got to pay more for faster service, just like in a French restaurant. C'est la vie.

So, how best to utilize your digital thermometer? On one of the more basic digital thermometers we ran the cord and external thermal probe around a wooden rod, making sure it was secure at least at three spots along the way with electric tape with the probe taped at one end. After drawing a rough sketch of the area on graph paper, walk along the room using the grid technique. For best results you should be grasping the display unit in one hand and gently sway the pole back and forth in the other hand as you walk across the designated area/room in a grid pattern. Remember; move slowly because you have to let your digital thermometer have a few seconds to register the ambient temperature. Go back and retrace your grid checking regularly for a difference in temperature from the external and unit thermal probes. Make sure you have a photographer near in case a severe drop in temperature is detected. Nod your head to indicate when you think a picture should be taken. Severe increases in temperature should be taken into account as well. You will be looking for a difference in temperature of at least 5 degrees from the internal probe. Got all that? Well, if you didn't at least you own the book.

Digital thermometers are also good tools for cemetery investigations. However, you will not be using them the same way there. Because of the nature of the great outdoors it would be impractical to try and measure temperatures in a grid pattern since airflow keeps the temperature moving constantly. In cemeteries, your best bet is to monitor the ambient temperature during the course of the investigation. Make a note every 30 minutes of the air temperature and mark it down. This will help you if something paranormal happens when you check your notes later. Remember to always make a note of everything you can.

## DIGITAL THERMOMETER/ PYROMETER

Okay, I admit it; these things have been around since the 1960's. However, they are the newest things in paranormal investigative equipment!

Basically, digital thermometer/pyrometers (DTP) are thermo-coupler thermometers like the digital thermometers mentioned previously, except slightly more advanced and specialized. They are also more accurate and faster. The DTPs manufactured by TIF™ Instruments, Inc. (www.tif.com) scans temperatures at three times a second. Depending on where you buy them from they range in price from $129 - $199 for the basic model which includes several different attachments.

The TIF™ Instruments, Inc DTP is the Maryland Paranormal Investigators Coalition's thermal scanner of choice. Designed primarily for automotive and refrigeration repairs, this DTP comes in a black plastic case and includes three attachments. Connected to the base unit via a heavy-duty phone cord are three separate attachments. The first is a surface probe, used to detect surface temperatures from -40° to +1999° F. A ceramic insulator "floats" a high temperature sensor near the tip of the probe that looks like a metal wand. By placing the probe against an object and pressing the side button you can get accurate surface temperatures. The second attachment is an immersion probe, used to detect liquid temperatures from -40° to +500° F. It has Teflon coated around a cord that is placed in the liquid you are trying to read. The third and coolest, most essential attachment is the air probe. The air probe is used to detect, well, air temperatures. It can detect air temperatures from -40° to over 1000 F. The air probe looks like a metal wand with a cylindrical tube placed horizontally at the tip. The tube is open at both ends and on top with visible sensor wires in the tube. The wires are only .004 inches thick (which is less than a human hair!) in order to provide rapid response times.

We fell in love with the DTP as soon as we saw it. It has all the qualities we paranormal tech nerds need. It looks cool, comes in a cool case and has three scientifically accurate attachments. We have found that it is best to give the wand a little shake with your wrist as you try to detect air temperatures. The wire sensors require some air movement in order to get the best readings. Otherwise it can be used like the digital thermometer using the grid method mentioned before.

## IT'S NOT THE HUMIDITY, BUT...

The main purpose for lugging all these gadgets into a location is to monitor the location's environmental conditions. This way you, or future investigators, can one day try to understand the nature of a haunting. What kind of conditions must there be for a ghost to appear? Since we are dealing with a probable type of energy when dealing with ghosts, we should utilize equipment that can best detect energy or environmental changes that can affect energy. Such a device is the relative humidity gauge.

You ever notice in winter months how you are twice as likely to get a static-electrical shock as in the warmer months? That is because of absolute humidity. Absolute humidity is the mass of water vapor divided by the mass of dry air in a volume of air at a given temperature. The higher the air temperature is, the more potential water it contains. Relative humidity is the ratio of the current absolute humidity and that of the highest possible absolute humidity depending on the air temperature. Total saturation of the air occurs at 100% humidity. At 100% humidity at high enough an altitude rain will probably occur. At ground level 100% humidity means the air is so saturated with water it prevents perspiration in humans by not allowing our sweat to evaporate and cool us down. This is why when the temperature is 75° it feels like 80°. Ah, air conditioning!

You get a static-electrical shock in the cooler temperatures due in part because of something called the triboelectric series. Essentially the triboelectric series is a chart of how different materials hold onto their electric charge. If a material is more likely to give off electrical charges it is more positive in the triboelectric series (such as human hands or fur). On the other hand, if the material is more likely to hold on to its charge than it is more negative on the triboelectric series (such as copper, brass, Teflon and plastic wrap. Steel is neutral.). When two non-conducting materials come in contact with one another adhesion occurs. The triboelectric series says that, depending on their position, these two materials can allow a charge to be shared between them. If the two materials are separated a charge imbalance occurs. The material that gained the charge is now negatively charged and the material that lost it is positively charged. When you separate these two materials, static electricity occurs.

The reason you don't get the BLEEP shocked out of you every time you touch a doorknob is because of the humidity. Humidity cuts down the resistance for electrical flow. If the material becomes coated in moisture the charges can reconnect and neutralize each other. In very dry climates like desserts the static charge can become dangerous. In Antarctica researchers have to contend with charges up to tens of thousands of volts!?

So, it is assumed by many that ghosts are some form of energy. Energy is a tricky thing and doesn't always behave well in certain conditions. This is why it is important to maintain accurate environmental records of a paranormal investigation. If a ghost appears or does something to show it's there, you will know exactly what the conditions were for the phenomena to have occurred. At the very least you'll have a good idea of what helped.

A relative humidity gauge comes in two primary forms. Both work under the same principles. In the first device, which you can get with a digital display there are two thermometers. One "dry" thermometer and one "wet" thermometer where the wet thermometer is kept wet by a cloth dipped in water. Low relative humidity will cause a lot of evaporation in the cloth and decrease the wet thermometer's temperature - the larger the difference between the thermometers, the lower the relative humidity. This difference is measured in percent. These gauges cost between $20 and $600+ depending on what fancy options you want. The higher priced options include a rotating paper wheel with a needle that records the information automatically. Cool, huh?

Significantly lower tech is a dial humidity gauge. It has human hair (yuck) inside that stretches when wet and shrinks when cool.

## THE PRESSURE IS ON

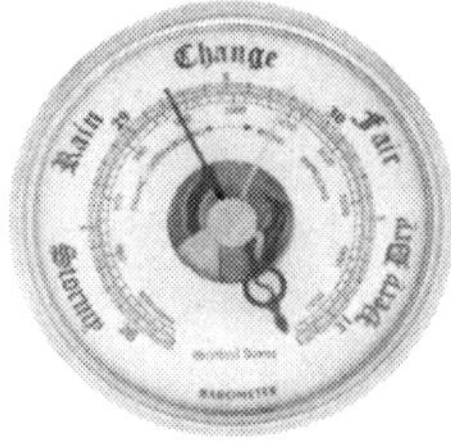


Another instrument in our meteorological arsenal is a Barometer. A barometer measures air pressure. Anything that can adversely change the conditions of the environment can and should be measured. Sorry if I sound like a broken record (or for the under 25 crowd a scratched CD), but this is important if you want to be taken seriously as a paranormal investigator. Due to the miles of cubic air that blankets the earth the average air pressure is 14.7 lbs per inch. You do not notice this because you have experienced it your entire life. You're just used to it. Hot air is less dense than cold air. Hot places like Florida have lower air pressure. The air is also less dense at higher altitudes. I wonder how this affects haunted mountaintop resorts.

In a barometer there are very small vacuum capsules that are devoid of any air. When the air density changes the capsule shrinks or expands and moves a needle or digital display. They range in price from $10 to $1200 depending on what options you want. Options include printouts, computer uplinks and even voice announcements. Barometers often come bundled with a thermometer and sometimes a humidity gauge as well. You do not have to use the grid technique with a barometer. It's detecting the pressure of the entire room so stationary monitoring of the barometer is fine.

## PART THREE: OTHER GHOST HUNTING DEVICES

Well, we have covered a lot so far haven't we? Now we're going to get a little more into the modern age with some devices many investigators haven't caught onto yet. Yes, everyone knows about trifield meters and video cameras, but what about Ion Particle Counters and IR Motion Sensors? There is a bunch of other stuff out there that definitely falls into the category of cool and useful. Devices like IR Motion Detectors are even affordable! At the conclusion of this chapter we will discuss low-tech alternative ghost detection techniques and some projects you easily do yourself.

Two of the most important pieces of equipment you will need are often not even considered! Caffeine and a hat! The caffeine will keep you awake and the hat (I recommend a wide brimmed safari hat or fedora) will keep cobwebs, insects, dust and even bat droppings out of your hair. I never leave home without my Tilley hat!

## IR MOTION DETECTORS

The concept of motion detection technology has been around in paranormal investigating since Harry Price's days. He used a bowl of mercury to detect vibrations. Well, I don't know about you but I try to avoid mercury whenever possible!

There are two main types of electronic motion detectors: photosensitive and passive infrared (PIR) sensitive motion detectors. The photosensitive models are useless in the dark because they detect differences in light and shadows. Therefore, we will be focusing on PIR motion detectors.

Also known as pyro-electric motion sensors, IR motion sensors are designed to detect the average infrared energy given off by a human being with +/- a few units for leeway. The components in a typical PIR motion detector utilize a crystalline material that generates a surface electric charge when exposed to temperature in the form of infrared emissions. When the amount of infrared striking the crystal changes, the amount of charge changes as well and is measured with a sensitive field effect transistor (FET) device built into the sensor. An FET is an electronic component for amplification and transformation of electric pulses. The sensor is sensitive to a wide range of radiation so filter window is placed in front of the sensor to block out all but the average IR emissions of a human being. When a person enters the room, a rapid shift in infrared energy occurs. If it tried to detect too slow a change, then your home's cooling and heating system would set them off. This is the technology used for those lights that turn-on when you walk past them at night in people's yard and on their porches. IR motion detectors are also used for home security systems. The home security models are the ones we're interested in.

Infrared detectors used in security systems are perfect for the average paranormal investigator as in they are high-tech, useful and relatively inexpensive. The least expensive PIR motion detectors on the market are available everywhere from hardware stores to drugstores and of course, online. They usually have a built in siren that can be as loud as 120 decibels. This type will run about $15 to $40 depending on what features are included. They are best used to make sure no one is walking into the area you are trying to investigate. Many models have an indicator light that blinks to let you know that it is active. They can also detect cold spot when no one is around. The problems with these are they have to be shut off manually for the most part. That means when the deafening siren goes off you have to run to the location and enter a code or flick a switch to turn it off and reset it. Some have RF remotes that can wirelessly turn them off though.

## GEIGER COUNTERS

Although useless for detecting ghosts at Chernobyl, these devices have been known to be useful in less dangerous situations of paranormal occurrences.

Hans Geiger developed the first Geiger counter in 1928. When the atoms of gases are ionized (lose orbiting electrons), they can conduct electricity. Herr Geiger used this principle in the development of his counter. His "Geiger Counter" uses a metal tube (called a Geiger-Müller tube) with a thin wire in its center and filled with gas to detect radiation. When Alpha, Beta or Gamma radiation knocks electrons off the gas' molecules/atoms the ionization creates an electrical charge that is sent along the wire to a meter, which registers the intensity and presence of radiation.

As mentioned before, any device that detects changes in the environment can be used to help detect paranormal phenomenon. Geiger counters register radioactive intensity in mR/hr, or milli-Roentgens per hour and the higher the milli-Roentgens per hour the greater the intensity. These devices range in price from $49 to $1,000 depending on features and where you purchase them. They are to be used to detect changes in background radiation and can be used with the previously mentioned grid technique. For more on radiation effects and causes, see Chapter Nine.

## ION COUNTERS

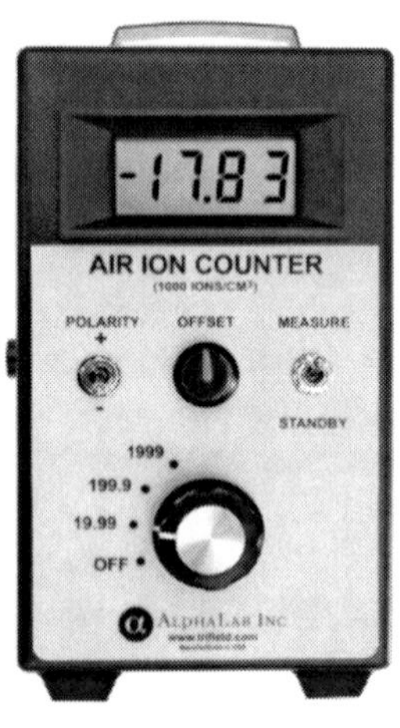


This expensive device can be used to count the number of free-floating ions in the air. They average about $515 to $700. Better save your pennies!

Ion Counters measure ion density in units of ions per cubic centimeter (ions/cm3). Ions are given off by radioactive decay, evaporating water, radon, open flames and red hot metal. It is believed by some researchers that paranormal activity can disturb the ion count in the air. Ions can be positive (as in the case of radiation) or negatively charged (as in the case of ghosts as some researchers believe). Air is pulled in through a slot in the top (via a fast moving fan) and blown out a hole in the bottom of the unit. While inside the meter, either negative or positive ions (depending on how the POLARITY switch is set) are taken from the fast flowing air and deposited onto an internal collector plate. The number of ions per second that hit the collector plate is measured (by measuring the electrical energy of the collector plate, which is connected to ground through a resistor). The case needs to be grounded with an included cord to avoid static charges. Several readings should be taken with an average reading determined since the ion counter has a +/- accuracy of 25%. So, if you take four negative ion readings that come to 130.5, 135.4, 133.2 and 140.6 you should have an average ion count of 134.9. Sorry about the math.

## OSCILLOSCOPES

If you have never heard of an oscilloscope I can assure you that you know what it is. You have seen them in garages, TV shows and hospitals. They are the cool view-screens with wavy lines and sometimes go "bleep, bleep"!

Oscilloscopes measure voltage and time. Much like in a television set, an electron beam is swept horizontally across a phosphorescent screen at a set rate. A signal sent from an external source changes the beam vertically. This is represented by a glowing dot or line on the screen that curves or jumps according to the input. This effectively gives you a graph of whatever you are trying to measure the frequency of. Although most households in the US have AC current that runs at 60 Hz, it may be a good idea to check that there are no devices about that run at different frequencies. Not only will this help detect sources of interference for your EMF meters that are calibrated at 60 Hz, but will also help find hidden devices in cases of fraud.

There are two main problems with an oscilloscope though. 1) It is very expensive with "cheap" ones running about $500 and expensive ones going upward of a couple of grand. 2) They are bulky and require external probes. They just are not easy lugging around your investigation looking for frequency changes.

## TWO-WAY RADIOS

In 2003 I did an investigation of the Judge's Bench in Ellicott City, MD. We had some success with EVP there before and were proceeding with a follow up investigation. Now, as a general rule, we have always had our team members to stay in pairs for safety reasons. To add an extra bit of precaution we give at least one member of each pair a two-way radio anything goes wrong. Mind you, we're not really concerned with the Blair Witch popping up and stealing team members. More so, we are worried about stuff like, oh, I don't know, someone backing up and falling down a flight of stone stairs and collapsing a lung. This is precisely what happened that night! Someone went outside to take a picture of the building and fell down some stairs. He had no radio to call for help either and was found 10 minutes later. What a story, huh?

Two-way radios are very good items to have for a number of reasons.

- They allow you to keep in contact with the rest of the team in case something interesting happens, like a ghost appears.

- If you fall down some stairs, you can radio for help.
- You can report your position to correspond with investigators around the location to prevent accidental interruptions.
- Radio interference should be noted, especially if it begins and ends for no apparent reason.

These modern day "walkie-talkies" are much more advanced than their ancestors. Ranging in price from $29 a pair to $300 a pair depending on features and manufacturer, you usually get more than your money's worth. Most come with about three-dozen channels for creating secure conversations and over a dozen sub-channels for creating an even more secure conversation between two parties. Price also determines the range of these radios. For a $29 pair you usually get a range of three miles line of site! They even have wristband radios! You can be like Dick Tracy: Ghost Detective!

## OUTDOORS

I have heard all too often of would-be ghost hunters trespassing onto private property and claiming to be a member of a legitimate organization that would normally never condone that sort of behavior. Don't trespass darn it! If you do not have permission to be on someone's property – stay off! That goes for cemeteries too.

Moving on then...

Believe it or not, in some cases, outdoors investigations will require more equipment than an indoor investigation. Not only do you need to bring all the equipment you would normally bring but also you have to take into consideration environmental conditions. For example:

- ✓ Bug repellent. Don't get eaten alive! I recommend a citronella candle (one of those big bucket ones) near the base camp and spray-on repellent for each investigator. This is very important to apply before beginning. Do not apply during an investigation as lingering fumes from spray-on repellents can interfere with photographs.
- ✓ Hats. Not only will a wide brim hat keep the sun out of your eyes but will keep ticks out of your hair in wooded areas.
- ✓ Flares. Mark trails with flairs or light sticks when going into wooded areas in the dark. Careful not to burn down the forest though. Smokey is watching!
- ✓ Tarps. A large plastic tarp will help your team if it had

rained earlier. Place it over any muddy area near home base.

- ✓ Raincoats. Don't use umbrellas. How are you going to carry an instrument or camera with an umbrella?
- ✓ Plastic zipper bags. If it starts to drizzle you can forget about taking pictures but you will still be able to take EMF readings if the EMF meter is protected in one of these.
- ✓ Portable screened-in gazebo. Yeah, this is a little extreme, but useful. You and your equipment will be protected against the elements and bugs. A few companies sell quick folding gazebos that set up in minutes.
- ✓ Extra medical supplies. Go to a local library and check out a book on the local wildlife and flora of the area you plan on investigating. Do you need snakebite anti-venom? What about lotion for poison oak? Bear repellent?
- ✓ Lanterns. It's always good to have a few of these around base camp. Careful though, they will attract insects.

## LOW-TECH TECHNIQUES

Harry Price used some pretty interesting techniques way back when. Although he was filthy stinking rich, technology just wasn't very advanced back then. Whether stuck in the past or cost conscious, sometimes low-tech works well.

## ENTICING THE DEAD

We were fortunate to have conducted an investigation of the Jennie Wade House in Gettysburg, PA in 2003. Jennie Wade was the only known civilian to have been killed in the Battle of Gettysburg during the War Between the States in July of 1863. She was struck by an infantryman's bullet as she baked bread for Union soldiers in her kitchen. The house is supposed to be haunted by Jennie and her family. It was here, in what is now a museum in her honor, which we were to conduct our first enticement experiment.

I noticed in the Jennie Wade House gift shop were reproduction Civil War era coins and paper money. Jennie Wade's father was a criminal we were told who was often in trouble with the law. What better to entice a thieving ghost than money! We placed the coins and paper money around the house and videotaped the areas where they were located. There was just one problem – the paper money was artificially aged with a vinegar solution. I am not sure if this is why we didn't get any results from the experiment (I'm not even sure ghosts can smell), but it does make a little sense (no pun intended).

Nevertheless, enticing ghosts out has resulted in some interesting phenomena. Mark Nesbitt of Ghosts of Gettysburg fame with the American Battlefield Ghost Hunters Society had also conducted research into enticement. Mark would yell out roll call orders and pay time orders and try to get EVP this way. It worked! Mark and ABGHS hope to record the first rebel yell in over 140 years! Money gets results sometimes. I found a place in Gettysburg that sells more realistic and less pungent paper cash and we use it every time we think there may be Civil War era spirits nearby. More recently deceased ghosts can be enticed with modern money and coins.

If you know enough to think you know the identity of the ghost, you can use personal enticements. If the deceased was an art critic, lay some paintings around. If he/she was a child, bring some toys. There are many ways to entice. You can even use your own team as bait! In a low-key investigation of the Old Stone House in Georgetown there is rumored to be a ghost that is rude and abusive toward women. Team leader Renée Colianni "volunteered" to act as the enticement for activity. Although we got some interesting pictures, Renée didn't experience a thing.

## TRACKING THE DEAD

Another popular technique is using talcum powder to track spirits and would-be meddlers. I recommend laying down a large piece of black poster board on the floor first. Then, using a metal sieve such as those used for baking, sift some talcum powder on the poster board so that it evenly covered. This should be done in hot spots near entrances in case someone tries to interfere with experiments or to detect the presence of a walking ghost. Write your initials into the powder too. This will help prevent anyone from messing with the powder and trying to fix it afterward. If the powder is found disturbed, take pictures since it may be necessary to purchase an additional piece of equipment as well, a handy-vac!

Another way to try to track the movement of spirits is too place obstructions in their way. You can use tacky putty (available at many arts and crafts stores) and attach paper party streamers to the ceiling. Have you ever walked into a room full of these before? Even the slightest movement will get them fluttering. Now if you have some time on your hands you can attach the ribbons in a pattern along the ceiling in a grid formation. They should all be at least 18 inches apart. Now you can aim a video camera at your arrangement (after making note of where all the drafts, vents and windows are) and see if they, the ghosts, move the streamers in the final movie. We will be talking more about how to check and mark natural and artificial sources later in the book.

## MORE DO-IT-YOURSELF GHOST HUNTING!

I will probably say it again later in this book, but I want to put emphasis on it – I do not want you to read this book and then say to yourself "well now I know everything". Actually, you will know more than I did when I got started and it is time for you to give back!

Learn and then create. Take these lessons and contribute back to the paranormal community. When you have made some of the devices listed in this section, create your own and then tell everyone about it!

## PKE TRIGGERS

PKE triggers are devices that demonstrate the influence of either ghosts or psychic activity. A good PKE trigger should be able to detect both. The criteria are simple – your trigger should be very difficult if not impossible to set-off without paranormal or super-normal influence. This normally involves an enclosure such as a glass jar and sound maker such as a bell. Visual alarms can be substituted for the bell as well.

## THE BELL TEST I: AUDIBLE

This is an oldie but a good oldie, a version of which Harry Price once used. In some versions of the experiment an electric buzzer is used, but this is unnecessary. I mean, what if your ghost predated electrical appliances? Then what are you going to do with your fancy electrical engineering knowledge?

What you will need:

1. A glass jar
2. A small bell
3. String
4. Plastic tape
5. A towel or cloth
6. A video camera

## STEP 1: GET A JAR

Glass works best. Go simple as well. Now, I am using a classic precision scientific bell jar. It is not necessary for you to do the same. Go to your local Target or craft store and get a glass vase used for candles or flowers. Turn is upside down on the surface you are using. A large pickle jar will suffice as well.

## STEP 2: GET A BELL

What size you ask? As long as it fits in the jar with some room to rattle you have a good bell. Suspend the bell from the top of the jar (which in some cases is the bottom when placed upside-down) with some string and tape.

## STEP 3: LAY DOWN A THICK TOWEL

Place a nice thick wooly towel or cloth on the surface you are using. Skeptics will say you are blowing under the jar to make the bell ring. This has happened! The towel will give you a nice seal.

## STEP 4: SET-UP VIDEO

Now aim a video camera at the experiment and begin recording. Make sure the whole experiment is within shot.

Some people like to watch the video later after leaving the room. Some like to stick around and ask questions like, "if there is anyone here, can you ring the bell?" If it works, try it!

## THE BELL TEST II: VISUAL

This is the visual version of the audible experiment.

What you will need:

1. A jar
2. A square piece of paper
3. A toothpick
4. A piece of Styrofoam
5. A towel or cloth

## STEP 1: SAME AS ABOVE

## STEP 2: FIND A SQUARE PIECE OF PAPER AND FOLD IT

Fold the paper corner to corner twice. Make sure the paper is not wider than the jar.

## STEP 3: PINCH THE CENTER OF THE PAPER

Use four fingers to create an umbrella-like shape or little pyramid.

## STEP 4: PLACE THE TOOTHPICK INTO THE CENTER OF A SQUARE PIECE OF STYROFOAM

Make sure the Styrofoam is not wider than the bottom of the jar.

## STEP 5: PLACE THE PAPER ON THE TOOTHPICK

Make sure the center of your pyramid is balanced on the toothpick. Place the jar over this set-up and then video record it.

If the paper moves in the jar without air currents, you may have a ghost on your hands!

## AUDIBLE LUMINOSITY VARIATION DETECTOR

Just about everyone has a laptop these days and I am designing this experiment around that. For those of you do not have laptops, don't worry, I have a variation for you as well.

As we mentioned before in this book any device that can detect variations and changes in the environment is a device you can use. This device detects light and with a slight modification detects IR light as well. Not many people know that LEDs (Light Emitting Diodes) detect light as well as emit light.

What you will need:

- ✓ A pair old headphones or 1/8" plug Y-adapter (you will never be able to use these again for the original purpose, so don't borrow someone else's!)
- ✓ An LED from radio shack (this can be just a regular LED or an IR LED which we will talk about later)
- ✓ Electric tape
- ✓ Wire cutters or really good scissors
- ✓ Audacity Digital Audio Editor (or comparable software) which you can get from www.download.com for free
- ✓ An audio recorder (digital or analog) for those without laptops

## STEP 1: CUT THE HEADPHONES FROM THE CORD

If you are using a Y-adapter you only need the male jack. Cut off the female inputs. Ex-polygamists may find this familiar.

## STEP 2: BARE SOME WIRE

Using the blade of your scissors or a utility knife, carefully expose about an inch of wire from the cords you cut.

## STEP 3: ATTACH THE LED

If you have some soldering experience you can solder the led to the cords. If not twist the ends together so that each cord is attached to one wire from the LED. Careful, LED wires are very fragile. After twisting them, use your electric tape to maintain the connection.

## STEP 4: TRY IT OUT

Wasn't that simple? Now plug it into your computer's microphone input and start-up Audacity. Turn the lights in the room on and off and see the audio spikes on Audacity correspond. You did it! Use an IR LED and detect Infra-red. Don't have a laptop? Use a voice recorder. Pitch variations in the static will correspond to light amplitude variations. Now your buddies will think you're a regular MacGyver!

While researching this book I came across another book by a guy who put electrical schematics for EMF meters and other devices in his work. I thought that was pretty cool myself since I have experience with such things. But many of my readers would not. I am trying to write a book that's accessible to everyone, not demonstrate how smart I am. Now get out there and design some ghost hunt experiments! Um, after you read the rest of this book of course!

## THE WRONG TOOLS FOR THE JOB

"All hope abandon, ye who enter here"
- Dante's Inferno (The Divine Comedy)

Don't worry, this is not a chapter dedicated to me bashing digital cameras and IR thermometers. No, this chapter is dedicated to much worse violations of common sense and scientific methods.

Besides cool gadgets, what else do ghost nerds buy in large quantities? Books of course! All the latest literature on Ghost Hunting and Paranormal Investigating must be yours. No matter how cheesy or expensive. No matter if it's current or decades out of date, the quest for more ghostly knowledge will go unabated. I myself have procured an impressive collection of books on the paranormal thanks to Prairieghosts.com, Amazon.com and eBay as well. But, how do you tell the crap from the cool and useful? Common sense. Of course that's easier said than done. You're smart, but no one can expect you to know everything there is to know about environmental science and physics.

We are going to skip the lit on the occult practices (Ouija Boards, Tarot Cards, etc.) since this is a book on technology and talk about how some ghost hunters have contaminated their own investigations.

## MAKING YOUR OWN GHOSTS

I'm not exactly Martha Stewart, but boy do I hate dust (or any air particles for that matter). Air particles can contaminate spirit photography. Most orbs on the Internet can arguably be some form of air particle, whether they are dust, water vapor/droplets or some other contaminate. We cannot remove all the matter floating in the air around us unless we're investigating a haunted Intel laboratory or a NASA clean room. The best we can do this is by being careful. Don't run around or create too much disturbance. I mean, who would want to attract more air particles than what are already present? Who indeed...

Earlier we talked about trying to entice ghosts into activity using very basic, non-technological means. In recent books published on ghost hunting several electronic enticement techniques have been suggested. The problem with the majority of these techniques is that they add contaminates into the environment being investigated.

## STATIC GENERATORS

Robert J. Van de Graaff, an MIT professor, developed the Van de Graaff generator in 1929 to do experiments with artificially created lightning and electricity and to power early atom smashers. You have seen them before on television and in science demonstrations. They're the big metal spheres that make your hair stand on end when you place your hands on them.

We discussed static electricity and its nature in Chapter Two. A Van de Graaff generator is essentially a static electricity maker. In most models there are belts and rollers that move to create a static electrical charge, which is outputted into a metal sphere at the top of the generator. Static electricity surrounds the charged sphere and will charge any matter nearby that is conductive of electricity. This is what causes your hair to stand on end. It will also attract anything to it and then repel matter away from its field - matter such as dust particles. Dust in the air will be attracted to the static-electrically charged sphere and then charge the particles and repel them. Any investigator using one of these will have created a bunch of orb pictures I'm sure.

Also, why would you want to fill any possibly haunted area with static electricity anyway? As stated several times before we do not know what ghost are exactly and what their composition is or what conditions are required for them to manifest. Filling the room with static electricity could hurt your chances. What if it prevents manifestations? If ghosts are some form of energy than you could be short-circuiting them. I even read one source that says you should use a dehumidifier to remove moisture in the room for a bigger charge. What if the ghost likes moisture?? Do you honestly know for sure?

## NEGATIVE ION GENERATORS

I admit, a few years ago I used a Negative Ion Generator in investigations. Negative ion generators are those air purifiers you see on TV all the time such as the Ionic Breeze. They claim all sorts of things besides cleaning the air. They also are supposed to make you "feel better". I dismantled an electric animal grooming brush that used a negative ion generator to collect dander. I read that these devices were supposed to attract ghosts. Boy was I mislead!

These devices work much the same as the Van de Graaff generator except they use electric fields as opposed to moving parts. Negatively charged ions are created in this fashion and attract positively charged dust particles. Without any moving parts you can actually feel the air flow through such devices!

So, the obvious problem here is – why would you want to pump more particles in the air? Well, maybe it's because of all the dust orbs you'll be getting in your pictures?

## VOICE STRESS ANALYZERS

It would be nice to know before I meet in person if the person who claims to have ghosts is being deceitful to me or not. It would be cool to just hook up a device to the phone and tell from the blinking lights if they were exaggerating or outright lying. A few companies claim to be able to do just that!

Also known as Tremolo Detectors these devices are said by their manufactures to be able to detect stress in your voice if you are lying. That sounds great if it works. Unfortunately, they don't. Researchers have been studying stress under pressure for years in order to detect honesty. Those wired "lie detectors" you see the FBI using detect electrical impulses from all over the body. They also detect blood pressure and heart rate. But do you know how most agents get the truth? The agent lies. Even these expensive and sophisticated machines are not fool proof. The agent usually tells the crook that the lie detector says he or she is telling a fib and the crook will break down and confess. Most of the time, the lie detector cannot tell the validity of the crooks story. So, how can a device that only detects voice stress do this? It can't. Scientists say the devices being sold on the Internet called voice stress analyzers are extremely inaccurate and untrustworthy. The voice stress modulations these devices claim to detect can also be caused by illness, anxiety or constipation. Better buy a laxative before taking that test man!

Even more importantly though is trust. People contact people like us because they need help. Yes, some people are cheaters and/or nut-balls, but you have to weed those people out without making the honest ones nervous and/or uncomfortable. Sticking a lie detector in front of someone will make him or her think you don't trust them or think they are crazy.

## WHITE NOISE MAKERS

What is white noise? It sounds like this: "Sshhhhhhhhhhhhhhhhhhhhhh" Turn a radio or TV to an "empty" channel (on older, analog models anyway) and you will hear what white noise sounds like. Now, there are devices out there that are called white noise generators. These devices are incredibly expensive for what they do. They make static noise for goodness sake and it is not much more complicated than that. The concept is that they create noise that covers all frequencies of sound from 0Hz to 22,050 Hz. For those who hunt ghosts, white noise generators are a means of blocking out ambient background sounds, theoretically keeping the background noise from interfering with your EVP recording. The problem is, sometimes background noise is EVP! I have heard furniture being moved around and footsteps on tape that were heard by everyone in the house from rooms no one was in. We caught that on tape. What if a ghost tells you to hush? That might get lost in the Sshhhhhhhhhhhhhhhhhhhhhhh sound of your white noise generator.

## BAD PROCEDURES

Because of a sense of professionalism on my part I cannot tell you the source of the information I am about to describe since it will embarrass another organization. The information involves a picture on their website that depicts their leader holding an EMF meter as it detects a strong EMF source. The picture has several "orbs" floating about the team leader in a dimly lit room and has the following caption above it, "This picture shows (team leader) with an EMF detector detecting ghosts nearby. You can see three 'orbs' near (his/her) head. It was taken with a (name brand) 3 megapixel digital camera." I have changed the wording just a bit so you can't "Google it", however I think you get the gist of it. But, it doesn't end there.

The team leader (who I have met once or twice) was standing in dusty and dimly lit room within three feet of a circuit breaker box! Sorry, but "LOL", I couldn't help but "LMAO" when I saw the picture.

There are groups out there who must find a ghost at every location they go too. A few of them do it for the attention. A few do this because they are naive and feel that ghosts are everywhere and will force the data to fit. Some lie to please the property owners and avoid a confrontation. Many are just plain unethical. I'm not sure how these people's minds work. Do they think people will really believe that they find ghosts at every location? I think ghosts are everywhere but not every place.

## THE OVILUS

The first time I encountered this device was during a tour/investigation of the Jennie Wade House in Gettysburg in March 2009. I was monitoring the basement of the house when some would-be investigators joined down there to attempt communication with their Ovilus. Now, I had heard of this gadget and was very interested in seeing it function. Suffice to say I was a little disappointed with the number of times it said "feet". Much of what was coming out of it was totally incomprehensible. Shortly afterward I decided to do a little research into this device.

Evidently what the creator of the Ovilus, Bill Chappell was trying to build with his invention was a device that would randomly select words (from a built in dictionary of 512 English words) and 71 possible phonetic sounds based on Electromagnetic Field Fluctuations. I should point out that on the website that sells the Ovilus (www.digitaldowsing.com) claims the device should only be used for "entertainment purposes" while also claiming it was designed for paranormal investigations! I guess the inventor wants his cake and be able to eat it too. Also on the website it says that the Ovilus does not include any additional computer algorithms that would interfere with the randomness of the devices responses. So, according to the creator, it does not and cannot cheat. But does it perceive or speak for, ghosts?

I have never watched any of the cable TV shows this gadget has been featured on, so I know little about how the public uses this. At the Jennie Wade House was where I first encountered the Ovilus directly. The "investigators" present seemed to be speaking directly at this so-called technological marvel. I asked them what was the theory behind this and they told me that the spirits could influence the electronics inside the Ovilus and make the words and sounds form conversation. Sorry, if I sound a bit skeptical, but I highly doubt that when someone dies they become electronic engineers. There is no data that suggests ghosts from decades past can learn to use modern technology. Interference notwithstanding of course. If ghosts cause a TV to act funny, it is more likely to be an unintentional side effect. However, the influence of probable outcomes is a regularly reported aspect of studies in psychic phenomena.

Now before I go and try to explain how the Ovilus could work, I should point out that it could be nothing at all. It is also possible the inventor knows that there is nothing to it. The website does say it should only be used for entertainment purposes. It could be your mind just trying to associate words with nondescript nonsense. More than half of the Ovilus downloads I listened to for this article sounded like absolute gibberish. Most of them had some text of what the poster thought it said, but I can only imagine they had very active imaginations.

Starting with experiments in the 70's, paranormal researchers did experiments into the effect of micro-pk (a form of psychokinesis) on probable outcomes. Using random number generators thousands of papers were written on very strong data that human observation can affect the outcome of events. I have yet to see any experiments with this device that shows that ghosts and not human influence is the deciding factor in Ovilus experiment outcomes. For that matter, I have seen no data to suggest it, and similar "talking boxes" are little more than just pricey toys.

## MULTI-TASKING

Laptops are quickly becoming essential pieces of gear for the intrepid paranormal researcher. Many places you may be going to investigate may have WiFi or some kind of hook-up for the internet. Indeed, you may even have a 3G compatible card in your laptop or netbook already. Now you can "wired" anywhere! That means you can record and catalog data and with an online server, save it virtually unlimited amounts of information. But, I am getting ahead of myself.

I am big fan of Pro-Measures, the manufacturers of the Mel-Meter, for their multi-tasking devices such as the before mentioned Mel-Meter. The model I have has an EMF meter, thermo-coupler thermometer and vibration sensor built into one tough and durable little unit. You know, if more people thought along long those lines, we would need a lot less equipment bags and smaller budgets.

Here is where I get back to the laptop, or more specifically, netbooks.

Netbooks are everywhere now and they are getting cheaper all the time. It is not uncommon to see a sleek Asus netbook on sale at for under $300. Although they usually do not have a built-in DVD or even a CD ROM drive, they are nevertheless not short on features. Tons of RAM and 250 gigs of HD space or more in many cases. Netbooks are the killer hardware app until the pad PCs catch on. Now let me ask you this: If you could have either a Netbook or a $300 voice recorder for EVP, which would you go for? Many of you may say, "The voice recorder! I already have a laptop." Sigh... With a netbook you can have all the goodies of that voice recorder plus MORE!!!

Think about it... If you bought a Behringer Podcast Studio setup and hooked it up to your new netbook, you would have the quality of a small recording studio in your carrying bag! Check it out:

- High-resolution 2 In / 2 Out USB audio interface with plug-and-play for Windows XP and Mac OS X operating systems.
- Studio-class 5-input 2-bus mixer with premium mic preamp and 2-band "British" EQ.
- Table microphone stand
- XLR microphone cable and 2 stereo RCA cables.

Get a full recording studio "out of the box" including USB audio interface, mixer, microphone, headphones, professional audio software!

Download the audio software Audacity for free and start

recording the best EVP you ever got! Use Skype to talk to colleagues and ask their advice. Even upload EVP to the web for the public's opinion (You have the original file, don't worry about people "stealing it"). With a small Aiptek HD video camera, you can upload and analyze data on the fly with a built in SD card slot.

Trust me on this, get a netbook or even one of the new tablets, you'll be happier!

# CHAPTER FOUR: ITC & EVP - VOICES FROM BEYOND

"Even though I am nearly deaf, I seem to be gifted with a kind of inner hearing, which enables me to detect sounds and noises, which the ordinary listener does not hear."

"Of all my inventions, I liked the phonograph best...."
- Thomas Alva Edison

## YOU DOWN WITH ITC?

ITC is communication from or with the dead via a device such as a phone, radio, television, walkie-talkie, etc. The acronym stands for Instrument Trans-communication. The concept is that living people can communicate with dead people via modern technology. Now, many people get the generalized term confused with experiments that fall within the parameters of the term. Technically though, ghostly phone calls from deceased love ones count as ITC. EVP is ITC to some degree. Hearing spirit message through the car radio is ITC too. Except for the murderous demon-ghosts the movie White Noise was an ITC instructional film!

The experiments I referred to in the previous paragraph involve placing a video camera in front of a television (turned to a channel with static, which would be hard to do with most modern TVs) or aiming two cameras at one another and waiting for something "weird" to happen. This usually comes in the form of vague images of faces or silhouettes of human or human-like figures. Way too many times to count we are really dealing with the natural human tendency to find familiar human features in random patterns. Even worse it could be a TV station that just isn't tuned in very well. I can hear it now, "Hey we just picked of these ghosts of some rednecks who struck gold and moved to Beverly Hills!"

To be honest, I do not have much experience with these types of ITC experiments. I have read many cases of ITC experiments though and think there may be something to it, but perhaps not in the way many researchers intended. We are all familiar I am sure with stories of ghosts interfering with electrical devices. Lights flicker and battery operated devices go dead even with fully charged batteries. I think ITC evolved from these types of stories. The assumption is that ghosts are energy and that their presence interferes with anything else using energy. Sound theory I suppose. But does interference equal a human face?

## EVP - I HEAR DEAD PEOPLE

EVP, or Electronic Voice Phenomena, is the concept that spirits or ghosts can be caught on tape or heard though electronic means. However, EVP has been documented to occur with video equipment, televisions and even phone calls from dead loved ones. That is why, instead of a separate division, many people consider EVP a sub-division of ITC. From time to time people will even receive calls from a dead relative who will leave a message on the answering machine. There will be no click from a phone being hung up and no traceable number. Now that I have given you a little background, it's time to get on with technical aspect.

Valdemar Poulsen invented the wire voice recorder in 1900. Engineers in Germany created the first tape recorders in the 1930s. These were based on the principles discovered by Thomas Edison's phonograph, which he invented in 1877. Edison himself said that he was working on a device that would allow human's to communicate with the dead! Edison said, "If our personality survives, then it is strictly logical or scientific to assume that it retains memory, intellect, other faculties, and knowledge that we acquire on this Earth. Therefore ... if we can evolve an instrument so delicate as to be affected by our personality as it survives in the next life, such an instrument, when made available, ought to record something." He, ironically, died in 1931 before he could complete it, leaving no notes. The first EVP is often attributed to Rev. Drayton Thomas who, in the 1940's claimed to have recorded his dead father at a séance. In the 1970's the Vatican was even involved when a priest became upset at recording his deceased father on a tape. It is a sin, according to the Catholic faith, to try to communicate with the dead. The Pope, allegedly, assured the priest not to worry, and that this technology may help to strengthen the faith of many Christians. Today EVP recording is an essential skill for any would-be professional paranormal investigator.

Not too long ago I had a discussion with Troy Taylor about the nature of EVP and how spirits are recorded. In his own ghost hunter's how-to book he wrote what seemed, at first, to be a valid argument for not using digital recorders. He said that since we do not know how EVP is made we couldn't assume that a digital recorder can pick up EVP. After all, we know that EVP is possible on tape. How do we know that it is not recorded directly to the tape, somehow bypassing the microphone and through electromagnetic manipulations or some unknown phenomenon recorded? Would such phenomena work with a digital recorder? Why switch to unproven technology? Nevertheless, I told him I thought it wouldn't make a difference what kind of recorder you use. Before I tell you why that is we must first understand how a tape recorder works.

The common every day tape recorder works just like everyone else's. From the technology used to tape Presidents and their interns to the same technology used to record EVP. The common tape used in tape recorders like the ones you buy at Radio Shack and play in older car stereos (yes, even eight-tracks) uses a thin plastic strip coated in an iron oxide (essentially rust) called ferric oxide. Ferric oxide is ferromagnetic which means it becomes permanently magnetized when exposed to a magnetic field. This is what allows you to record and erase the tape over and over again. A 90-minute tape is 443' long.

Inside the tape recorder are two electromagnets that receive a signal from a microphone and translate the signal into a magnetic flux (a measure of the strength of a magnetic field over a given area) that is "remembered" on one half of the tape as a stereo audio signal when it spools by at 4.76 cm per second. When you flip the tape over, the other half of the tape will be used to record the two stereo channels. During the playback of the tape the magnetic field is amplified to play through the speakers.

The recording mechanics inside most tape recorders is where the theory of a direct recording to tapes by paranormal means falls apart. As the capstan and pinch roller help pull the tape across the magnetic head, a bulk erase head erases any information that may have already been on the tape to make room for the new audio input! This means that if a ghost were trying to get it-self recorded, it would have to know to send its "signal" directly after the bulk eraser or on or after the recording head. Also, the spirit would need to know the precise magnetic flux to transmit at and at what field strength. Otherwise the tape will be completely erased. So, unless you learn the basics of electronic audio recording immediately after death, it would seem that the only logical place an EVP could be recorded would be the microphone!

That means, whether you use tape or digital recorders, you don't have to worry about if the kind of recorder you use will interfere with recording EVP.

I was in a haunted mansion in a remote part of Maryland with Mark Nesbitt (author of *The Ghosts of Gettysburg Series and The Ghost Hunter's Field Guide: Gettysburg and Beyond*) and Patrick Burke (president of *The American Battlefield Ghost Hunter's Society <ABGHS>*) and a team of investigators (including Scott Fowler president of Beltsville Ghosts and Daryl "Smitty" Smith of ABGHS) (Jeez, too bad I don't get paid by the letter!) when I experienced some of the most amazing EVP (Electronic Voice Phenomena) yet.

Mark was using a digital voice recorder on the uppermost floor of the mansion. He was conducting the third part in the ASQ (which we will discuss shortly) technique for conducting EVP experiments. In part three of ASQ you ask questions of the ghosts who may be present.

Mark started by asking a few questions in regards to the family that once lived there years ago. In this instance the recorder was in his hand. He would ask if a certain family member was there and then wait three of his breaths for an answer or about 15 seconds. If the ghost was answering you were able to see the red indicator LED on the recorder blink. It blinked often that evening.

We asked Mark if he wouldn't mind placing the recorder on a tabletop so to prove for the record that his hand was not interfering with the recorder. It was not. The light blinked and responses were recorded. But how is this possible? How can a ghost, that is usually assumed to be somewhat intangible, create sounds that can be interpreted as EVP? Let's hypothesize some more, shall we? But first, we will need to know how the human voice works. Hey, I'm not big fan of biology either, but bear with me.

Creating the sounds that we call our voice is very complicated. It is one of the miracles of human biology, or in the case of Gilbert Godfrey, a curse. The most important parts of our vocal anatomy are the larynx and the vocal cords. The process of voicing your opinion or reading this out loud requires you to move air up from your lungs and past the edges of your vocal cords. This vibrates the loosely touching vocal folds of the vocal cords. The regular air movement causes the fold to open and then snap back. This excites the larynx creating a tonal sound. The series of events will repeat itself 110 times a second for the average male and 200 times a second for the average female (there are several very sexist jokes in there that I refuse to touch). The tones created by your larynx and vocal cords are formed into words by your lips in conjunction with your tongue controlling the passage of air. Of course none of these would be any use without any air. Not only would you be dead from asphyxiation but your last words would go unheard without the medium to carry them: air.

Sound is a sequence of waves of pressure. In order for sound to be heard it must be transmitted through a medium that will carry it to our eardrums. Sound speed in air is normally 1,130 feet per second at 68° F. Imagine a rock dropped from an outstretched arm into a sandbox. When the rock reaches the sand it will create a series of ripples from the shock-wave emitted from the impact. Likewise if we drop the rock into a pool of water the water will ripple out from the spot where the rock impacted and broke the water's surface. Without a medium to transmit the vibrations of a sound wave, sound cannot reach our ears or even be recorded via normal means to a recorder, albeit tape or digital medium.

Most every microphone that is readily available to the general public is a dynamic microphone. A dynamic microphone uses a thin plastic diaphragm that when introduced to sound vibrations vibrate a magnetic element and coil that, by changes in the positions of the coil and magnetic mass, sends an electric signal to the tape recorder. The microphone that is built into most tape recorders is usually a dynamic microphone. The best dynamic microphones are Neodymium dynamic microphones. They are more sensitive, smaller and more powerful.

Whether or not ghosts can generate the needed sound vibrations to vibrate the diaphragm in a microphone is unknown. It is possible they can directly influence the magnet and coil through electromagnetic energy. Perhaps the same electromagnetic energy that sets off EMF meters.

So, how can a ghost, that has no tangible vocal system, create the necessary sound vibrations to be recorded on an electronic device? Most times the investigators present during an EVP experiment cannot hear anything but their own breathing. Taking it for granted that the before mentioned theory that ghosts can manifest a shell of electromagnetic energy is true, perhaps they can also manipulate enough of this force field to vibrate the elements of the microphone. The ghost would do all this without thought of course. I'm sure everyone doesn't become an electronics engineer when they die. There is another possibly though.

Perhaps the ghost uses electromagnetic resonance to manipulate the magnetic coils of the microphone. Possibly what happens is a ghost sends out a magnetic pulse that effects the coils much like sound vibrations do. This is an interesting concept, but how can it be tested?

In a vacuum! If a ghost uses EMF (Electromagnetic Fields) to manipulate the magnetic elements inside a microphone as opposed to vibrating a diaphragm (which is how sound is carried normally) then air would not be necessary to record EVP.

So, here is how the experiment will work. Using a basic bell jar (the kind you would get from a scientific parts distributor) placed on top of a vacuum pad and hooked to a vacuum pump, we run a microphone into the jar through a rubber stopper placed through the plughole on the top of the bell jar. You can use grease or petroleum jelly to make sure you have a tight fit, but a properly measured stopper should do just fine. Then all you have to do is pump out the air and leave the setup in a location (preferably a known haunted one) to see if you record EVP. Easy and makes a great science project for the kids!

If you record any voices during the experiment you know it must be a ghost since no sound vibration could possibly be reaching the microphone.

Extensive experimenting has been done with this setup since I came up with the concept on 2004. I recommend purchasing a metal vacuum pump or brake-bleeding pump (same thing) instead of the plastic ones that are available on some websites. Also, use an empty pickle jar instead of a bell jar to put a small micro-cassette recorder in or digital recorder. You would think an external microphone is not needed for this experiment since vibrations from winding gears cannot be heard anyway, however I have detected an electric hum from an Olympus digital recorder and the same hum from a Panasonic. So, I recently purchased a small external microphone that fits perfectly in the pickle jar I have been using. The microphone is normally used for lecturing and fits on your shirt or lapel.

Why use a pickle jar? The top of the jar is shaved off to be level for a more secure seal. I did manage to find a decorative bowl used to put over dried flower displays. It was cool because it made the experiment look like a crystal ball! However, my cat Teddy knocked that over and broke it. He's fine though.

Okay, now where were we.... The fact that EVP must start at the microphone also explains how EVP can be recorded on different formats like videotape audio. A local reporter here in Maryland once told me about a local access show that did a Halloween special on paranormal investigating in the late 1980s. The show had a popular psychic on who, with a reporter and cameraman, went to a local bar called the Charm City Inn. The inn was and is notoriously haunted. When they descended into the basement the sensitive woman suddenly became overwhelmed. She exclaimed that there was a presence there. The spirit told her that there was a body beneath the basement stairs! She told the owner that he had to dig up the cement floor as soon as possible to put the restless spirit to, uh, rest. To which the shaken owner replied, "Do you know how much that would cost?" Later, when the film crew returned to the studio, they played back the tape and heard, at that fateful time, a voice say, "Dig it up... Dig it up!"

EVP t the microphone would also explain why microphones in separate rooms than the recorder still pick up EVP. Some might say that there is a possibility that the ghost sends a "paranormal energy" down the cord to the tape. Well, as farfetched as that is, the ghost would still have to know exactly what wavelength to broadcast at and what field strength or risk erasing the tape.

## SO, HOW AND WHY DO GHOSTS GET PICKED UP ON A MICROPHONE?

Most every microphone that is readily available to the general public is a dynamic microphone. A dynamic microphone uses a thin plastic diaphragm that when introduced to sound vibrations vibrate a magnetic element and coil that, by changes in the positions of the coil and magnetic mass sends an electric signal to the tape recorder. The microphone that is built into most tape recorders is usually a dynamic microphone. The best dynamic microphones are Neodymium dynamic microphones. They are more sensitive, smaller and more powerful.

Whether or not ghosts can generate the needed sound vibrations to vibrate the diaphragm in a microphone is unknown. It is possible they can directly influence the magnet and coil through electromagnetic energy. Perhaps the same electromagnetic energy that sets off EMF meters.

## RECORDING EVP

I have heard of all kinds of false EVP incidents in which non-paranormal sounds were mistaken for EVP. Everything from creaky doors to flatulence has been mistaken for EVP. You can't eliminate every possible false EVP, but you can help limit them.

## STEP ONE: USE AN EXTERNAL MICROPHONE

Okay, take your tape recorder and hold it up to your ear and with a blank tape inside press record without an external microphone plugged in. What do you hear? Winding and spinning noises coming from the tape player I bet. Now, play the tape back. What do you hear? A bunch of winding and spinning noises again, right? You are recording the noises from the gears and mechanics that run your tape player. External microphones eliminate this issue when used right. Even digital recorders suffer from this ailment in that you can hear white noise sometimes from the recorders electrical output. When using a digital recorder you must remember to adjust the recorder for the lowest level of compression! Audio compression is when software removes bits (or pieces) of information from a file in order to save space on the device it is being saved too. Setting the compression level very low (if this feature is even available) will cause you to lose record time but gain sound quality.

Make sure the external microphone is a good distance from the tape recorder and not on the same surface as the tape recorder. If the tape recorder and external microphone are, for example, on the same table top the microphone will hear the sound vibrations from the tape-recorder's gears through the tabletop. I find that hanging the microphone works very well. You can hang it from a doorknob, chandelier, lamp or tripod. But make sure that it hangs freely and doesn't bump against a flat surface like the wall or a door. Otherwise when you walk into or near the room your footfalls will be caught on the tape with a tap, tap, tapping noise from the microphone banging against the surface.

## STEP TWO: SPEND AT LEAST $20 ON A NEW MICROPHONE.

You get what you pay for. I bought a microphone recently that looked okay and seemed professional enough. So what if it was $6.99. Well, it worked like crap because it was crap. All I heard was white noise. It was as bad as having no microphone at all.

## STEP THREE: WHEN USING A TAPE RECORDER, BUY HIGH DEFINITION TAPES.

You get what you pay for. Better quality and better sound. Duh.

## STEP FOUR: USE ONLY NEW TAPES RIGHT OUT OF THE WRAPPER.

This way you can keep track of your recordings better and have better quality sound since reused tapes have sound degradation.

## STEP FIVE: USE ONLY ONE SIDE OF THE TAPE.

Yes, I know, this will cost you more tapes, but its better this way. It's easier to keep track of where on a tape the EVP is if you only have to worry about one side.

## STEP SIX: FOLLOW PROCEDURES!

Procedures for recording EVP on a paranormal investigation:

Before you begin your investigation be warned, EVP recording is very time consuming. It also takes a lot of effort. Not only setting up but also finding time to listen to the data you have recorded. In regards to what kind of recorder to use I recommend one with VOX (or voice activation) capabilities. Voice activated tape recorders will start to record as soon as they hear sound when the play/record buttons and pause button is depressed. However, do not use this feature for EVP! It has to detect noise to start. That means you miss a fraction of a second when it records due to the tape having to start. That fraction of second could be important. The reason I recommended VOX recorders is because they often have a light indicator to alert you to the fact they are recording. The light will flash when the microphone is detecting sound vibrations. In this way you can be alerted to EVP when it is first recorded. If the room is silent and the red light flashes, it a may be paranormal.

As I said before, doing EVP is time consuming. If you can, wait until a follow up investigation before doing EVP at an initial investigation. That way you can spend more time on collecting data and making sure it is worthwhile. Ask the owners or witnesses where the "hot spots" are. Did they hear any voices? Where? Did they hear any unaccountable noises? Where?

Once you have settled on a location and properly arranged the microphone and recorder you are ready for ASQ (pronounced "ask"): Phase one is when you leave the setup Alone. Phase two is when you supervise. Phase three is when you do a little Q&A. ASQ.

### ASQ PHASE ONE: ATTEMPT ONE: ALONE

This is simple. Leave the room where the EVP setup is. Go as far away from it as possible. Let it run until the end of the tape (about 45 minutes) or with a digital recorder, about 90 minutes to whenever. Your level of patience will decide.

### ASQ PHASE TWO: ATTEMPT TWO: SUPERVISE AND TAKE NOTES.

Here's the hard part - sitting still for 45 minutes while the tape runs and waiting for the little red light to hopefully blink. Take notes if anything at all changes. If you make a single noise, make a note of it. Something like:

EVP: Investigator Ciara C. sneezed at 10:42 pm.

## ASQ PHASE THREE: ATTEMPT THREE: ASK QUESTIONS.

Sometime in early 2004 I did an investigation of Bertha's Mussels in Fells Point, an area in Baltimore, MD and possibly one of the most haunted areas on the Eastern Seaboard (the last part's an inside joke; you'll have to ask me about that sometime). We had a visiting investigator from New Jersey with us who wanted to see how other groups conducted investigations. When we got to this part of the investigation she refused to take part initially. Why? Because, she explained, her group in New Jersey does not partake in necromancy. Necromancy is defined as an attempt to communicate with dead through supernatural means. Magical conjuring if you will. I have to admit I was taken aback at first. Necromancy? I explained to her that what we were doing is based firmly in scientific methods. If we were dealing with any intelligent ghosts than the best way to elicit a response would be through Q&A. This has been a tried and true method and has worked on many documented EVP cases. We are not casting spells here.

Now it's question and answer (hopefully) time. Start asking questions. This is especially important if you are dealing with a suspected intelligent haunting. Avoid asking questions that pertain to the ghost's death! One popular theory is that some ghosts don't know they're dead. The investigation will end pretty quickly if the ghost finds out from a bad question. So, avoid questions like "when did you die?", "what's it like on the other side?" or "how did you die?" Ask questions like, "what year is it?" "What is your name?" "How old are you?" "Who is the president of the United States?" If you think you know who the ghost or ghosts may be, use specific questions that would cater to what you know of the person. For example, if the ghost is George Washington, you might ask about crossing the Delaware. Write these questions down as you ask them and what time you asked. Don't ask the questions too quickly. Take a pause between each question to allow for an "answer". I also think it important, and this may sound silly to some, to plan your Q&A away from the area the EVP will be recorded in. You know, just in case "someone" is listening in.

When you are done collect your tapes and/or files, and assign one person to review them. Have him or her listen to them with earphones on at a comfortable volume. Large earphones that cover the ears completely are best for this. If you have one, use a line double-ended phone jack to attach your recorder to a laptop and use readily available software to load your EVP sample to a computer. This technique might help you "see" something you may have missed when listening. Alternatively, you might have a handy USB capable Digital Voice Recorder. If your tester has found what may be an EVP, have them play back the sounds/voices for the group. Have each member of the team write down on paper what they think the sounds might be. Do not announce what you think was said on the recording. Your opinion will influence everyone else's opinion. Try to determine if there is a more logical explanation for the sounds. If not, you may have recorded real EVP!

I myself have begun using my laptop to record EVP. I use a Radio Shack portable equalizer attached via a USB audio input device. I load the files I record into a piece of software called Audacity. Audacity can be downloaded from the popular website www.download.com. Since Audacity has a visible waveform during recording and playback, you can "see" the EVP. With this setup you will be able to skip to bits where there is sound without having to listen to, possibly, hours of nothing.

There are other techniques for EVP investigations out there. One such technique recommends videotaping your EVP sessions with equipment (EMF detectors, thermometers, etc.) in camera frame to see if they are activated by whatever is making the EVP. This is a really good idea, as long you don't have any equipment in the room that makes noise. You could have the ghost of Howard Hughes saying, "There's a million bucks under the..." "Deet-deet-deet-deet-deet..." goes the tri-field meter.

# CHAPTER FIVE: SAY CHEESE: SPIRIT PHOTOGRAPHY

The sleep and the dead are but as pictures...
- William Shakespeare's Macbeth

Now, since I wrote my first book GHOST SCIENCE, my opinion of digital cameras has changed. My opinion changed because it had too. Digital cameras are here to stay and there will be a day, sooner than I thought a few years ago, when there will be no more film cameras. As of the writing of this book Polaroid will no longer be making instant film. So, no need to mention those now. Don't bother stocking up either. Film does expire so we'll just have to get use to these changes. So, you won't hear me bashing digital cameras anymore. They are so advanced now that many of the issues I used to have with them are no longer valid.

## A BREIF HISTORY OF PHOTOGRAPHY

What has become modern photography is based on technology that has been in use for hundreds of years. Ibn al-Haytham (Alhazen) (965–1040 AD) is credited with inventing the camera obscura (Latin for 'dark chamber') and the pinhole camera, although, Chinese philosopher Mozi (470 BC to 390 BC) wrote about the principle behind the pinhole camera earlier still. Ibn nonetheless built the first practical model known. A pinhole camera works by light shining through a small pin-sized hole into dark room or box. The light will shine through and form a cone that will project anything on the other side of the hole into the room or box. Varying the size of the hole will increase and decrease sharpness and brightness. Later lenses would give better control over this. It is theorized that many artists used this technique to make more realistic pieces.

In 1825 French inventor Nicéphore Niépce made the first permanent photograph on a polished pewter plate covered with a petroleum derivative called bitumen of Judea. Eight hours after exposure to bright sunlight and voila! Obviously, progress in photography advanced exponentially after that.

## IMPORTANT TERMS TO KNOW ABOUT YOUR CAMERA

I have always said that paranormal investigators should know every aspect of their equipment or at least as much as they can. I am always surprised when ghost hunters know more about tri-field meters than their most basic piece of equipment –their camera!

**APERTURE** – In most cases an iris diaphragm that opens to let light into the lens (think of the opening of every James Bond movie). The letter F followed by a number represents the aperture size (ex.: F/18).

**AUTOFOCUS** (AF) – Cameras with autofocus will automatically adjust themselves to the object being photographed.

**F-NUMBER** – The size that a lens will open too in relation to its focal length. For example: f/1.4 means that the focal length of the lens is 1.4 times its diameter.

**F – STOP** (f-stop) – A lens aperture setting calibrated to an f-number.

**FILM SPEED** – The sensitivity level of film to light. The faster the speed, the less exposure the film needs to light. For most paranormal investigations an ISO (Short for International Standards Organization, the internationally recognized system for measuring the light sensitivity of film and image sensors.) of 400 is more than enough.

I highly suggest going the library and getting some books on photography. Those IDIOT'S GUIDES are very good. Don't be offended by the name.

## A HISTORY OF SPIRIT PHOTOGRAPHY

A fellow named William Mumler took the first spirit

photograph way back in 1861. He claimed that a self-portrait contained a picture of his father. Of course this all happened around the time of the spiritualist movement and is subject to conjecture. Nevertheless, the genie was let out of the bottle.

There are only theories and conjectures about how ghosts end up on film. No one really knows for sure. Suggestions include the idea that ghosts are a different wavelength of light that only can be picked up by cameras sometimes. Maybe they project their image onto the film. Perhaps the camera can glimpse higher dimensions when the moment is right. We may never know in our lifetimes. But you know we're going to try anyway, right? To understand how ghosts can appear on film or digital media we must first understand how a camera works.

## HOW DOES A FILM CAMERA WORK?

Most cameras have a glass convex lens that directs light onto a point. In film cameras the lens directs the light source or sources onto the negative. Where the point or points meet is a real image. This means, what you see is what you get. Well, except in the cases of spirit images. The proximity of the lens determines focus by changing the angle that light enters the lens. This is why you must focus the camera before taking a picture. Cameras with auto-focus do this for you. Have you ever seen an auto-focus camera try to focus in on an object that isn't there? Could be a ghost...

Light sensitive materials on the camera's film undergo a chemical reaction when exposed to light. The cameras shutter opens to expose the film as quickly as possible. If the film is exposed to long it will have a blurred look from any motion of the camera.? When you take the film to be developed chemicals are added to bring out the light activated materials. With black & white film brightening light areas and darkening dark areas do this. With color, a three-step process is needed to expose the reds, blues and yellows. This is done with chemical dyes.

The two main types of film cameras are point and shoot cameras and SLR (Single-lens Reflex) cameras. The differences between these two types encompass more than just price mind you. A basic point and shoot camera has a viewfinder to view what you are taking a picture of. That means that you are not seeing what the lens is seeing. Kind of like in a rifle, you look through a site on a rifle and not through the barrel. In a SLR camera you see what the lens sees. A series of lenses, small mirrors and a prism directs the light coming in from the lens to the viewfinder. You almost always get better pictures with an SLR camera.

Regardless of which type of camera you use, it is important to consider film speed in your investigations. The speed determines the light sensitivity of the film. You can determine the speed of the film by looking at the box it comes in. It is measured in a standard of ASA (American Standards Association) or ISO (International Standards Organization) in increments of 100 and 200. Faster film is good for photographing moving objects and low light situations. The trade off is the fact that the light sensitive materials on the film are larger on faster film. This gives the photo a grainy appearance. This will always effect enlargements. However, because many times in taking pictures for paranormal investigations you will be working in the dark, you do not want too slow a speed either. I recommend, as do others, 400-speed film. It's not too fast and not too slow. Slower than 400-speed and you pictures may be too dark and any faster than that and they may be too grainy.

Now, I could go into all the details of how film cameras work exactly and talk about film emulsion, the complete mechanics of the camera, the chemistry of film negatives and a ton of other technical aspects, but that would take up most of this book! Besides, it's already been done with books that are only on spirit photography. I think we can cover just enough to give you a head start without bogging you down with too much photography mumbo-jumbo. Also, this chapter is here to talk about the differences between film and digital cameras and which is better for you.

However, you cannot completely ignore costs unless you are very wealthy. So, use your instant camera sparingly. Use it only when you detect something on your instruments or if you feel you should. It also can be used to map out a location. Take some pictures of the house or cemetery and use them as a guide to your investigation.

## THE DIGITAL REVOLUTION

Before the digital revolution most everything was analog or fluctuating waves. Analog phones, film cameras, tape recorders, TV, etc. Sound waves, light waves, waves and more waves were the norm for the longest time and suited us just fine. Lately we have learned that for better quality we need digital. No more fluctuating waves, now we have ones and zeroes carrying our information. The more ones and zeroes, or bits, we can squeeze into the format we are using the better the quality of, well, whatever. I watch baseball in High Definition now and will be getting a Blu Ray player very soon. My MP3 player fits in my shirt pocket and has over 300 songs on it. My new digital camera can take pictures that can be blown up to poster size before it even starts to look "pixilated". I used to have film cameras that didn't even need batteries and now every time I want to take a picture I use a digital camera that, essentially, has a small computer inside of it. Yes, my battery budget has increased but it is worth it. As I am writing this book, film is still king in picture quality, but how long will that last?

Although utilizing highly sophisticated electronics and the latest technology, the digital camera has a much simpler process when it comes to capturing images. Instead of the chemicals and dyes found in the composition of camera films the lenses (which are pretty much the same as those in film cameras) in digital cameras focus light onto a semiconductor (a material that conducts a small amount of electrical current), which sends the data to an analog to digital converter that converts light into electrons. This digitized data is then sent to the storage device (either an internal, non-removable device or removable storage disk such as Memory Sticks and CompactFlash Cards). By attaching your digital camera to a computer via cable or docking port or inserting your memory card into a card access port you can transfer your images to your computer or, in some models, directly to a printer. These days you can even take your memory cards into your local photo lab and have your pictures printed for you!

Digital camera models very significantly, the main differences being quality and price. The better the quality, the more you're going to pay. When we're talking about quality, we're talking about resolution. The resolution is measured in pixels (The individual dots that are used to display an image on a computer monitor or sensor). The more pixels your camera uses, the better the resolution. Anything less than 2240 x 1680 pixels are unacceptable for use in an investigation. The quality just isn't there. 2240 x 1680 pixels equal four mega-pixels. Four mega-pixel cameras or higher are preferred.

There are two competing types of sensors used in digital cameras – CCD (Charge Coupled Device) and CMOS (Complementary Metal Oxide Semiconductor). Both cameras turn light coming in from the camera's lens into an electrical charge, however they do each do it in a different way. The CCD camera has to convert the signal from analog to digital. A CMOS camera uses several transistors to do the same job and is already digital, therefore it does not need an analog to digital converter (ADC) like CCD technology does. In olden times (circa 2005) CCD was king of quality, but not anymore. CMOS has matched, and in some cases surpassed, CCD in quality and clarity. Although some people hold out for one "camp" or another you shouldn't worry about which to buy. CCD and CMOS are both good quality, but, on the other hand, CMOS is a little cheaper.

The benefits of digital cameras are enormous and cannot be ignored.

- You get instant access to what your picture will look like thanks to the now standard LCD (Liquid Crystal Display) screen on today's digital cameras. No more waiting for film processing.

- Unlimited pictures at little or no cost! Carry around a USB compatible laptop and you could upload tens of thousands of pictures if you have a decent hard disk on it.
- No need to scan pictures for your cool ghost hunter website! Upload them right from the camera.
- Did I mention it's cheaper than buying film?

These reasons are enough alone to explain why digital cameras have become so popular to modern paranormal investigators. Just about every ghost hunter group in the country uses them.

## HOW TO USE DIGITAL CAMERAS IN A PARANORMAL INVESTIGATION

One of the draws of digital cameras is also one of the setbacks – ease of use and virtually unlimited photos. People tend to get very click-happy on investigations. I have seen ghost hunters on investigations take hundreds of pictures in just a span of two – three hours. Well, what's the problem with that you ask? When it comes to cataloging data the more the merrier, right? The problem is, unless you live in the home, how are you going to know later where and when those pictures were taken? It is important that you have some sort of PHOTO LOG SHEEET to keep track of every single picture taken. Log the time, place and reason for the picture. That way if something interesting comes up you will know the conditions of location when the picture was taken.

The larger the camera, the better! When a flash is too close to the camera's lens it will illuminate microscopic particles floating in the air. This what most "orbs" are.

## HOW TO USE FILM CAMERAS IN A PARANORMAL INVESTIGATION

I know what our thinking, "Look at hot spot. Take picture of hot spot." Well, it's not that simple my friend, especially when you have to take into consideration different cameras, different film and different situations. We haven't even discussed infrared film yet! But first...

## WHAT KIND OF CAMERA?

The best camera for the job would be a SLR camera like the ones we discussed earlier. The cameras come in a wide variety of styles with many different options. You are looking to spend at least $300 on a decent one. Although I have been seeing digital SLR cameras on Amazon recently for less than $200. These cameras take really good pictures and are great because the flash is not to close to the lens. Even in film cameras, the proximity of the lens to flash can contribute to false positive orbs.

A basic 35mm camera is just fine most of the time. If you can, get a model where the flash is at least 2 ½ inches from the lens or more. Some models even have flip-up flashes that exceed this limit. Use at least 400-speed film but no more than 800 when using these cameras. I would suggest spending at least $50 on one of these cameras. The auto-advance features on the more expensive models are very convenient when you need to work fast.

## HOW TO BEST UTILIZE YOUR CAMERA

I was at a website recently where there was a picture of a so-called "vortex". The black vortex had a caption below it that said, "This is not a camera strap like my brother says it is." This lady's brother was a very smart man. I could tell right away it was a camera strap. I have seen it dozens of times. When the flash is on you will get a white "vortex". The plastic coated woven straps on most cameras will reflect the flash and give it a white appearance. Due to the fact that the camera is focused on a distant object when the strap falls in front of the lens the strap will seem blurred. This will give it a smoky appearance and look vaguely like a tornado. I would say 99.9% of all vortexes on the Internet are camera straps or hair. I haven't seen the other .1% yet. Keep your hair tied back or in a cap. Do not use a camera strap! Please, trust me, no matter how careful you are; eventually the camera strap manages to get in a picture. Also, be careful of loose clothing and make sure you clean the lens with a lens cleaning cloth. Humid areas can cause fogging on the lens too.

I have seen pictures with snow on the ground with "orbs". I

have seen pictures of dusty roads with orbs. I have seen pictures in the rain with orbs. I have even seen people running through a colonial era house that hasn't been dusted since George Washington slept there (I'm telling you, that guy got a round!) with orbs! That's my dusty office in this picture and the only thing paranormal about that is the litter box for my cat Monty. Suffice to say, be mindful of air particles.

I hate it when people use the term ectoplasm to describe photos like this picture. In the case of this picture we have a match and smoke. So, NO SMOKING ON AN INVESTIGATION! I have gotten lots of pictures like this by email from people who have asked if they had a ghost on their hands. I would ask if anyone was smoking and would get responses like, "Yes, but we were really careful." Doesn't matter, you have contaminated the objectiveness of the investigation. Please don't smoke, okay? Anyway, when you do take a picture and get an image that's not cigarette smoke, your breath on a cold day, a match or candle or exhaust from your car (has happened) then please call it a paranormal mist or paranormal fog or something like that. Don't call it ectoplasm because that's not what it is.

Another piece of advice is to be mindful to avoid pareidolia. Pareidolia is a type of illusion involving seeing something distinct in something non-distinct. Like looking into a garden salad and seeing Elvis in your ranch dressing. One of the most common forms of pareidolia is when people see the Virgin Mary in objects like windows and tree bark. It is commonly believed that orbs and paranormal mists are unformed ghosts or energy given off by the attempted manifestations of ghosts. If you look into an orb and see a face, you're looking too hard. I understand it's easy to do. I used to do it myself. If you look into any random pattern long enough you will see familiar objects very quickly when you let your imagination run off with you. Try it with wood grain, clouds or used chewing gum and see for yourself. Especially easy to do is to see faces and figures. The knowledge to recognize the human face is in your brain as soon as you're born. You are hardwired to do so from birth. The trick is to be objective and rational when it comes to analyzing spirit photos. Remember; avoid seeing faces and figures in non-distinct forms and orbs. After all, you can't have the word analyze without anal.

## OTHER TYPES OF FILM

Alright then! Here's where we get into some serious paranormal photography investigating.

## BLACK & WHITE FILM

Black and white film can be purchased at a few drug stores

around the country but your best bet is at a photo store like Ritz Camera Center. Affiliates using Kodak Premium processing will get you the best results when getting your conventional B&W pictures developed. When I say conventional I mean there are two types of B&W film: conventional and chromatic. Chromatic B&W film doesn't require any specialized processing like conventional B&W film does. It gets developed the same way color film does. With chromatic you get more details and finer grain too. Now they even have one-time-use chromatic B&W cameras!

You know we want to avoid false positive orbs and the risk of lens reflection right? Lens reflection is the flash reflecting off a reflective object like polished metal or a mirror. What's the best way of doing this? Turn off the flash of course! B&W film is good in low light conditions because it is sensitive to ultraviolet light.

## INFRARED FILM

This film is not for the amateur ghost hunter. This is one of the most difficult pieces of paranormal equipment you are likely to use on any investigation. Not to mention to find! Film is fast going out of style due to digital technology finally catching up with film in quality. Many manufacturers do not produce this kind of film anymore.

IR film is very specialized and may not be available easily in your area. Number 25 red filters are recommended for cameras using infrared film. This is because IR film is extremely sensitive to violet, blue and red light. By limiting the film's exposure to the red and infrared regions of the color spectrum you also might be limiting the chance of taking a picture of a ghost. Some experts such as Dale Kaczmarek (author of Field Guide to Spirit Photography) suggest not using filters.

It is recommended that you use a SLR camera when using IR film. Do to the extreme sensitivity of the film it is important that no light whatsoever comes in contact with it at any time. Although cheaper point-and-shoot cameras may seem absolutely closed to incoming light it may not be the case with infrared light, which is at a higher wavelength. In fact, the film must be loaded in absolute darkness. When you receive your IR film it will be either packaged in dry ice or given to you directly from a freezer. It must be kept cold during transportation. So, it is recommended that you call ahead to photo lab to see if they have any in stock. Then bring a cooler with gel ice packs, not ice cubes. Keep the IR film cool until about one hour before use. Then find a room that's completely dark. Stuff towels under the door to make sure there is no light getting in. This will take some practice but you will have to load the film in the dark. Take your pictures without the flash. The flash will create artifacts on the pictures.

When you are done taking your pictures with IR film, take it out in the dark room and seal it in the container it came in. Tape up the container and seal it in a Zip Lock bag. Then place the film into the cooler with frozen gel packs (not ice). Have the film processed as soon as possible! Make sure you take the film to a photo processor that is experienced with developing IR film.

Due to the amount of effort that goes into using IR film, I recommend using it only in cases where you have an established haunting. After you have visited a location two or three times and have already found some interesting phenomena, then it would be okay to go through the effort of using IR film.

## I GOT YOUR ORBS RIGHT HERE!

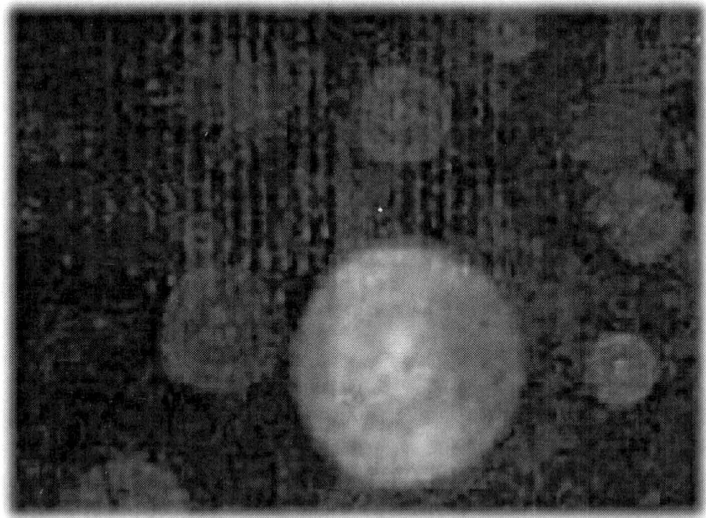

Okay, let me level with you, whenever you go to a convention or book signing and a long term, well known paranormal investigator looks at your orb photos and says, "Well, that's very interesting," he or she is pulling your leg. They are being very polite of course, but they are still thinking otherwise. Too many paranormal investigators have been researching this for many years now and, let me honest with you, orbs are bunk. I laugh out loud (LOL) when someone shows me orb photos with different colored orbs and says something like, "Look! A red orb! That means the ghost was angry!" Who makes this stuff up? I would conservatively guess that 99.99% of all orb photos are NOT GHOSTS or even paranormal. They are particles in the air illuminated by the camera's flash. You know, dust, moisture, bugs, dandruff, etc. I had a person come up to me and tell me that she was in a museum doing an investigation and the place she took pictures in had an industrial air handler to prevent contamination during art restoration.

Therefore the orb picture she took surely must be real! I then asked if she was wearing some sort of contamination suit. "No," she replied. "Then how did you keep your own dust out of the picture", I asked. Most of the dust that accumulates in your home is from dead skin cells from you and your family. Even in a seemingly dust free environment you can make "dust orbs". Sometimes I get a picture from someone that has an orb hiding halfway behind something. Sometimes the orb will be peeking out from behind someone's head. That must be a paranormal orb, right? Nope. When the person took the picture, distant objects were in focus while the dust (or whatever small particle) was not. The sharp contrast will give the illusion that your head or another object is partially blocking a big ball of gooey light.

Okay, but what about that 0.001%? In, what will become the famous "Entity Case", the scientists who investigated that case actually saw the orbs of light first and then took pictures of them. That's how rare real paranormal orbs are. Anyway, why even worry about it? Let's say, for example, you see a paranormal in origin orb of light floating in a cave. You rush and take a picture and when you look at the shot you just took – there are hundreds of orbs! All the dust in the cave got in the picture too. So since you cannot tell the difference (don't argue – you cannot tell the difference), why bother? If you want to be taken seriously as a paranormal investigator or amateur parapsychologist, get off orbs. Focus on photos of apparitions as was intended with spirit photography. Sorry to say, those kind of photos are very rare, so good luck!

# CHAPTER SIX: RESEARCH AND INTERVIEWS

Copy from one, its plagiarism; copy from two, it's research.
- Wilson Mizner (1876 - 1933)

If we knew what it was we were doing, it would not be called research, would it?
- Albert Einstein (1879 - 1955)

One has a greater sense of intellectual degradation after an interview with a [doctor] than from any human experience.
- Alice James

Now you have already learned a lot if you have read this book all the way to this page. If you have just skipped to this page, stop cheating and go back. If you think you are ready to hit the pavement and do some serious research and start investigating homes, then please continue.

This book can only help you start ghost hunting, however there is more to know that cannot be covered in just one book or many books for that matter. You have to be very inquisitive and occasionally suspicious when doing paranormal investigating. Regrettably there are people out there who are ready to deceive you for juvenile fun. There are those who have serious personal issues like drug and alcohol addiction, mental dysfunction, etc. Still there are people who just want attention or have nothing wrong at all and have misdiagnosed their problem (i.e., it ain't ghosts). I am pretty sure I still have not covered all the possibilities that can erupt from the complex human psyche. Above all it is important to be professional and courteous. There are a lot, and I mean a lot, of ghost hunters out there who don't know anything about being professional. Take the following example from the Associated Press Newswire:

> (West Haven-AP, Aug. 17, 2005 7:30 AM) West Haven police say they arrested more than a dozen people who broke into an old factory looking for ghosts.
>
> Police say the group broke into the old American Buckle Company factory on Campbell Avenue early Monday. The building is apparently on some Web site that describes the factory as one of the city's most ghost-ridden buildings.

Police say it wasn't getting into the spirit of things that led to the arrests. Some of the ghost hunters apparently got into some spirits, stealing liquor from a closed restaurant next to the factory. Now you can argue that these people were not ghost hunters or paranormal investigators. But does it matter? The press didn't care, did they?

Now, many ghost hunter novices out there think that if they have a vast array of "evidence" they will be taken seriously by the public. EVPs that sound like gurgling alligators and lots of orb pictures may get you on the six o'clock news on October 31st, but do they make you look professional? Knowing about all the research out there can help you if you do not have a lot of convincing evidence yet yourself. All you have to do is make double sure you credit the original source. Feel free to use the following quote when asked by a would-be client or a Halloween-time reporter:

Although our group does not yet have a lot of convincing evidence ourselves, I should point out that what is considered legitimate evidence by the paranormal investigative community is very rare. Many long time ghost hunters do not even accept orbs as paranormal evidence anymore due to the high probability it is merely dust, moisture or some other air born contaminant. Despite their rarity, our group is focused on picture evidence that shows human-like figures, EVP that is clear and not subject to interpretation and experimental evidence acceptable to scientific scrutiny.

We would be happy to go over our procedures and techniques with you and discuss what evidence has been uncovered so far by well established colleagues in the paranormal investigative community.

Feel free to use these comments verbatim on your website.

## RESEARCHING A LOCATION

When researching the history of a location (outside of what the owners can tell you) there are always some very valuable resources usually in your own town. The local Hall of Records and Historical Societies are always good places to start. Even the local library, the main branch being the best, can help you find important details. At the library you can usually find newspaper archives for the local papers in your area that may reveal details of why the location you are investigating might be haunted. Ah, I will never forget the hours spent with my colleague Jaime Lee Henkin in the Maryland Historical Society looking up info one of Baltimore's most haunted places. I will never forget nearly passing out from exhaustion!

Anyway, another valuable resource that may be easier than hovering over documents at the library is the internet. The website www.newspaperarchives.com has helped me out countless times. You can find birth, death and marriage information at www.ancestry.com as well. Yes, you will have to pay to access these sites, but usually you have to pay a small fee for unlimited access for a year. It is very worth it!

## RESEARCHING GRAVEYARDS

One of the hardest locations to uncover information on for investigations is small graveyards. In Baltimore we are privy to a wealth of knowledge on two of the most well known haunted graveyards in the world – Greenmount Cemetery (est. 1839) and the Westminster Burying Grounds (est. 1786). We know a great deal about these locations and indeed they have been investigated many times. However, there are many smaller graveyards that are much more mysterious. If the graveyard is fortunate enough to have a curator, you can start there. Of course you have to make sure you have permission to investigate that graveyard to begin with. While asking for permission, you can quiz the curator or property owner on any info they may have on the area's history. Otherwise you may have to rely on books on local haunts.

## PRACTICE MAKES PERFECT

First and foremost you will need some experience and training first. I recommend browsing the internet for places in your area to investigate - national parks, haunted bridges, etc. You need not even meet at known haunted places. Your own home or backyard can be a good place to practice. Once you have gotten some practice using this book, you can start getting some more practice! Sorry, I'm not going to make it that easy! Many towns have well known haunted taverns, hotels and other businesses. Since these are public locations that can benefit from any kind of publicity they won't mind you investigating their property and then talking about it on a website or blog. This will help with your "ghost hunting resume". Don't, I repeat, don't start a website or Facebook page to publicize yourself and begin your training by investigating private homes. That is careless and irresponsible. All you will do is, no offense, is bumble around and embarrass yourselves and the paranormal community. Practice makes perfect. Frequent meetings and group discussions on application of techniques will save you from starting your group on the wrong foot.

## HOW TO GET INVESTIGATIONS

The best way to get your name out is with a website. This is the 21st Century - everyone has a web presence of some sort now. I recommend Bravenet (www.bravenet.com) for your website needs. It is relatively inexpensive and very full featured. When you begin designing your website - KEEP IT SIMPLE! Bells and whistle will only distract from the goal of your website of your group. Try to have no more than five link buttons on your site. That means your site should be no more than five pages deep. I recommend the following pages:

- HOME – This is your main page. Its file name has to be index.html or index.php and must be in the main folder of your site. On your main page it should explain what your goals are and why you are qualified to be the investigative team of choice.
- ABOUT US – Friendly pictures and bios of your team can go here. This page should have your "mission statement" on it too. The mission statement will explain your team's goals and criteria for operation.
- CONTACT US – Here is your contact info. The email address of the person who handles interviews and decides on what investigations you will go on, goes here.

Really, that's it. You can add a links page if you want and page that discusses public places you have been to with the permission of the establishment, but I wouldn't do too much more than that. Remember; keep it simple and straight-forward. For those with limited budgets try www.facebook.com.

Something else that might help you, actually will help you, is your own contact number just for the group and investigations. Do not give out you personal phone number! You will be harassed by nutcases if you do. You can use online services like www.skype.com as well. Skype is a VoIP (Voice over Internet Protocol) service that allows you to take calls over the internet and make them as well. It also has voicemail.

Alternatively, you can get a cell phone just for your group's services. Many phone services like Boost Mobile have unlimited service for about $50 a month.

## WHEN CONTACT IS MADE

So, you are ready to investigate a private residence. Before you begin it is important to understand something you may not be comfortable with. The most important thing when it comes to investigating someone's home is the people that live there, not the ghosts. Real living people with their own emotions, problems and lives will be contacting you in fear and angst. They don't know what to think about what is happening to them. Sometimes it can be terrifying. They are confused and do not know what to do. In some cases they may have already contacted someone else who did not show any level of professionalism. Now they are truly desperate. Part of your job will be being a paranormal counselor. Don't make promises you can't keep but be reassuring. To the best our knowledge no one has been hurt by a ghost or haunting since the Bell Witch.

Before setting up a face to face interview it is important to conduct a phone interview first. Even if they insist on a face to face as soon as possible, do not give in. Explain that you have tried and true procedures based on techniques developed by experienced investigators from around the world. Do not bend on this.

## WHAT TO ASK

To open your conversation, try to make the person you are talking to as comfortable as possible. You want to tell them a little about yourself, your group's objective and exactly what these questions you are about to ask will accomplish. For example:

"Hello, my name is ______________. Thank you for calling the ___________________________. Just to reassure you, I have been doing this for quite awhile now and have studied the techniques of many even more experienced paranormal investigators. Our investigators are very professional and dedicated. I am going to need to ask you some questions - quite a few actually. Please be assured that although some questions may seem direct and very personal, they are based on standardized questions used by investigators around the country. Everything you say is completely confidential. Your answers will better help us understand what you are going through."

The first part of this Q&A session is pretty straight forward.

Make sure you have a pen and paper ready for notes. If you have the ability to record phone conversations, remember to get their permission to record. After asking them if it okay to record them, ask them again after you have begun recording so that you have a record of their permission. Check local laws on this delicate subject. Here's what you will need to begin:

- Name and age of contacting individual and their relation to others in the household (i.e. wife/mother, husband/father, etc).
- Name and ages of all in the household and relations to one another including pets.
- Job descriptions of all those in the household.
- Grade level finished of those in household (high school, college, etc).
- Names and ages of regular visitors who may have been witnesses to what is happening.
- Age of home and how long have residents been there.

You can get a complete list of questions for download free at www.ghostscience.net.

Be wary of "haunted dorms"! College students will ask you to "investigate" their haunted campus for their amusement. They will also use you as a topic for a paper they are writing on us "goofy ghost hunters".

## PARANORMAL-HYPOCHONDRIA

Years from now when everyone is talking about paranormal-hypochondria, remember I discovered it first. Some of the questions you will ask will deal with what movies and television shows the homeowner watches. Why, you ask, because I am seeing more and more cases of the psychological condition known as paranormal-hypochondria. This is a condition that afflicts dozens of Americans each year and the epidemic is getting worse each month. A clinical hypochondriac is someone who believes they haveserious diseases without objective evidence. Hypochondriacs will read up on all sorts of exotic illnesses and swear they have it. Paranormal hypochondriacs (or as Loyd Auerbach and Dr. Barry Taff suggested, para-condria) watch too many ghost hunting shows on cable television and swear they have a haunted house. I hate to get a phone call from someone saying they recorded some weird EVPs in their home and they need our help. "Oh, and by the way, are you a member of the TAPS family?" (Don't get the wrong idea; Jason and Grant are great guys) When I first started, no one knew what EVP was. Now everyone thinks they're an expert. Since the beginning of the "ghost hunting boom" every time someone hears a creaky board they think there's a demon in their house! Ironic since I usually tell people to never investigate their own house if it is not a serious issue. I mean, you do have to live there after all.

## WHAT YOU NEED TO KNOW

It is with regret that I have to inform you that perhaps 75% or more of you cases will not involve ghosts. Unless someone let Gozer out again (Ghostbusters reference) there just isn't that much real paranormal activity in the world. Anywhere can be haunted, but not everywhere. When I hear of investigators claiming to find ghosts at nearly every home they investigate, I usually assume that something is not right. Either they are poorly trained or they are lying. Some individuals lie to themselves!

They want to find ghosts so bad they will conclude that every EMF reading is a spirit. Through the phone interview process you are trying to at least determine the following. Make this a checklist for when you do your interview:

- ✓ Is the person you are dealing with imagining the haunting (i.e., the ghost is really raccoons in the attic for example)?
- ✓ Is the person you are talking to crazy?
- ✓ Is the person on drugs?
- ✓ Is the person trying to scam you for personal gain?
- ✓ So they can get out of rent/mortgage/etc. (yes, this does happen).
- ✓ So they can get on television news.
- ✓ So they can write a book.
- ✓ For personal attention.
- ✓ Is the person some sort of practical joker out for a good laugh at your expense?
- ✓ Are the kids faking it?

These are just some of things I have come across or have heard from someone else about. You must be cautiously skeptical at all times, especially when you meet face to face.

## STARTING A CASE FOLDER

As you take on cases you will need some sort of filing system. It is important that you keep your cases organized for future reference. Even the phone conversations that go nowhere (yet) should have a folder started before you dial the number. They may be relevant later.

I use tabbed manila envelopes for every case file and I keep them in a steel file cabinet. File boxes will be fine though as long as you keep them somewhere safe. Next to the furnace or in the basement that floods all the time are usually bad choices. When you go out and buy your manila envelopes get some tabbed file dividers as well. The dividers are for cross referencing your cases. For example, if John A. Smith lives at 100 S. Main Street you will have a folder under S for Smith, John A. and a divider under M for Main Street, 100 S. Since I do a lot of investigations out of state I have my cabinet divided alphabetically by state and then regional county/city. The hierarchies looking a bit like this:

Also, for each street address there would be a divider present. Each file will have all the paperwork and evidence collected about what you are doing in reference to the case. This would include film negatives, EVP and digital pictures (burned to CD of course). What's the pay-off for all this work? Real research that can be shared with other organizations is the pay-off. I highly encourage you to make doubles of everything as well. Once thing many researchers including myself are working on is a centralized location where all data can be stored.

## THE FACE TO FACE INTERVIEW

There are two things you must remember first before the initial face to face interview: (1) never, ever go by yourself. What if the home owners are cannibals? How many ghost hunters have been eaten by going out by themselves? We may never know. (2) Never take more than four people with you. You want the home owner to be comfortable, not stressed by having a bunch of people hovering over them. Before we go on, I would like to share with you my favorite story about what can go wrong when you go by yourself.

My good friend and occasional collaborator Ed Okonowicz is beyond any doubt the best story teller I know. Before you read his true story, I would like to tell you a little about him first.

Ed Okonowicz, a Delaware native, worked as an editor and writer at the University of Delaware, where he continues to teach courses in folklore, storytelling, communication and writing. He earned a B.A. in music education in 1970 and a M.A. in communication in 1984, both from the University of Delaware. A professional storyteller, Ed presents a number of programs throughout the Mid-Atlantic region. He is a member of the Delaware Humanities Forum Speakers Bureau and Visiting Scholars Program and the Maryland Humanities Council Speakers Bureau. He has served on the Maryland State Arts Council Traditional/Folk Arts Advisory Panel. He is the author of 24 books. They range from biographies and oral history to short story collections about Mid-Atlantic ghost stories, legends and folklore. He also has written two murder mystery novels set in the fictional state of DelMarVa.

Now onto Ed's story...

Haunted objects. It's not the first thing that enters into one's mind when someone mentions the paranormal. More likely, people think about ghosts, spirits, demons and urban legends. Sometimes Bigfoot and the Loch Ness Monster pop into your head.

But haunted "things"?

Usually, objects are well below the radar. At least, this was my initial reaction when a "ghoster" suggested I write a book on the subject. Well, I was wrong.

Two books about Possessed Possessions: Haunted Antiques, Furniture and Collectibles, and scores of stories later, I'm much more aware of the topic. In fact, I've met a fair number of people that believe certain "items" may have a "life of their own."

The theories for this active state are wide ranging. From weapons used in battle or during the commission of a violent act, to treasured, hand-crafted heirlooms passed down through generations — some suggest the essence of the evil (in the former example) and love or affection (in the latter case) may have become attached to the piece and remain with it. Occasionally, this mysterious, unseen energy may cause the object to move, make sounds or affect the new, unsuspecting owner.

It was during the search for more stories for the second volume of my possessed series that I encountered Sailor. This grumpy retiree said he owned an authentic voodoo doll, and I made an appointment to record his story and see his prized paranormal possession.

During a rather long, extended interview—during which Sailor consumed a third of a bottle of Jim Beam and delayed my entry into his basement "museum"—my host shared the circumstances surrounding his acquisition of his miniature "monster," as he called it.

About 90 minutes into my note taking, Sailor's mood changed. Suddenly, he snarled at me and said: "Ya know, I could make a voodoo doll of you! I would go through your garbage and get an old shirt that has touched your skin. I'll go to your barber and scoop up some of your hair. I'll sit outside your house and take your picture. Then I'll make a little doll, put a shoestring around your neck and stick pins into you every night until you're walking around with a cane!"

That comment got my attention.

As I remained silent and stared at Sailor, he abruptly burst into a fit of laughter and shouted across the kitchen table, "Just kidding!"

Right, I thought, wanting to finish the interview, view his

voodoo doll and exit Sailor's lair.

Eventually, he led me down the stairs of his South Philly row house. Above a desk hung the small, Gumby-like "monster," only about five inches high, with a black and white man's photograph attached to the figure's cloth head. The back end of more than three dozen rusted pins protruded from the tiny creature.

"Somebody musta really hated this guy," Sailor said.

It was only a moment later, when I looked to the left, that I saw a half-dozen large, eerie collectibles in my host's narrow cellar. Lined up in front of a side wall where full-size tombstones — one about five feet high bearing a cross at the top. They sat there, in full view, for any visitor to see. Before I could and an obvious question, Sailor glared at me and uttered two words: "Don't ask."

Nodding, I turned toward the stairs, to make a slow but steady escape from the strange man's eerie collection. My mind told me that the 100-mile distance separating my home from Sailor's was enough to insure our paths would never intersect again.

So far I've been lucky.

I haven't bumped into the voodoo doll owner, the collector of tombstones, the stranger with the threatening tone and bizarre sense of humor.

But when I do recall that evening, I wonder if the neighbors on his block, especially those in the two adjacent row-homes, know about the marble and granite monuments lined up in Sailor's cellar.

How did he obtain them?
How did he get them into the bowels of his home?
Why would he want them?

Who helped him move them, and who else knows about his odd collection of funeral architecture? But then I recall Sailor's advice: "Don't ask." And I shove my natural sense of curiosity aside — confident that I'll live to write another day.

END

In my humble opinion, Ed was lucky. Never take risks like that yourself. He would tell you the same.

## THE INTERVIEW

Now that you are ready to meet the home owner (or business owner) I can only assume that you have reached a point through the phone interview that you are comfortable meeting this person. Set up a day and time to have the interview at the place in question and bring with you at least one other person, but no more than four. This can be considered your initial investigation. Remember, although this person made it through the telephone interview, that doesn't mean you're in the clear. Whatever you do, do not bring all your gear with you. Here is my recommended list:

A camera for surveying the property and to later formulate your follow-up investigation.

- ✓ One EMF meter for taking base readings.
- ✓ One thermometer for taking base readings.
- ✓ One voice recorder for recording the interview- not for EVP.
- ✓ Notepads and pens/pencils for taking notes (duh).
- ✓ Forms.

That's it. You are not there to intimidate the people you are trying to help. That's why you will not need more than four people. As a matter of fact, when one person (the team leader) interviews the home owner and/or the family, the rest of the team (1-3 others) will be pre-occupied taking pictures and base readings. The main reason this needs to be simple and short is in case something goes wrong. Years ago I was interviewing a man who said his house was haunted who managed to pass our phone Q&A.

When we got there we brought dozens of pieces of equipment in big tote bags. While interviewing the man he brought out huge stacks of photo albums filled with prints he made with his digital camera of floor tiles and shower curtain patterns. "Look, look," he said, "faces!" Alrighty then! I knew it was time to go. However, this guy expected a full on investigation. We were already there with so much equipment after all. So, we went through a basic session of cataloging EMF and temperature readings for two very uncomfortable hours. After that we adopted the minimalistic approach. From that point on, we always told the person or people we would be interviewing that the initial investigation and interview should take little more than an hour. If anything interesting and paranormal does happen, we can do a huddle and decide then if it might be worthwhile to ask if we can stay a little longer. This approach also guarantees, in the cases where it is justified, a return visit. Remember, it is more impressive to visit one location a dozen times than a dozen locations one time.

When actually sitting down and interviewing the person or persons involved there are a few things you can do to make it a little more comfortable for you and them. As you enter the threshold of the location in question, try to say something nice about the property or about the person that is greeting you. Introduce yourself and all the members of your team by first names. Have everyone shake hands and mention how pleased all of you are to have the opportunity to be there. Mention also why it was such a wise decision on the part of the person who contacted you that they didn't contact someone else. This is where you tell them how professional you are, how you try to go by the scientific method as much as possible, blah, blah, blah. At this point the rest of team should begin taking their base readings while you prepare or the interview. Have the interview in the living room, kitchen or dining room – whichever is cozier. If they offer you a drink, always say yes as long as it non-alcoholic. Having drinks together creates a sense of camaraderie. As you proceed with the interview, slowly emulate the sitting position of the main person you are interviewing. This will create a subconscious feeling of familiarity and subsequently a higher level of comfort.

# CHAPTER SEVEN: FINALLY, THE INVESTIGATION

Any doctrine that will not bear investigation is not a fit tenant for the mind of an honest man.
- Robert Ingersoll (1833 - 1899)

Art is born of the observation and investigation of nature.
- Cicero (106 BC - 43 BC)

The first duty of a man is the seeking after and the investigation of truth.
- Cicero (106 BC - 43 BC)

The magic number for an investigative team is six. Trust me on this. Less than six and you will not have enough help when doing a full scale investigation. Worse still is having more than six members on your team. There is a group here in Maryland that not only charges investigators for the chance to investigate with them; they have been known, on at least one occasion, to bring as many as 30 investigators with them! With more than six you run the risk of losing control of your investigators. Remember a team works as one and to succeed you will need a lineup of cooperative individuals who won't clash with each other's personalities. Besides, as I have said before, you do not want to intimidate the property owners and bringing a crowd of people into someone's home will do that.

After your initial interview and basic investigation you and your team should meet somewhere and discuss your findings. Some local libraries have study rooms you can use or you can get together at a team member's home. I find that planning these things on weekends is usually best since most people have jobs the rest of the week. Also, you don't have to plan investigations or interviews necessarily at night or even in the afternoon. Evidence suggests that ghosts haunt all the time. The exception is of course if there is strong evidence that the ghosts are appearing at regular intervals. In those cases you want to get there around the time the events might be occurring. We were told by one person that her infant son was being visited by a dark figure around 10:30 – 11 o'clock pm. The figure didn't appear for us, but we did get some really weird readings with the EMF meter and we also detected a cold spot in the area of the crib. That was definitely one our spookier cases.

Confidentiality Agreements As a standard procedure with our team, we sign, with the property owner/manager, a confidentiality agreement. In it we agree to accept responsibility for any damage and to a certain level of anonymity for the people involved. A copy of this form can be downloaded at www.ghostscience.net.

During your phone interview you should have learned how many rooms were in the house. Knowing the size of the home as far as square footage is concerned might be helpful as well. This information will aid you when you begin mapping out the location. On our website at www.ghostscience.net you can download a ROOM GRID FORM that will serve you well in this regard. Alternatively you can use graph paper. Either way, you want to log the location of furniture in relation to magnetic north. This will help you with EMF readings. Then you want to mark locations that might give false readings like air vents, drafty windows and doors, electric outlets, stereo speakers, ceiling fans, etc.

## THE BASE LOCATION

There is almost always a location where the property owners will say there is little to no activity on the property. That is where you should set up your base of operations. Call it your command center if you want but whatever you call it, it is where you will centralize your team and equipment. Everything you bring will remain at base until needed. This helps prevent leaving equipment behind. I pack everything very carefully in wheeled collapsible plastic totes I bought at the local office supply store. Lately I have also been bringing with us a large plastic tarp to lie on the floor. This keeps us from scuffing certain floors and also aids in cases where we have dropped items around the base location.

Something else to factor in when choosing your base of operations is availability of electricity. If you are to the point where you will be filming video, you will need a convenient power source for your audio/video equipment. In cases where an outlet is not readily available a lamp or lighting fixture usually is. I always bring with me an AC 110 Volt screw-in adapter. These are usually available everywhere. I just take out the nearest light bulb, plug in the adapter, replace the bulb and there you go!

It would be a good idea to map out the location and take some base readings during the initial interview. Discuss a signal that will tell your companions if something goes wrong and you should get out ASAP. From your base location systematically map out the entire house room by room. Take base reading of the location and mark the ROOM DATA & INFORMATION FORM (1&2) and ROOM GRID FORM accordingly. You will be walking through each room in a grid-like pattern. An assistant should be standing nearby with a pad and paper taking notes. Walk in straight lines, back and forth and very slowly. Take your time and get it right. As you take your readings announce to your teammate if anything out of the ordinary shows up on your device or even if you feel a little weird (ROOM DATA & INFORMATION FORM 2). After one person is done that, or another team member, should go back into the room with an assistant and another piece of equipment. You will be surprised how quickly and efficiently you will be able to cover the entire house. This also keeps investigators from bumbling into one another between rooms since they will all be within a reasonable distance of one another.

## THE FOLLY OF THE ALL-IN-ONE INVESTIGATION

What I call the "all-in-one investigation" is what one usually sees on television. The ghost hunting team gets a call about a possible haunting and they set out to investigate. Not having any previously discussed game plan they arrive with every piece of equipment they have. While one or two people talk to the owner, each person goes off in several directions to spook themselves every time their EMF meter beeps. Throughout the evening the ghost hunters take virtually no notes while attempting EVP and other experiments. While half the team focuses on EVP, the other half is making a racket upstairs. At the end of the "investigation" they go home and never contact the property owners again. Sound very professional to you? By taking your time and revisiting a location you will be able to better ascertain the situation.

By being more systematic in your approach you will gain respect from your peers and make far fewer mistakes.

While investigating a home or business it is important that you and your team cooperate with and understand one another. Remember you are dealing with real living people and they can be easily stressed. Already they think their property is haunted and surely they were apprehensive about calling in others. Allocate all questions and comments to your team leader at all times. It is alright and of course encouraged for your team members to have differing opinions. However, each team member represents the team and in such it very important that you are all on the same page while conducting an investigation. Questions about the nature of the case should be exclusively handled by the team leader. If other members have something to add or say, it should be discussed in private conversation, not in the open. This helps prevent confusion and sometimes even panic on the part of the people you are attempting to help. This tactic is also wise when used around the few times you may have to interact with the press.

Here is what I recommend as far as a residential investigation is concerned when it comes to systematic investigating. Assuming everything checks out with the people involved and you have strong, credible reasons to believe that paranormal activity is present, proceed as closely as possible to the following bullet points:

- Contact is made and followed by a detailed phone interview. The people involved in the case are told to keep a journal of everything that happens.
- A face to face interview is scheduled. Any journal entries are analyzed. Base readings are taken (EMF, temperature, etc.) and the building layout is recorded. Pictures can be taken.
- The team meets and goes over the interview and base readings. A follow-up investigation is scheduled.
- At the follow-up investigation the team leader goes over any additional journal entries with the persons involved. Meanwhile, more base readings are done. Additional equipment to take readings can be used. EVP can be recorded. No video. At the conclusion, all film and forms are turned over to the lead investigator.
- The team meets later to go over the evidence. If warranted, another investigation is scheduled.
- At the third investigation the team leader goes over any journal entries with the persons involved. Meanwhile, more base readings are done. Additional equipment to take readings can be used. EVP can be recorded. Video surveillance can be done. At the conclusion, all film, tapes and forms are turned over to the lead investigator.
- The team meets later to go over the evidence. If warranted, another investigation is scheduled.

Remember, it's not how many places you visit or what cool

haunted places you go too, it is how much information and evidence you manage to collect. With the right motivation behind you, ghost hunting can be taken beyond a hobby. You can be more than a ghost hunter, more than a paranormal investigator. You can be an amateur parapsychologist and usher in a new era of paranormal research. Wow! That's pretty deep for me!

Despite my deep reservations for all-in-one investigations, sometimes you will have no other choice. In rare instances when the property is about to change ownership, about to be condemned or demolished, is preparing for extensive renovations or exists in some other similar state where you may not be able to revisit, then, and only then, is okay to do an all-in-one investigation. It will be a very long day and night though. I suggest starting either early in the morning or as early as you can in the afternoon. Essentially what you will be doing is splitting the day into separate investigations. First conduct the interview and take some base readings, and then take a break. During the break discuss any journal entries since the phone call and what your next move will be. Then you can take some more readings and do some EVP. Take another break and when you return you can begin video surveillance. These breaks are important in that they will help keep you alert. Keep in mind that in cases like this, caffeine is a paranormal investigator's best friend. More efficient than coffee runs, we normally bring a carafe of coffee or one of the disposable boxes you can get at Dunkin' Donuts (I am drinking some now as a matter of fact).

## ENDING AN INVESTIGATION

Even after you have visited a place several times and filed your reports, does and investigation truly ever end or is a case really ever closed? In cases of paranormal phenomena, for the moment – no. After your interview the property owner you should ask, "when we are done, what do you think will be the outcome" or "what do you want from us?" Most of the time they will say that they just want to know they are not crazy. Many times, even if a house is haunted it is at least livable. Sometimes though, they will ask if you can get rid of the haunting. The team I train does not try to rid houses of ghosts. However, we can recommend a few things.

Here are few things that have worked in some cases. Although, and stress that, you should mention this to whomever you are dealing with, nothing is guaranteed.

## RIDDING A PROPERTY OF RESIDUAL AND INTELLIGENT HAUNTINGS

I recommend using these in the order they appear here.

Sometimes though, the property owner/manager may insist on one over the other.

## THE SCIENTIFIC APPROACH

A theory that many researchers have, is that ghosts require certain environmental and atmospheric conditions in order to manifest. So changing the conditions of the environment may make it impossible for the haunting to continue. Some experimenters have tried using multiple humidifiers in haunted homes. The theory being that the extra moisture in the air will prevent energy from collecting in one place.

## THE DIRECT APPROACH

Believe or not this has worked in some cases. Just have the property owner walk around the house and yell, "Get out of my house! This is my house now, not yours!" No one knows for sure why this works.

## THE METAPHYSICAL APPROACH

This includes smudging (burning a pungent material wrapped in cloth and twine, to cleanse a location), burning incense, performing a séance, chanting mantras, etc. We usually recommend Googling a local shaman for this.

## THE "GOD HELP US" APPROACH

Call the clergy. This should be done on the personal beliefs of the property owner/owners. Although I do not recommend you "lie" to the denomination they pick, I do recommend not saying something like, "Hey my house is haunted, can you bless it?" Simply ask for a blessing.

## POLTERGEIST AGENTS ARE HARDER TO GET RID OF

Poltergeist Agents are people and therefore none of the previously mentioned suggestions will work, unless you're a jerk, and then can try the Direct Approach. What will usually work for a poltergeist agent tends to be lots of kindness, patience and therapy.

# CHAPTER EIGHT: TEAM WORK

> One man alone can be pretty dumb sometimes, but for real bona fide stupidity, there ain't nothin' can beat teamwork.
>
> - Edward Abbey (1927 - 1989)

> When you're part of a team, you stand up for your teammates. Your loyalty is to them. You protect them through good and bad, because they'd do the same for you.
>
> - Yogi Berra (1925 - )

There is an illusion I am going to have to bust for a few of you. Forget about any Utopian ideas of your team not having an actual "leader". I know, it sounds really nice doesn't it? Everyone is equal and you vote on everything. Well, I have tried this and teams I know and work with have tried this. It doesn't work. Unless you have a team composed of sextuplets, it can never last indefinitely. In every case someone's personality and leadership skills will outshine everyone else. There will be resentment in most cases unless most involved in the group have enough sense to acknowledge the obvious - it didn't work.

In order for a team to truly succeed as a team, you will need a guiding force known as the Team Leader. The team leader is your representative. He or she is the one that makes sure your team's charter and core foundation is upheld and remembered. Try to remember your American History. You need a team leader with veto power. Most of the time the team leader will go along with whatever the team wants, but sometimes they'll have to put their foot down. Think of the leader as the Electoral College. Many times the team leader and the founder of a group are the same person. In these cases they are also dictator for life. Hey, if your team founder is a schmuck, found your own team. A poorly run organization won't last long anyway.

It is usually okay to have another team leader or co-captain if you will. However, you are just asking for trouble to have any sense of hierarchy beyond that. I know a lot of teams have co-captains and a tech specialist and a treasurer, etc, etc. The co-captain is in case the founder/team leader is not able to make it and also the one in charge when the team is taking base readings while the team leader if doing the interview. The team leaders are just there to keep focus. You can have a team with individual responsibilities without having to label them. Who wants to be the treasurer anyway? If you think about it, many teams give out these "titles" just so the team members can feel good about themselves. "Look at me! I'm the director of operations! Not just another investigator!" What's wrong with being an investigator? Your performance and character will set you apart more than a label ever will. I remember the days when I was always worrying about hurting someone's feelings instead of worrying about the next case. Not so fond memories!

## MAINTAINING A SUCCESSFUL TEAM

I know some people are going to read MAINTAINING A SUCCESSFUL TEAM and laugh knowing that I wrote that. This is because I have gone through several teams over the years. Many members left due to differences in opinions, illness, injury and loss of interest. Actually, now that I think about it, that does cover every case of a team member leaving. Regardless of the reasons, you can almost always expect to lose members over the course of months and years. Only a handful of people in the world have the dedication and patience to stay with a ghost hunting/paranormal investigative team long enough to watch it grow into any degree of success. For most part, people have lives outside of ghost hunting and some prioritize their day job over researching ghosts and hauntings. Many get tired of the fact that the majority of the cases they investigate turn up nothing. Some are even embarrassed out of it when people scorn them for have such a silly "hobby".

Let me tell you one thing I know separates this author from the authors of other "ghost hunting books". I actually have a team I go out ghost hunting and investigating with. Yes, other authors will tell you in great detail how your team should behave and write chapter after chapter on the dynamics of the ghost hunt, but few well known ghost hunters even ghost hunt anymore. They are either promoting the embarrassingly stupid "Frank Box" or too busy with self-promotion to even care about keeping a team together. At least one well known author hasn't been with a team of ghost hunters on an investigation outside of a paid tour since at least 2004. Hey, for the sake of full-disclosure, I do paid tours too (such as at the Eastern State Penitentiary in Philadelphia, PA), but they are few and far between and I still do real paranormal investigating. I hope that never changes for me.

One thing that will separate the hobbyist from the true amateur psi field researcher is dedication to the team. Meetings held on a regular basis will help weed out those who are not as dedicated as others. Most information and scheduled investigations can be handled via email or conference calls, but showing up at actual meetings is very important as well. It a rule with my team – if you do not show up for meetings on a regular basis, you will not be able to investigate. At each meeting we discuss past investigations, new recruits, current and new techniques, etc. I have meetings every single week for the most part. At least twice a month would be okay for most teams. Places you can have meetings include:

- Libraries. Many local libraries have meeting rooms you can exploit.

- Community centers.
- Picnic grounds and parks – weather permitting.
- Restaurants. However, you will be obligated to buy food.
- Your home.

I am very reluctant to use a home as a meeting place. If you are recruiting new investigators, you may not want to give your personal address out to someone you have never met.

## CHALLENGES YOUR TEAM MAY FACE

I am going to use personal experiences and the experience of others to try to convey some of the many challenges the modern paranormal investigator may face.

### COMPETITION

What a sad world we live in where everyone "just can't get along". Regrettably, many groups out there will consider you and your fellow team members – competition. Yes, when we should be sharing information and acting like one big ghost hunting family, others are more worried about what they consider their "turf". These people will harass you and badmouth you due to them lacking tact in any form whatsoever. No matter how little experience they actually have, they will always claim to have more than you. The best thing you can do is be better than them and most importantly IGNORE THEM. Engaging them will only make it worse.

### THOSE WHO ARE HOLIER THAN THOU

A few years ago a colleague of mine ejected a troublesome team member from his group. I am not sure of all the details except this former team member did not handle ejection well. He went out and started a Yahoo Group (essentially a free online community service) and began badmouthing his former team leader and everyone associated with him. He claimed he was going to "police the paranormal community". Sounds nice at first, but what he really created was a slander site. Cease and desist were issued, but I understand he is still making trouble.

## FINANCING

This belongs in this section as it is a challenge to bankroll a ghost hunting team, but I have a better place for it coming up.

## INNER TEAM TURMOIL

Sometimes folks just don't get along. Occasionally it will be someone taking the devil's advocate position one too many times. "I don't think we should do that and here's why..." It could be someone who just revealed a viewpoint that completely differs from anyone else on the team. "Ghosts are really dead psychic aliens." from time to time you are going to have to deal with disagreements within your own team. If you are already a member of a team of ghost hunters, you may disagree with your team leader. Most of the time you can compromise and sometimes you can't. Whatever you do be civil about it and don't lose your cool. Since we can agree that there will be disagreements, I always recommend having discussions while on a case away from the family or property manager/owner. It is never a good idea to show confusion or seem like you are not clear on your procedures in front of the people you are trying to help.

## GHOST HUNTING AND DEAD PRESIDENTS

1. Sony HandyCam with NightShot - $399
2. AC Tri-Field Meter - $139
3. Natural EM Tri-Field Meter - $229
4. TIF Digital Thermometer - $149
5. 35 mm and Digital Cameras - $99+
6. Actually catching a ghost on film – Priceless!

The list above is composed of some of the most sought after devices used for 'ghost hunting'. This list uses the average price for each item with a little leeway for shipping and taxes. Just five pieces of equipment and you will be paying over one grand. Ka-ching!

Now, for the beginner ghost hunter there are alternative techniques that are both inexpensive and worthwhile. A compass (a nice camping compass for around $10) is a great alternative for an EMF meter! A digital thermometer from Wal-Mart, although slow to react, will get you through your investigation with very accurate readings. Finally, as long as your flash is more than 2 inches away (or more) from the lens of your cameras, you will be OK! Spend wisely. A new ghost hunter on the scene once asked me at a conference what types of equipment I used on investigations and where did I get them from. I gave him a list and a week later he bought over $400 worth of equipment that he didn't even know how to use! I understand he still calls a tri-field meter a "tricorder". I may be the author of a book called Ghost Tech, but even I know that fancy gadgets do not an expert make. C'est la vie! I'd hate to think that his wife and kids had to eat microwave dinners because Dad needed ghost-hunting gizmos so quickly.

Well, in case you haven't figured out yet, this section is about money – specifically raising money for your ghost hunting team. Equipment, gasoline, and film – it adds up! Where does all that money come from? Usually – You! Now what we're going to discuss is different ways to raise money for your group honestly and legally. But first...

## GIVING GHOST HUNTING A BAD RAP

In an article for Ghost Hunting 101 that I plan on writing very soon we will be talking about sharing information with other investigators and teams. What good is having all that acquired data if you cannot share it with other investigators? If we are going to solve the mystery of what ghosts and hauntings are then we need to have some better standards. For example at the official Ghost Tech website (www.ghosttech.net) you can download forms that will help you document nearly all aspects of an investigation. Developed by the Maryland Paranormal Investigators Coalition these forms are believed to be some of the most comprehensive in the country. The best part is they're free!

There is a group or two out there who are charging new investigators for accessing data from their website. For a yearly fee you can download their videos and pictures. How is the field of ghost hunting going to move forward if there are people like that? Although it is important to receive recognition for hard earned research it is never acceptable to charge for data that should be available to the public and peer scrutiny. Call me self-righteous if you'd like.

I did an article once for Ain't It Cool News (www.aintitcoolnews.com) for the movie White Noise. It wasn't favorable. Regardless the moderator for the site was a little excited about getting an honest to goodness ghost hunter to do the review. The sites message boards were a little less "excited". Some of the comments were about how all paranormal investigators were rip-off artists that preyed on troubled people who thought they had ghosts in their houses. They sounded like Walter Peck from Ghostbusters! Who can blame them though? There are people out there like that. In the Midwest there are groups that charge as much as $2000 to investigate your home. Scoundrels! That's what they are. It is an honor to be invited into someone's home and to charge to do investigation is deplorable. You can say that you will accept a donation for gas and film development, but that's all. Most of the time the homeowner will insist on feeding us or at least making us coffee and that's enough. Usually bad coffee, but it is the thought that counts. If it were a long distance to travel though, it would be okay to ask for lodging of some kind.

When we tried to create a local Baltimore group here in Maryland I would talk to other, more experienced ghost hunters around the country for advice. This is when I found out that Maryland had an appalling reputation for serious research. Evidently there are groups that are claiming to train investigators for a "price". They would have investigations with up to fifty people then charge each person for attendance! How can you control fifty investigators? All running around at the same time with their EMF meters and digital cameras and not a minute of good training! So much for real research!

## DON'T BURN YOURSELF!

Williamsburg, VA – 2005. The Queen Mary – 2005. Two examples of ghost hunting conferences gone wrong - Really wrong... Have you ever been to a ghost conference before? Some are very good and have been around (such as the American Ghost Society Conference in Illinois) for a long time now. Some are new and have yet to prove themselves, but have proven talent behind them (such as the Ghost World Conference [www.ghostworldconference.com] in 2007 [Please excuse the shameless self promotion]). On the other hand though, there are conferences that are simply awful or simply not well planned. Let us talk about the ones that are not well planned, shall we?

In 2005 a few colleagues and I were invited to a ghost conference in Williamsburg, VA. Williamsburg is well known for its colonial era hauntings and all involved were genuinely excited about going. So, the conference got closer and closer and closer. The updates from the conference planners became fewer and fewer and fewer. Then, just three weeks before the date of the big Williamsburg Ghost Conference we got an email. The planners were not very good planners as it turns out and had driven themselves into bankruptcy. We would later find out that these people had invested so much money into the conference that they lost their house having not made enough money from projected reservation sales. Many who had bought reservations still have not gotten their money back. Yes... Ouch.

That same year a huge and exciting conference was planned on the famously haunted RMS Queen Mary in California. They were going to have hundreds of people attend, dozens of famous ghost hunters and special events like investigations of the ship's more infamous ghost stories. They planned on using money from a documentary of the ship's ghosts to help pay for the conference. Their contract stipulated that they had to rent the entire ship. Too bad the Queen Mary said they couldn't film there. The proceeds might have saved them from going into debt and having to cancel their conference.

In 2004 the Maryland Paranormal Investigators Coalition headed by yours truly decided they would have their own conference in Baltimore. We had some truly great speakers and only 75 out of a planned two hundred person conference bought reservations. I personally lost about one thousand dollars that year. We thought we were doing it right. We researched and planned and asked for advice from other conference planners. Perhaps we should have listened. Most conference planners said don't do it!

Since 2004 we have done five additional significantly more successful conferences for the Paranormal Investigators Coalition. Each one was called the Eastern Regional Paranormal Conference and each one about doubled the previous year's attendance. Not all planners are so lucky. Even if you have a great conference your 1st year doesn't mean you will be so lucky the next year. We had other issues as well of course. We couldn't help but notice that we were so busy planning conferences three months out of the year we were neglecting our duties as paranormal investigators and subsequently creating a backlog of investigations that needed to be done. Also the stress of the conference caused all sorts of conflicts among our inner circle. Life goes on for us as we focus on our goals to advance research into ghosts and hauntings.

In the past few years the country has become saturated with ghost conferences. Just Google "ghost conference" and you'll see what I mean. Are you willing to take the risk we did and those poor (now literally!) souls from California and Williamsburg? You may find your conference lost in a teeming sea of conferences or worse you may find yourself in bankruptcy court. Trust me fellow ghost hunters, there are better, safer ways...

## THE BETTER, SAFER WAYS...

So, the questions at hand is, "how do I raise money for my ghost hunting group honestly and without putting my family out on the street?" There are several ways actually.

### DUES

This is the simplest, easiest way to earn money for your ghost hunting gear, film development and gas for the Mystery Machine.

However, careful consideration should be made as to how dues are collected and how often. Your team should have regular, monthly meetings. These meetings can take place in a home, park, library, restaurant, etc. Your group, preferably, should have some kind of regular traditions and/or practices. Reciting your team's mission statement at the beginning of each monthly meeting creates a strong sense of purpose and dedication amongst the team members. For example, the Paranormal Investigators Coalition has the following mission statement:

Our mission statement:

- To provide leadership in United States through the application of scientific research of the paranormal.
- To provide education, assistance and resources to new and existing paranormal organizations, the public and the media.
- To foster and create new paranormal organizations throughout the country.

As far as how much dues are, this is up to the budgets of your average team member. I recommend no more than $10 per member per month. Money can also and should also be collected on a per investigation basis. Try to calculate how much it will cost for gasoline per vehicle (carpool if possible!), how much film development will be, how much new audio tapes will cost, etc. Then, at the end of the investigation collect the divided total from each investigator (Example: Film, gas, tapes = $30. Six Investigators = $5 per person).

## FUNDRAISERS

This one is not so easy. If you already have a full-time job you're probably not going to like this one. Fundraising requires real hard work. You are pretty much limited to bake sales, car washes, candy bar sales, etc. You will have to go to your co-workers to hock your stuff.

"So… What are you selling the Christmas wrapping paper for? Your kid's school? Band?"

"Uh… Actually it's for our ghost hunting team. Do you like peanut brittle? It comes in a decorative can…"

The other negative of course is you usually have to sell a lot to get a little.

## GHOST TOURS

The best ghost tours in Gettysburg are Mark Nesbitt's Ghosts of Gettysburg based on his best selling award winning Ghosts of Gettysburg book series. Many of the most famous (or at least very well known) ghost hunters in the country do ghost tours. There's Troy Taylor in Illinois, Dale Kaczmarek and even myself from time to time. Starting your own ghost tour has many advantages besides making money from something that you enjoy doing.

There are many ghost tours out there that are not exactly accurate in either history of ghost tales. In my own hometown of Baltimore there is a ghost tour in Fells Point that is horribly inaccurate in its telling of Edgar Allan Poe legend and lore. Know your history first before planning your ghost tour! Years, names and dates always impress your customers. Look for the bloody, gory and grisly murder stories too. They're always popular!

If you can, only report eyewitness accounts of ghosts. Documented cases are even better. There is a famous B&B in Gettysburg that rhymes with 'barn's girth' that has many exaggerated stories associated with. Exaggerated is a nice way of saying made up. People (especially ghost hunters) will try to prove you wrong, so it's best to keep honest.

The problem with starting your own ghost tour is competition. When I first started doing ghost tours in Baltimore there were no other tour companies out there doing haunted history tours. Now there is at least four in Maryland that I know of. They were started by people trying to emulate me. I would have been flattered if they weren't such obvious rip-offs by going to the same places I was. Now I don't do so many tours.

## WORKSHOPS

This is where we separate the kids from the adults. Well-planned workshops can serve your group well in many ways besides earning spending money. They can also help you find only the most dedicated investigators to work with your team.

First of all, you want to make sure your core group is well on its way to being established. I recommend that you don't try doing workshops until you are at least a year old having done multiple investigations. Also, it would be good if you are well read in the latest techniques and perhaps have attended some other workshops or a well-established conference.

Although they can be done practically anywhere, an indoor location is best for your workshop. Scope out the your town for a place that is willing to host a group of ghost hunters. The best possible place of course is somewhere known to be haunted. Look at libraries, dance halls, theatres, bookstores and restaurants. Restaurants with private rooms work well. Tell them that if they let you have your workshop there for a few hours you will encourage your team of would-be investigators to eat there as well.

Privacy is a factor to consider as well. If you are conducting mock investigations and/or hosting a course on the proper use of EMF meters snickering patrons who don't appreciate your line of work can be very distracting.

Once you have established a location you should try to have one on a regular basis. At least once a month is perfect. It is essential to establish regularity if you are going to have the public ascertain your team as professional and reliable. Each month should focus on a different aspect of ghost hunting. Topics can include "Ghost Hunting Technology", "Spirit Photography How-to's", etc.

Now it's time to establish price. A well-run workshop should be no more than $10. This is a fair amount to charge individuals. If the location you are having the workshop has a mandatory entrance fee than you can talk about upping the price.

A good way of getting better attendance would be to have local authors and well known ghost hunters. I myself will gladly help out as long you are within four hours of Baltimore and don't mind me bringing along some copies of my books (hint, hint).

Well, whatever combinations of fund raising you decide to do, I really hope you do it honestly. You will definitely get my respect for it.

If you have any other, honorable ways to raise funds for ghost hunting groups other than what I have mentioned in this section, please tell me about it in an email. Write me at vince@ghosttech.net.

## WHEN THE MEDIA CALLS

We have already touched on the media several times already and this section will cap that subject off.

It is important to realize that the media is not your friend. Oh, they talk sweet and claim to be totally respectful, but forget about it. They want a good show. They want entertaining video that will get viewers attention and therefore ratings. A scientific survey done in a very systematic fashion may not be what they looking for.

Almost always the press will ask the following questions:

- Do you have any evidence we can see?
- Can you take us to a real haunted house?
- Can we speak to a psychic?

They will ask about your equipment too and procedures among other things, but these three questions are significant. The reason is that they cut into your credibility and trustworthiness depending on what you provide them with. The first question can compromise the location and privacy of the people and property you investigated if you are supplying them with video or photos. Would you want the inside of your home on television or in a newspaper?

In regards to the second question, the media will almost always want to see into someone's home. Obviously this would be very questionable ethically. Try to take them to a known haunted restaurant or other location friendly to media coverage instead.

Question three will be the trickiest to work around. If you do have a reliable psychic on the team, you may feel guilty about not giving them the attention they deserve for all their hard work. Nevertheless, the reporter will only exploit your team member for entertainment purposes. You will find the other team members relegated to the background as all the focus is made on getting the most sensationalist quotes possible from your sensitive. So, what do you do? Simply insist that any sensitives on your team are anonymous.

# CHAPTER NINE: THE FUTURE OF PARANORMAL RESEARCH

I never think of the future - it comes soon enough.
- Albert Einstein (1879 - 1955)

Where a calculator on the ENIAC is equipped with 18,000 vacuum tubes and weighs 30 tons, computers in the future may have only 1,000 vacuum tubes and perhaps weigh 1.5 tons.
- unknown, Popular Mechanics, March 1949

I look to the future because that's where I'm going to spend the rest of my life.
- George Burns (1896 - 1996)

Amateur Parapsychology may catch on or it may not. I hope it does since it may be one of the things that takes paranormal investigation, specifically ghost hunting, that much closer to being taken seriously by the rest of the scientific community. Ironically, I imagine that when it does, I will probably have to find another field of study! Why?

Imagine what would happen if someone actually caught a Bigfoot. They turn the creature immediately over to the proper authorities and it is confirmed as authentic. From that point on every amateur Sasquatch researcher in the country will be forgotten and ignored. Primatologists with actual doctorate will move in and take over research. All those thousands of hours of research and study made by average citizens will be ignored as the real "professionals" take the reins. Scary thought, huh? All your hard work and ghost hunting taken over by stuffy scientists is not something I would look forward to either. Regardless of this possible outcome of proving the existence of ghosts, the work is very fulfilling.

## TECHNOLOGY

It is my belief that in the near future we will see an increase in custom devices for paranormal investigation. Now, unfortunately I am not talking about Egon's PKE meter (although that would be awesome) but something more on the lines of a specifically calibrated EMF room monitoring device. Several companies are already making data loggers that store information electronically without the need for supervision. These stand alone devices are already available widely on the internet and I foresee them very soon be incorporated into a ghost hunting monitoring system device. A monitoring system has already been developed by several would-be ghost hunters with limited success so far. Sometime a few years ago Stan Suho developed the Geophysically Equipped Instrument of Scientific Testing otherwise known as G.E.I.S.T. What Suho had done was design a computer-based monitoring system capable of monitoring, recording and testing the environment without the bothersome presence of human beings. Using a "polling device" Suho was able to attach multiple instruments (EMF meters, Geiger Counters, Thermometers, etc.) to a single laptop. A few years ago Justin Faulk of www.ghostgadgets.com went one step further.

Justin developed ARCADIA or the Analog Reading Computer Aided Digital Input Analyzer. From Justin's website:

"There have been several other scientific based groups that have interfaced computer logging systems to natural field meters before, but ARCADIA takes it a step further. All previous systems of its kind have only logged continuous streams of data, leaving hours of digital or analog data to sort through. Personally, I hate data review, so I have someone else do it for me - the computer, in real time. Data from each channel is sent through a device specific algorithm, developed from hundreds of hours of control runs. With this algorithm, Arcadia can actively distinguish what should naturally occur in a given field (static magnetic fields, temperature, humidity, etc.), and therefore can ignore the data in a stable environment. When an anomaly becomes apparent to the system, Arcadia will log the data from the anomaly digitally, which can be further analyzed later." Mr. Faulk adds, "Now, Arcadia has been modified to log everything for specific time blocks, do various types of DSP on the data sets, and calculate statistical data for each block (standard deviation, mean, range, etc.). That way, a true mathematical analysis can be implemented, including probability values, etc., for submission to peer reviewed journals."

Another promising technological field that may help future ghost hunters is robotics. I have recently completed our 3rd generation articulated robot for our team. It has an arm for grasping objects and treads for scaling obstacles. Built onto the arm is a wireless video camera that can be cabled if necessary. The reason I designed and built this little guy (we consider "him" a member of the team and refer to him as a he) was to go into places that would be much too dangerous for a person to go into. Now, I don't mean the dark closet where Max Shrek's Nosferatu is hiding in and waiting to attack an innocent ghost hunter. I mean weak floorboards, small crawlspaces and unsafe mines. I have also built a Blimp-Cam to go on investigations where locations may be even too rough or inaccessible for Robo-Cam 3.0. It is composed of two 4 foot by one foot oblong Mylar helium filled balloons with a remote controlled propeller system underneath for locomotion. It can go up, down, left, right, forward and reverse. I got the idea for the Blimp-Cam from a location in Maryland's Ellicott City (not necessarily the most haunted city in the Mid-Atlantic area). The Patapsco Female Institute is supposed to be haunted by a little girl who died at the school. She is said to stare out the second story window with dark, sad eyes. However, as you can see from this picture, there is no second floor! A fire gutted the institute years ago. What better way to investigate a non-existent second floor than with a flying remote controlled video camera! We have only used it on the USS Constellation as of yet.

## PSI RESEARCH

Paranormal researchers need to return to their roots when it comes to the scientific study of PSI phenomena. Psychical research has really suffered as of late due to the sensationalism of certain factions of this field of study. Regrettably even the Rhine Institute has suffered a hit in credibility with their recent acceptance of more pseudoscientific and metaphysical methods. Whatever happened to Ganzfeld experiments guys?

## COOPERATION

The startling lack of true cooperation among paranormal investigators around the country is truly mindboggling. Attempts have been made by long term investigators to try and remedy this issue with limited success. Online sites trying to encourage shared data are largely ignored and community sites generally degrade into little more than MySpace rip-offs. Many so called "leaders in the field" are always decrying that we need to band together while doing very little in the way of actually pulling this off. Getting together for a ghost conference every once in awhile is nice, but they usually end with everyone going their separate ways and certainly not "keeping in touch".

We need to start changing the way we do things now. Part of the problem is we have no centralized location. An issue I am working on now. As of this writing I am scouting locations for the purpose of establishing an institute of paranormal studies, a place where all information on ghosts and hauntings can be sent to for safe keeping and analysis.

## PROFESSIONALISM

Once again I would like to point out that yes, ghost hunting can be fun. It can also be very fulfilling. However, if you are using it to get attention or to profit (or both) then please quit now or at the very least call yourselves the Fun and Profit Ghost Hunters Society or something like that. Remember, making a career out of paranormal investigation is tricky at best, especially if you want to do it honestly and scientifically.

One of the things I have been encountering more and more is reports from people that they have had their house investigated already and that the people that came to their house were less than proficient in the field of paranormal investigation. In one recent case, the woman involved told me that a previous team of investigators told her she had angels, her dead mother and a portal in her house after spending just two hours in the home. Once again, what am I doing wrong? All this equipment I lug around with me, more than ten years of experiences, four books authored and I never pick up stuff like that! Which device picked up the angel? If it was a psychic, what is her phone number? Why doesn't the government have this person locked up in lab in Area 51? She could have found bin Laden already! Don't tell me it "doesn't work like that" either. If you can walk into a home and talk to dead people, find evidence of someone's Guardian Angel and hone in on dimensional portals, then you should be able to help with the War on Terror. Anyway, the previous groups succeeded in making the situation worse by scaring the current residence with a bunch of oogey-boogey terms. Always explain to the person that manages or owns the property you are investigating that you are there to learn about the nature of the ghosts and hauntings. You are researcher of the unexplained, not an exorcist. Never tell them they have cosmic entities or portals to hell in their house unless you can really demonstrate that. The worse thing is when someone says stuff like that and then leaves them hanging with more questions than they had and then never returning.

Another aspect of professionalism is keeping your opinions to yourself. Yes, there are awful people out there that are doing a lot of damage. However, many of them are smart and clever enough to often come out smelling like roses despite their dubious deeds. So criticizing many of them in public will only end up with you smelling like... well, not rosy if you know what I mean. You have to be diplomatic about your opinions even with those you may completely disagree with. The rest of the world will come around.

# CHAPTER TEN: IN CONCLUSION...

There are more things in heaven and earth, Horatio,
than are dreamt of in your philosophy.
- Hamlet

When writing this book I tried to put as much as I could into it and still did not add as much as I would have liked. C'est la vie! However you reach a point where you realize that enough is enough. I would have liked to have included a section on pop culture and paranormal activity. I guess I will have to save that for a future edition down the road.

It was only a week before writing this chapter that I was talking to a colleague with big plans for his career in paranormal investigation. He wanted to publish a paranormal magazine. I suggested some names for him to get in contact with and he didn't even know who some of the people were. All he knew of were those guys on cable TV. I was justifiably astounded. I would like to ask the reader to please try and learn as much as you can about the foundations of paranormal research.

For paranormal research to survive the current "fad" more people are going to have to really sit back and ask, "Why am I doing this?" I asked myself that and concluded it is the same reason that got me started - curiosity. If it's for money or fame, get out and join a circus. I almost quit several times for different reasons and I keep coming back because even though I have made mistakes, in my heart I know my endeavors are honorable.

# APPENDIX I: HAUNTED PLACES I HAVE BEEN

I have been to dozens and dozens of supposed haunted places over the years. Most of them are private residences which I cannot mention here. However, I can mention the following locations being that they are public locations and already well known as haunted places. These are definitely my favorite places to visit. In 2009 I plan on adding the Winchester Mansion, Alcatraz Island and the Stanly Hotel to this list.

## BERTHA'S MUSSELS

Ever seen a bright green bumper sticker with EAT BERTHA'S MUSSELS written on it in white capital letters? No, it isn't a dirty joke that you're not in on. This bumper sticker has been seen in an arctic research center and the Congo in Africa. "My husband said not to put the location's name on it (referring to the infamous bumper sticker). He said no, it wouldn't be any fun," says Laura Norris, co-owner of Bertha's Mussels. He was probably right.

Most of Bertha's was built in the 1770s with additions added in the 1820s. At different points in the building's history it was an inn, a private residence, several pubs and restaurants and even a brothel. Its last incarnation was that of a rough seaman's bar called the Lone Star in the 1960's and early 1970s before being purchased by Laura and her husband in 1972. They had originally planned on turning the Lone Star into a music room for chamber music. As fate would have it, a zoning law created in 1971 made live music in Fells Point illegal. So out with the Music Room, in with Bertha's Mussels!

Tony, Laura's husband, had obtained from a junk dealer three stained glass windows that obviously came from a church. Written on one of the stained glass windows was the name Bertha E. Bartholomew. After her husband came up with the bumper sticker they decided to name the new restaurant Bertha's.

Bertha's first cook Bill Arnott (pronounced Arno) designed the first menu for Bertha's and drew the first conception of Bertha for that same menu. Later the image evolved into the one that is present on today's menu and the famous painting of Bertha that hangs out over the corner of Broadway and Lancaster Street.

Bertha's I famous not only for its bumper sticker but also for its food! Make sure you get a heaping plate of their famous mussels. The crab cakes and shrimp salad are also great with the house Pinot Grigio.

Employees, diners and would-be ghost hunters have reported

many strange things at Bertha's over the years.

My team, the Baltimore Society for Paranormal Research, has done many investigations at Bertha's over the years. During one such investigation we recorded what sounded like laughter from the upstairs kitchen area. During a fund-raising tour we did we had around a dozen or so out-of-towners (none of whom knew one another) who saw some really kinetic activity take place.

On your way to the rest room upstairs you may run into the "woman in black". She glides effortlessly down the staircase - feet unseen! Once you reach the top look to your left and running by the fireplace may be the ghost of a little girl. Is it the ghost of the daughter of one of the "ladies of the night" who once walked those same floors? Once, while training new ghost hunters, I became part of a new story. Near the Women's Restroom door is an old trunk near a window. Three witnesses, none previously knowing each other before that night, came rushing in the room I was in. The trunk it seems was moving and bouncing on its own!

Heading back downstairs watch the windows in the front dining room. Out of town diners saw a man in 19th century clothing sitting by a window there smoking a pipe. When next they looked - he disappeared in a puff of pipe smoke!

## FT. MCHENRY

Baltimore has hosted many battles since colonial times, including the famous battle at Fort McHenry on September 13th, 1814. During that battle an American imprisoned (actually a British "guest" according to the Fort's current park ranger staff) aboard a ship in the harbor would see the U.S. flag waving amongst the constant bombardment. Alone in his cabin, a 35 year old Francis Scott Key would write the poem called The Star Spangled Banner. Of all the areas in the National Park System, Fort McHenry is the only one designated a national monument and historic shrine. It is also, by many accounts, very haunted!

The Battle for Baltimore in 1814 was one of the most important moments in US history. We stand a free nation today in part of the brave actions of the men who fought for the defense of Baltimore, of America, of liberty.

The star shaped fort served the harbor well. While bombarding the British ships out in the Chesapeake Bay (while being bombarded itself) the British ships were prevented from advancing due to voluntarily sunken merchant ships that prevented movement into the Inner Harbor.

So successful was the defense in fact that with the thousands of bombs and rockets being thrown and fired at the Defenders, there were only two deaths on our side - Lt. Levi Clagett and Sgt. John Clemm. A bomb fired from a British ship hit the third bastion (or point on the star). After that the area was henceforth called "Clagett's Bastion".

Reports of a soldier, not a re-enactor, walking back and forth in Clagett's Bastion have been around for years. The soldier is always seen wearing 18th Century colors.

Near the statue of Orpheus (weird choice to commemorate the centennial of the writing of the Star Spangled Banner) has been seen a man suspended high in the air. The reason for this haunting? Perhaps it has to do with location. The statue now stands in the original location of the fort's gallows. Many other spooky stories have been reported over the years as well.

## GOVERNORS BRIDGE

When I first started doing anything that resembled ghost hunting, it was here at Governors Bridge in Bowie, MD. My high school friend Reneé Colianni was really getting into these adventurous "urban legend hunts". She had already been doing them for several months before telling me about her excursions. Evidently, she was fearful that I would think she was weird! If anything, I was upset she didn't tell me sooner! Soon we were learning all about ghostly legends and paranormal activity all over Maryland. Within months I was investigating houses and businesses with new equipment like EMF meters and digital thermometers.

Governors Bridge is known as a "Crybaby Bridge" in urban legend circles. In fact, it may be America's first Crybaby Bridge. A Crybaby Bridge is a bridge which has, as a paranormal event, the sound of baby that will cry at a certain time after a certain act is done. Most states have at least one. According to legend a woman has a baby out wedlock during a time in the nation's history when that was unacceptable. In a fit of desperate depression she throws her baby (in some versions of the tale, herself too) over the side of bridge into the rushing water below. From that night on, if you drive your car up to the bridge at midnight and honk your horn three times you will hear the sound of a crying baby.

Now, we have been there dozens of times over the years and have never heard any babies crying, however, we have experienced some weird things. At different times we have experienced sensations such as extreme energy drains. For no reason members of the investigative team will begin to feel as if all their energy was being sucked from their bodies.

On another occasion we had photographed figures that that seem to hang in the mist surrounding the area and seemed almost magnetically clinging to the metal superstructure of the bridge itself.

Research has shown that the area was occupied by the local Iroquois and Shawnee tribes for many years before the arrival of

Europeans to these shores. Residents further up the road sometimes reported seeing people walk by in traditional Native American clothing and saw and heard "little Indian children" playing in the fields. We used flashlights to survey the land around bridge as well. After the first few visits we became mindful to always bring with us back-up light sticks and sometimes road flares as well. Electrical equipment did not always perform for us. While exploring the deep dark woods (which strangely even appeared dark in broad daylight) we came across some beaten down old shacks that seemed to be occupied from time to time. These macabre ramshackle makeshift dwellings were further distinguished in their grotesquery by the hand painted satanic imagery which adorned the walls, floors and ceilings of the abodes. Suffice to say, feelings of dread and discomfort shortened out visit to the shacks. Certainly these domiciles are what gave credence to the rumors that there were satanic cults and even a Church of Satan in this area. By the way - did I mention this is the area where Maryland's *Goatman* is said to dwell?

## GETTYSBURG

The turning point in the War Between the States was here. The bloodiest battle in American history and, perhaps, its most famous – The Battle of Gettysburg. This small Pennsylvania town would forever change US History in just three fateful days.

More than 51,000 people lost their lives due to the battle. As famously stated, it was "brother against brother". Many people believe that acre for acre Gettysburg is perhaps the most haunted town in the world.

Now, I am going to try to keep this short. I am in Gettysburg (just 85 minutes from Baltimore) at least once a month or more and have investigated so many areas in that town I will no doubt be able to write a book just on that one day. In the meantime there are few hotspots I would like to point out.

Triangular Field is just around from Devil's Den. Free maps to battlefields are available at most places in town. You can always go online too. In Triangular Field EMF meters tend to go haywire and batteries drain in seconds. I had a tri-field meter bury its needle at the entrance for over 20 minutes. Investigators have caught some pretty notorious footage here as well. Video of a spectral soldier has made its way onto YouTube.

One of the funniest experiences in my career happened here. I was testing a new technique for walking with a tri-field meter by going parallel to North and South. My friend and colleague Robbin Van Pelt was holding the meter as I held a compass to keep her straight on course. As we made our way up the field, we walked past another group of ghost hunters (they're all over the place there) and one of them says, "I hope you're not walking with a tri-field meter! Haven't you read Vince Wilson's GHOST TECH?"

Another great place to try to do some ghost hunting is the Jennie Wade House. It is located right next to the Gettysburg Battlefield Holiday Inn. Jennie was the only civilian killed during the Battle of Gettysburg. A stray bullet came in through a door and killed Ms. Wade as she kneaded bread dough for Union Soldiers and her family staying in the duplex two-story home. Visitors have reported unusual occurrences here for decades. If you call and try to schedule an investigation, tell them Vince Wilson sent you!

## HARPERS FERRY

At the very least he was one of the most interesting figures in American History. Mostly though, he was a madman who lit the fuse that began The War Between the States. Since I am talking about Harpers Ferry, I must be talking about none other than John Brown.

John Brown considered himself an abolitionist. If you want to compare John Brown's cause to any modern movement, think of the controversy over abortion rights. Most "prolife" advocates are content just protesting peacefully with signs, marches and letters to politicians, however, every few years or so you get a lunatic who shoots an abortion doctor. John Brown is a lunatic like that. He decided he wanted to free the slaves by force since the peaceful way wasn't working fast enough. Some might argue that is very noble. Brown's actions though were anything but noble. He got together a crew of about 21 men and began a march of bloodshed from Kansas to Harpers Ferry, WV where the US Armory was. He claimed that God told him to do this. He was going to use the Blue Ridge Mountains as cover for guerilla warfare tactics against slave owners and eventually free enough slaves to rise up against the South. The bloodshed is from his frequent stops along the way to Harpers Ferry. What Brown would do that was so monstrous was to stop at the homes of people he thought were sympathetic to slavery. Although none of the people he visited were slave owners in his warped mind they were sympathetic to the wrong cause. So, Brown would drag the father of the family out in front of the women and children and he or one of his men (no one is sure about this detail) and disembowel them while their kin watched. What a hero, huh?

When John Brown finally got to Harpers Ferry on October 16th 1859 he managed to seize the armory and several other strategic locations around the town. His small victory was short-lived however when the townsfolk violently rose up against him. Within 36 hours reinforcements led by, ironically, Lt. Robert E. Lee arrived and put down most of his men. His son dead and he wounded badly, John Brown was captured the next day. On December 2nd he was hung by the gallows after a brief trial in nearby Charles Town.

Sympathy from the North for John Brown's raid enraged the South. Did the North really feel such hatred for the Southern States? Did those Yanks really wish such contemptible violence upon their neighboring brothers and sisters? Although most people, from both the North and South, condemned Brown for his actions there was enough of an outpouring for his martyrdom that the South felt they had a genuine case for succession based on this and other threats of change directed at Southern policies. Thus began the War Between the States.

When the War Between the States finally did come it hit Harpers Ferry as violently as any other town touched by those trying times. Not only was there much physical devastation, there was economical chaos as well. Harpers Ferry would switch back and forth between the Southern and Northern forces eight times over four years. After the battle of Antietam the North returned to Harpers Ferry they fortified the surrounding heights to protect the railroad and what was left of the town.

One such fortification still exists at Harpers Ferry's KOA Campgrounds. According to employees I interviewed there, figures have been see in the darkness near the embankments even in the off season when there wouldn't be any campers. Of particular interest is the camp store. Both shadowy and luminescent figures have been known to appear in the store after hours. The store's alarm will go off from time to time and when someone comes to investigate, there is no one there. Electronic malfunctions will plague the office in the morning then quickly disappear. In the movie theatre next to the store, staffs have told me they would shut everything off in the evening and come in the morning to find a film playing. Additionally they have found items mysteriously stacked in the middle of the store.

Dale Brechlin, the campground's general manager, had allowed us into the store after hours to do an investigation. During the course of the night around 2 o'clock in the morning, we got some very interesting EVP. It sounded very much like a woman screaming "get out!" We keep this EVP on our Ghost Science website at www.ghostscience.net.

Another popular haunted location in Harpers Ferry is the famous Hilltop House Hotel (currently under renovations as of this writing). The Hilltop House is an American monument to the ideal that, through hard work and perseverance, anyone can be successful in these United States. Former hotel manager and prominent African American Thomas S. Lovett built the Hilltop House Hotel in 1888. Twice, in 1912 and again between 1918 and 1919, the Hilltop House burned down and each time Lovett managed to rebuild her from the ashes.

I am not sure how room numbering will be when the hotel's remodeling is done, but I do know the most notorious room at the Hilltop House was Room 66. No, not 666. People have reported seeing the apparition of an old hotel maid in a classic black and white maid uniform standing at the base of their bed at 1 o'clock in the morning. There used to be a painting of a little girl in a blue dress in the room that would weep real tears. The painting has since disappeared. A local ghost hunting team had caught a picture of a disembodied and in the hall mirror. My own team has gotten EVP of a crying in the hallway outside of Room 66. Archaeological evidence hints that the property the Hotel stands on may have been a Native American burial ground.

Possibly the most incredible paranormal event that has ever happened to me happened to me in Harpers Ferry. It was along the Appalachian Trail and just past the amazing natural formation known as Jefferson's Rock. Jefferson's Rock's name derives from Thomas Jefferson, who stood there on October 25, 1783. He found the view from the rock so impressive that he wrote "this scene is worth a voyage across the Atlantic"

It was here at Jefferson's Rock, while walking to a mountaintop graveyard, that all of our 12 member team's equipment malfunctioned at once. It was nearing dusk and the sun was setting behind a distant mountain. We had EMF meters, flashlights and Sony Handycams all running during our accent up the mountainside. Just 20 paces or so past Jefferson's Rock every electronic piece of equipment we had shut down at once. Even our watches! Even stranger is when it all came back on. Anyone who has ever handled a video camera knows that when the power is shut off you have to manually turn it back on. Yet, after we had walked, or more accurately stumbled, about in the dark for what was most likely just 3 minutes, but felt like 20, all the electronics came on exactly where they went off.

## THE EASTERN STATE PENITENTIARY

It was supposed to be the time of Enlightenment in the Western World. When a group of powerful men of Philadelphia met at the home of Benjamin Franklin in 1787 they convened with hope in their hearts to replace the hopeless prison system with something revolutionary. It was with good intentions that the members of The Philadelphia Society for Alleviating the Miseries of Public Prisons came up with idea of creating a true penitentiary, a place where criminals will actually learn right from wrong and be humble before God. Instead what they created was hell on Earth.

Inspired by the Quaker concept of penance (hence penitentiary) and punishment through isolation the prison was built in hopes that self-reflection would inspire the prisoners into reformation. In 1831 Alexis de Tocqueville and Gustave de Beaumont visited Eastern State on behest of the French government. In their report they wrote:

"Thrown into solitude... [the prisoner] reflects. Placed alone, in view of his crime, he learns to hate it; and if his soul be not yet surfeited with crime, and thus have lost all taste for anything better, it is in solitude, where remorse will come to assail him.... Can there be a combination more powerful for reformation than that of a prison which hands over the prisoner to all the trials of solitude, leads him through reflection to remorse, through religion to hope; makes him industrious by the burden of idleness.."

Many did not agree with this assessment. It wasn't long before its completion in 1829 that the outside world began to learn of the horrifying failure that was ESP. In 1842 Charles Dickens visited the prison and had this to write about it:

"In its intention I am well convinced that it is kind, humane, and meant for reformation; but I am persuaded that those who designed this system of Prison Discipline, and those benevolent gentleman who carry it into execution, do not know what it is that they are doing....I hold this slow and daily tampering with the mysteries of the brain to be immeasurably worse than any torture of the body; and because its ghastly signs and tokens are not so palpable to the eye,... and it extorts few cries that human ears can hear; therefore I the more denounce it, as a secret punishment in which slumbering humanity is not roused up to stay."

Many inmates went insane while staying at Eastern State Penitentiary. The years of solitude were just too much for the fragile human psyche of many of the convicts kept here over the years. Even today, when you enter Eastern State, despite state of rot and decay, it drips with the impressions of suffering souls and leaves one with a sense of foreboding mortals most likely only feel on the onset of the entrance to Hell.

We have conducted three investigations at Eastern State since 2007. We walked its depressing corridors as they extend out from a central hub like the spokes of a long rotted wagon wheel. Electricity is scarcer than the laughter of inmates must have been outside of madness. We have never captured anything on camera yet, but we have captured what appears to be the sound of suffering during EVP sessions. When we played back the recording we heard the faint and seemingly distant sounds of moaning and screaming.

## THE WAVERLY HILLS SANATORIUM

Now, of the places I have been over the years, this is the place that scared me the most.

The main building was constructed in 1923 to replace an older wooden structure for tuberculosis (TB) patients. It remained in operation for 51 years. Before an antibiotic was created in 1943, many victims of TB went to Waverly simply to die. Little was known about what was called "consumption". The best they knew to do was wheel your bed out to the balconies on one side of the building (to this day, still exposed to elements). Fresh air was all they could give the patients to try and help them.

I have read some greatly exaggerated statements about the number of people that died at this place. Some accounts claim 63,000. Clearly, that is impossible. More likely it was around 6,000, still, a very large number indeed. It is hard for many people to fathom when you talk about so many people dying in a single location despite the buildings impressive dimensions.

In 2006 I visited the Sanatorium before lecturing at a conference in Louisville. I was there with some other authors and well known paranormal investigators. Our team of five was allowed to spend an hour at a time on each of the five floors. Earlier that day I was on the phone with the conference organizer, who happened to be very experienced with Waverly, and was instructed by him to bring a laser pointer. I asked why, but "you'll see" is all he would tell me besides that I should point it at a distant wall and wait. Before going to the sanatorium we stopped at a store and purchased a laser pointer and during our investigating we tried the experiment he suggested. It was on the third floor that I learned what supposed to happen with this device!

It was about 2 o'clock in the morning. I was pointing the red laser dot at the far end of the hall like I was instructed. We were on the third floor and we had done this experiment on every floor going up from the lowest level. At this time there was no electricity and no lighting but for our flashlights (which were off) and the moonlight coming in from the open side of the building where they used to wheel out the patients. As our eyes became more and more adjusted to the light we began to see movement in the shadows around the area the laser was pointed at. We knew we were the only ones on that floor since the only entrance was behind us. The far wall was about 50 feet from where we stood and we were seeing, what appeared to be, human silhouettes. Actually, what we saw was just heads and shoulders, scuffling in the dark corridor. We were so focused on seeing more details that we almost didn't notice the dot was getting bigger and bigger. It had struck one of the figures and that figure was walking straight at us! 50 feet. 40 feet. 30. 20. Then it was at 15 feet. We were getting nervous. It is one thing for a ghost to walk through a wall and disappear near you, but when it is coming right at you... 12 feet and I turned on my flashlight... It was gone!

In addition to the places listed above I have also been to following:

**THE MYRTLES PLANTATION**. I had visited this famous southern paranormal hotspot with an Orlando based ghost hunting team. There was a lot of activity with a psychic and in my own room the bathroom faucet turned itself on and off repeatedly.

Many of the stories associated with this place are either made up or very exaggerated. Keep that in mind if you're looking for Chloe.

**THE BROOKDALE LODGE.** This place was amazing with its dining room having a stream running right through it! This rustic former Hollywood celebrity hangout has seen better days from tinsel-town but it still stimulates the imagination to conjure up daydreams of yesteryear with things like its still functioning mermaid pool.

I set up one of my more elaborate video set-ups ever here. Once again I was invited by the Orlando team I mentioned earlier. I took the above picture with a night-vision camera. We caught what seemed to be a figure moving across one of the video clips and many of the team felt very emotional while in the dining area at night.

**MOUNDSVILLE STATE PENITENTIARY.** This is brick by brick even creepier than Eastern State, although not nearly as well known.

The team I was helping with this case didn't really get much in the way of evidence, but we did manage to reproduce and debunk a famous picture taken here of what some thought was an apparition but was more than likely the photographer's shadow.

**THE ALAMO.** Admittedly, I never actually had the chance to investigate the Alamo, however I did interview many of the staff and one of the park rangers there. They showed me pictures that have been sent in over the years. Many of them were just dust orbs though. Nevertheless, there were a few that appeared to be shadowy apparitions. Many of the people that work there have reported hearing gunfire and cannon fire at night and have seen figures in period clothing walking about as well.

**THE LEMP MANSION.** This is another case of a place I have been, but not really had a chance to investigate. I love the history of this place though!

The Lemps were a bunch of crazy rich beer merchants that couldn't seem to go from generation to the next without a suicide. They built an underground entertainment room complete with a stage and swimming pool beneath the mansion and brewery using a system of natural caves. Now that is decadence! These people were insane and their ghosts, according to people who work and have stayed there.

# APPENDIX II: BIBLIOGRAPHY AND FURTHER READING

A Change of Heart, by Claire Sylvia and William Novak 1998

Aliens Above, Ghosts Below, by Dr. Barry Taff 2011

Bell Witch Haunting, by Pat Fitzhugh 1999

The Concise Encyclopedia of Western Philosophy and Philosophers 1991

Ghost Detective - Confessions of a Parapsychologist, by Dr. Andrew Nichols 2011

Ghost Tech: The Essential Guide to Paranormal Investigation Equipment, by Vince Wilson 2005

The Ghost Hunters Guidebook, by Troy Taylor 2004

The Ghosts of Gettysburg Series, by Mark Nesbitt

Ghosts on Film: The History, Mystery & How-to's of Spirit Photography, by Troy Taylor

Ellicott City's Guide to Haunted Place, by Russ Noratel 2008

The Encyclopedia of Ghosts and Spirits, by Rosemary Ellen Guiley 2000

Esp, Hauntings and Poltergeists: A Parapsychologist's Handbook, by Loyd Auerbach 1984

A Field Guide to Demons, Fairies, Fallen Angels, and Other Subversive Spirits, by Carol K. Mack and Dinah Mack 1999

The Fourth Dimension: A Guided Tour of the Higher Universes, by Rudy Rucker 1984

The Enchanted World - Ghosts, by Time Life 1984

Flatland: A Romance of Many Dimensions, by Edwin A. Abbott 1854

Field Guide to Spirit Photography, by Dale Kaczmarek 2002

The New York Public Library Science Desk Reference - 1995

Quest for the Unknown: Ghosts and Hauntings, by Reader's Digest 1993

The Real-Life Entity Case, by Dr. Barry E. Taff 2004

The Ghost Hunter's Guidebook, by Troy Taylor, 2004

The Handy Science Answer Book, by the Science and Technology Department of Carnegie Library of Pittsburgh 2003

Hyperspace: A Scientific Odyssey Through Parallel Universes, Time Warps, and the Tenth Dimension, by Michio Kaku, Robert O'Keefe (Illustrator) 1995

In Search of Schrodinger's Cat: Quantum Physics and Reality, by John Gribbin 1984

The Paranormal, by John Spencer 1992

Parapsychology, Introduction to and Education in, by Parapsychology Foundation, Inc 1999

Parapsychology: The Controversial Science, by Richard S. Broughton, Ph. D. 1991

The Parapsychology Revolution, compiled by Robert M. Schoch, Phd., and Logan Yonavjak

Photography for Dummies, by Russell Hart 1998

Poltergeists: Examining Mysteries of the Paranormal, by Michael Clarkson

Season of the Witch, by Troy Taylor 2002

Sneakier Uses for Everyday Things, by Cy Tymony 2005

What is Deep Ecology?, by Chris Johnstone 2002

# APPENDIX III: QUESTIONS TO ASK

I was greatly pleased when Loyd Auerbach gave me permission to reprint this entire chapter from his groundbreaking book ESP, Hauntings and Poltergeists. I recommend going over these suggestions with would-be case studies. They may just help you weed out any crazies or scam artists.

## WHAT DO YOU ASK?

The following questions are suggested for certain investigations of apparitions, poltergeists, and hauntings. Keep in mind that these questions may have to be chosen according to whether they are applicable to the experience reported and to the family (or office) situation. For these questions, besides some of my own composition, I have drawn on those suggested by William G. Roll and Dr. J. G. Pratt (published in Roll's book, The Poltergeist, first printed in Theta, the Journal of the Psychical Research Foundation, Number 16, Winter, 1967), and a questionnaire developed by Cynthia Siegel and Sharon Solfvin.

Also, remember to ask the applicable questions not only of the people directly involved (those who actually witnessed something or who live or work in the situations)but also throw them at any secondary witnesses (e.g., neighbors or police or priests) who may have learned from the what was going on.

## INITIAL QUESTIONS (TO HELP DETERMINE WHETHER AN INVESTIGATION IS WARRANTED)

1. Please give a general description of the occurrences.
2. Please list the names and ages of all those living/working in the situation where the disturbances have taken place.
3. Please list the relationships of all those in household/office to one another (their place in the family in relation to everyone else; positions in the office and works with whom; etc.)
4. Are there any pets?
5. What are the occupations of those in the location who are or have been working?
6. Please give educational background of all those in the location.

7. Where have the occurrences taken place? Address and specific locations within the premises, please. Describe the premises, please.
8. How long have you lived/worked there?
9. Any disturbances noted at previous addresses?
10. When did the current disturbances begin?
11. What sorts of things went on at the beginning?
12. What did you think of them?
13. When was the most recent incident?
14. Would you say the occurrences are frequent? Are they occurring with any apparent regularity?
15. Have the disturbances been increasing in frequency and severity since they first began?
16. Who are those people directly involved? What did they experience?
17. Any witnesses from outside the household/office? Please give their names, occupations, and phone numbers. What did they experience, as far as you know?
18. Is there a pattern of any kind to these disturbances that you've noticed (i.e., when the events occurred, what sorts of objects were affected, what locations were involved, who was around at the time, etc.)?
19. Have you looked for ordinary, normal explanations? What makes you sure the events are paranormal?
20. Have you or any of the others involved had any psychic experiences in the past?
21. Have you (or anyone else who witnessed the events) been interested in psychic phenomena for a while? Has family discussed psychic phenomena in the past? If so, in what context?
22. Does anyone involved have a theory as to what may be going on?
23. Have you contacted any "experts"? (Such as, obviously, a parapsychologist, or psychologist, police, priest, rabbi, psychic, etc.)
24. If so, what did/do they have to say?
25. What kinds of books or articles have you read about psychic phenomena or the occult/supernatural/unsolved mysteries?
26. Have you seen films like Ghostbusters, Poltergeist, The Entity, The Amityville Horror, The Sixth Sense, The Others, The Exorcist, White Noise, Paranormal Activity, Carrie, etc.? Which ones?
27. What did you think of them (in terms of how they

portrayed psychic experiences/disturbances)?

28. How about others involved? Reading? Films? TV shows?
29. What are your feelings/beliefs regarding psychic phenomena or the spiritual world? Religious background (both family and your present religious status)?
30. Have you ever taken any courses on parapsychology, the occult, or any self-development or psychic development courses? The others?
31. Have you or any of the others ever been to see a psychic?
32. Has there been any publicity of these events? In other words, has the press found out about what's going on? If so, which members of the media, and how can we contact them? If not, can you be sure there won't be any publicity (can you keep this quiet... the press tends to disrupt investigations)?
33. What would you like done to help you?
34. Would you allow me and perhaps some colleagues to do a serious investigation of the occurrences in your home/office?

The above questions should give you a good handle on the beliefs, background, and thoughts of at least the person being initially interviewed (which we generally do by phone), and a general idea of what the psi disturbance might be. The answers to these questions will certainly give you enough to decide whether or not to go ahead with an investigation. Again, you might want to ask some of these questions of the others involved, when you get to them. In addition, the background questions in the above group will help you assess the kind of people you're dealing with.

## WHO/WHAT/WHEN/WHERE/HOW

These questions will help you narrow down the general patterning of the disturbances/experiences. You could, of course, ask these questions from the start, but you may get a better handle on what's going on if they are asked when you are actually in the location where the incidents are occurring. In some respects these questions do duplicate some of the aims of the above questions, but it helps to ask some of the same questions in different ways, since by doing so you can often pick up different pieces of the puzzle (in other words, the answers may differ slightly).

1. Have you connected the disturbances with any particular people witnessing or living/working in the

location? With any particular visitors?

2. If there is an apparition seen, does the apparition represent anyone identifiable (does anyone know "who" the apparition represents)?
3. Are there particular activities going on when the incidents occur (such as eating, watching TV, arguments, etc.)? Explain.
4. Are there certain times during the day or night when the incidents appear to be more frequent? If so, when are they?
5. Are the events seen to occur more in one spot (or in more than one place) than in others (certain rooms or parts of the room)? Where are these places?
6. Are certain people seemingly more affected than others? Who? What reactions do the people in the situation have when confronted by one of the disturbances?
7. Do all witnesses to the events have to be around for anything to happen? If not, give examples of such incidents where not everyone was around, and who was there.
8. Have any disturbances been noted to occur when no one was around (i.e., has anyone noted the after-effects of a disturbance that may have occurred with no witnesses, perhaps by objects having been moved)?
9. Has any one person appeared to be very close to the starting points of moving objects? Do you think there's any chance that that person could have physically thrown or pushed the objects to simulate a paranormal event?
10. Is there any reason to think that someone in the home/office might fake the events?
11. Have you thought about normal explanations for some or all of the events? Have you taken note of outside sounds, vibrations, etc. (such as a truck rumbling down the street) when the occurrences happen?

## THE PHENOMENA

These questions will help you got a good picture of the actual goings-on. Remember not to jump to any immediate conclusions about the events being paranormal. Always look everywhere for normal explanations for the events, whether considering fraud or problems with the electrical system or earth movements, before making a "paranormal" judgment. Also, I want to say not all of these questions are applicable to any one situation, given that many of them relate to physical disturbances (like those in a poltergeist case) or to a haunting where there may or may not be noises heard or objects affected.

1. Please describe the disturbances/experiences in terms of what you actually observed. (Note: this should be asked of everyone involved, both in separate interviews and later in the presence of all witnesses.)
2. Were there any unusual feelings or emotions associated with the disturbances/experiences?
3. How often do they occur?
4. Who first noticed them? When were they first noticed? Under what circumstances?
5. Please describe the experiences/observations of the others to the best of your knowledge.
6. In terms of movement of objects, describe the movements and what was unusual about them. Did objects seemingly take flight or visibly move by themselves? Were there unusual flight patterns (in other words, did they move like someone had pushed or thrown them, or did they make unusual curves in the air or on a surface, such as making right-angle turns)?
7. Could someone have been near enough to an object to move, push, or throw it, either purposely or by accident?
8. Did objects hit their final resting point with unusual force?
9. Did they make unusually loud noises when they struck something?
10. Were breakable objects seen to move and strike something without breaking?
11. Were heavier objects seen to move or rearrange themselves (such as furniture being piled up, especially in such a way that one person could not have done it)? Describe, please. Were these objects seen in motion, or were they simply discovered in rearranged fashion after had been moved?
12. Has anyone seen an object start its motion? In other words, have there been any witnesses to an object disturbance beginning with the point just before it took flight or began to move?
13. What were the objects affected? Any particular kind of object affected more than others? Any particular single affected more than others? If yes to either one, are any relationships between the object(s) and any of the

people in the household/office?

14. Have you noticed any metal objects particularly affected? Bent silverware, for example? If yes, are you certain no one could have had access to the pieces and bent them normally? Any chance that the pieces of metal/silverware could have already been bent through normal use (and that you simply never noticed the bends)?
15. Have there been any unusual electrically related effects? Have appliances, TVs, stereos, lights, or computers been affected? If so, to what extent and how frequently? When any particular person(s) were around?
16. If certain persons were associated with the appliances/ devices, what are their attitudes towards the function of those devices (i.e., if a vacuum cleaner, does the person hate housework? If a computer, does the person dislike computers)?
17. Have there been any occurrences of unusual noises? Have these sounds been found to have a cause connected with them, or have they occurred with no seeming cause? Describe the sounds and why you think them unusual.
18. Have any of the sounds been connected in any way with the movement/disturbance of physical objects?
19. When the others who have witnessed the events had their first experiences, were they aware of previous encounters or observations or experiences by those who first noticed them? What did they know about them, if anything?
20. Have there been instances where one or more persons saw an apparition (ghost)? If yes, please describe what was seen.
21. If nothing was seen, yet you (and others) are sure there is something there (a presence or "entity" or "force"), what makes you so sure?
22. Have voices been heard, either with or without the appearance of an apparitional form? Were attempts made to see if the voices had a (living or mechanical) source?
23. Have unusual smells been noticed? What was unusual about them? Have

1. they appeared at only certain times or only in certain areas? Have they been localized, yet mobile (confined to a specific area in the air, yet that area has been

observed to move about)? Were attempts made to find a natural source of the smell?

24. Who has been around in each instance of a visual apparition? Of voices? Of unusual smells?
25. Have you or anyone else gotten unusual feelings in a particular place or at particular times (example, do you sense a "presence" or get "cold chills" under certain conditions/in certain locations)?
26. Has the temperature of the location been affected unusually? Have normal causes been looked at as being behind such effects?
27. Have there been times when apparitions/ghosts, smells, voices, footsteps, or odd noises have been experienced by only some of the people (or just one person) and not by others at the same time? Please describe these instances.
28. Have the images been associated with particular people or events? Have they been associated with particular people who are witnesses to the events or whom you know (example, maybe the ghost is that of your Uncle Harry from Cincinnati)? Were these images connected with the past (the past of the people present or of the house) or with the present (could the images represent living persons or current/future events)?
29. How about the noises or the smells (if present)? Could they be connected with persons not present (living or dead)? Or can they be connected with the house or building (past or present)?
30. Did the witnesses who had the experience of seeing/hearing a ghost know about that person (whom the ghost represents) before the experience?
31. In the case of images seen, did everyone who saw something see the exact same thing, or were there the kinds of differences one would expect if the apparition had been a living person, there in the flesh? (In other words, if one person stood in front of where the apparition appeared, and another behind it, did the people see the figure from the proper perspective [front and back] or not?)
32. Describe the behavior of the apparition(s). Does the apparition repeat the same activity every time it appears? Or does it seem as if it is aware of your presence as well?
33. Is there attempted communication on the part of the

apparition? Have you or

2. anyone else who has experienced the apparition tried to communicate with it? Any results (like communications back, reactions on the part of the apparition, changes in behavior of the phenomena, etc.)?
34. Would you say the apparition seems to be one that is conscious or aware of its surroundings, that it is an intelligent "entity"?
35. If not, would you say that the experience might represent a past event repeating itself like a video "instant-replay"?
36. What is known about the house/building? Previous owners? History of the location it stands on?
37. How did you feel just before the experience(s) (physically, mentally, and emotionally)? Any common factors between each of the experiences?
38. How did you feel while the experience was actually happening?
39. How did you feel/react after the experience(s) was completed?
40. Did you discuss the experiences with anyone (witness or not) just after it happened? Describe the discussions.

The above questions should give you a fairly complete picture of the phenomenon itself, what may be going on, paranormally or otherwise. Keep in mind that all witnesses and others connected should be asked their opinions and given the chance to answer all relevant questions, so as to help form that complete picture. Interactions and Symbols Given that I have talked about looking at the incidents as symbolic of underlying psychological and interpersonal dynamics, more or less viewing the disturbances as dreams come to life (but dreams nonetheless), you should try to pick out the symbolic meaning of the experiences. I have a few suggested questions below, but really one needs to explore the lives of the people involved, the relationships, their history as a family or work group, to get that overall picture of how to deal with the phenomena.

1. Do you see the events as representing any emotions or tensions that you or others may have at the moment?
2. Have there been any changes in the daily routine/ lives of the people involved (such as new job, new, school, divorce, marriage, death of relative or friend, etc.)? If so, what are they? When did they happen in relation to

the disturbances?

3. Do you see the way the disturbances/experiences are happening as being symbolic of anyone's emotional state or thought processes?
4. Are the events perhaps symbolic of any problems that may be going on between people in the affected group (here, not just direct witnesses, but all those with relationship to the people having the experiences)?
5. If you were to pretend this were all happening in a dream, what would you make of it (the "dream," that is)?
6. Are there any visible problems between the people having the experiences and anyone else?
7. Is anyone particularly tense or frustrated or under some stress? What do you think this may be related to (job, friendships, housework, sexual relationships, school, lack of leisure time, etc.)?
8. What would you say your overall health (both physical and mental) was before the experiences began?
9. What would you say your overall health (both physical and mental) has been since the disturbances started?
10. Are you taking any medication or non-prescription drugs? What are they?
11. Are you drinking alcohol, drinks with caffeine, or taking in a lot of sugar, or smoking tobacco? Which one(s), and how much?
12. Was there any change in your diet or use of the above substances before the initial experiences?
13. Has there been any change in your diet or use of the above substances since the disturbances began?
14. Are you or any of the others currently under the care of a doctor or psychological counselor/therapist?
15. Do you practice: yoga, meditation, self-hypnosis, biofeedback, relaxation exercises, or physical exercises?
16. Would you be willing to work on any social, psychological, or physical problems that may be related to the incidence of the disturbances?
17. Would you be willing to see a counselor, therapist, or doctor if that is the most
1. positive way to help deal with the experiences?
18. Are you interested in participating in future parapsychological research, or in learning more about the field?

There you have it. If you apply these questions to the

experience and ask the appropriate ones of all involved, you should have an excellent idea of what may be going on, not only as far as potential paranormal events are concerned, but also as far as the underlying problems are concerned.

Gertrude Schmeidler and Thelma Moss came up with a way to help understand what may be going on in haunting cases (whether there's an apparition or not): that is, to have a group of psi sensitives each give independent assessments of what they think is going on. They came up with a list of activities and adjectives to help pin down the apparition/haunting. The use of this checklist, which I have added to, is appropriate for everyone involved in the situation, whether witnesses to phenomena or not. One can take all independent lists and see if the perceptions of what is going on are similar or not.

The list was first published in the Journal of the American Society for Psychical Research (Volume 62, October 1968) in an article entitled "Quantitative Investigation of a 'Haunted House' with Sensitives and a Control Group."

Instructions: Circle those descriptive terms that seem to relate to the ghost's activity or intent. Cross out any terms that are opposite to what you think relates to the ghost or presence. Those terms that are not applicable you can just leave alone.

Afraid
Angry
Annoying someone
Attacking someone
Bored
Building something
Cautious
Cold/nonfeeling
Compassionate/warm
Cooking something
Communicating
Crazy
Crying
Dancing
Depressed
Eating
Fearful
Floating above the ground
Flying in the air
Fun-loving
Gesturing in a specific way
Getting rid of someone/something
Happy

Harassing someone
Helping someone
Hiding himself
Humorous
Insulting someone
Intelligent
Laughing
Lonely
Loving
Lying down
Mischievous
Mocking someone/something
Musing
Nonthinking
Obnoxious
Pacing restlessly
Passive
Peering around
Playful
Playing a musical instrument
Playing a game
Protective (of someone or something)
Purposeful
Pursuing someone
Puttering around
Reading
Repairing something
Resting
Restless
Running
Sad
Sarcastic
Searching for someone or something
Sensual
Serious
Sewing
Shy
Singing
Sitting
Standing up
Stealing something
Stern
Talking
Threatening someone
Trapped

Vengeful
Violent
Walking/moving in a definite direction
Wandering aimlessly
Writing

In addition to the above list, you might add a few more descriptive adjectives that relate to the activities the images or presences or ghosts are carrying out, or to the accompanying emotions or behavior.

Also, you may ask all to take down physical descriptions of sights, sounds, smells, and their own feelings.

# APPENDIX IV: ULTIMATE GHOST HUNTING GLOSSARY

## A

**ASQ** (pronounced "ask"): The three phases of an EVP investigation. Alone. Supervise. Ask.

1. Leave the recorder alone until the tape runs out.
2. Supervise the recording area while it records.
3. Ask questions to check for an intelligent haunting.

**Atom**: The smallest possible piece of any pure element that still has the properties of that element. Atoms are made of smaller particles including electrons, protons, and neutrons. Differences in the numbers of these particles create the differences between the elements. An atom is about 500-billionths of an inch, or one hundred millionths of a centimeter across. (As quoted by the PBS Glossary website)

## B

**Barometer**: Any device that measures air pressure.

**Black Hole**: An object that has gravity so strong that not even light can escape from it. Has infinite density.

## C

**Chaos Theory**: A branch of mathematics that studies long-term change, which is sensitive to initial conditions, so that small initial changes cause great differences long-term.

**Clairvoyance**: Seeing beyond normal sight. Sometimes called "second sight". See also ESP.

**Classic Haunting**: Also called an "**Intelligent Haunting**" or "Traditional Haunting"; rare, a sentient spirit that can manifest itself into an apparition and communicate with the living; the ghost responds to outside stimuli like questions and statements; it can be friendly or hostile and will let you know the difference; they are sometimes capable of opening and closing doors and windows and moving objects like furniture around.

## D

**Dogma**: A blind belief in things to be unquestionably true, often without a material base.

**Dynamical energy systems theory**: Suggests that all dynamical systems store information and energy to various degrees.

## E

**EMF**: Electromagnetic Field.

**EMR**: Electromagnetic Resonance.

**Enticement Experiment/Technique**: Using objects from different time periods (money, toys, antiques, etc.) or reenacting events from the past (playing poker in a haunted casino or shouting a roll call in a battlefield for example) to "entice" reactions from ghosts.

**ESP (Extra-Sensory Perception):** Paranormal abilities such as precognition, telepathy, and clairvoyance.

**EVP (Electronic Voice Phenomena):** The recording of spirit voices through electronic means.

## F

**Frequency**: the number of times that the current goes through a complete cycle per second.

## G

**Gauss**: the preferred unit in the United States for measuring magnetic field exposure; also the German mathematician who developed the theory of numbers and who applied mathematics to electricity and magnetism and astronomy and geodesy (1777-1855).

Ghost: From Anglo-Saxon gast, from a root word seen in Icelandic geisa, to rage as fire, and Swedish gusa, to ferment. Believed to be a remnant of the human consciousness.

## H

**Hall Effect**: A way of measuring magnetic fields. A current in a suitable semiconductor experiences a sideways force, in turn creating a measurable voltage, proportional to the magnetic field.

**Hawking Radiation**: In physics, Hawking radiation is thermal radiation that is created by black holes due to quantum effects. It is named after British physicist Stephen Hawking who worked out the theoretical argument for its existence in 1974. Hawking's discovery became the first convincing insight in quantum gravity. However, the existence of Hawking radiation remains controversial.

**Hypercube**: A higher dimensional object that is impossible for our 3D minds to visualize.

**Hyperspace**: Higher dimensional space.

## I

**Intelligent Haunting**: see Classic Haunting.

## K

**Kinetic Energy:** Energy possessed by a body in motion.

## M

**Memory Possession**: Through electromagnetic resonance, or other means, a person is taken over or possessed by the memories of persons and/or events of the past. Someone experiencing a memory possession will experience one or more of the following:

- Emotional duress. You will feel emotions outside of what you felt before entering the "memory possession zone". The emotions can be pleasant or unpleasant.
- Feeling of being watched.
- Feeling of being touched. Many who have been in haunted locations have claimed physical sensations of being touched or handled. The question is, are you being touched or are you experiencing the sensation of someone from the past being handled?
- Witness of apparition(s). Are you witnessing a ghost manifest itself, or are you viewing the memories of someone from the past?
- Viewing of past events as eyewitness. In this more rare case of a very powerful memory possession a person will be completely immersed in events from the past. They may feel as if they are someone else and even hear another person's voice come from their mouth. Would be like a "waking dream". Ex.: A person walks in the fields of Gettysburg and is carried back over 140

years to the Battle of Gettysburg. The subject will take on the role of a soldier and will witness the battle as it takes place. They will not have control over their actions in most cases and will literally "reenact" events that transpired. If the soldier's memories are of being shot, then the subject will feel the effect of being shot.

**Molecule**: Smallest portions of a substance having the properties of the substance.

## P

**Pareidolia**: (from the Greek para- amiss, faulty, wrong and eidolon, diminutive of eidos appearance, form): Seeing defined objects in non-defined subjects. Example: seeing the Virgin Mary in a tree stump or the devil in a fireplace. Also called, although inaccurately, simulacra.

**Platonist/Platonism**: (As defined by Wikepedia.com) Platonic idealism is the theory that the substantive reality around us is only a reflection of a higher truth. That truth, Plato argues, is the abstraction. A particular tree, with a branch or two missing, possibly alive, possibly dead, and initials of two lovers carved into its bark, is distinct from the form of Tree-ness. A Tree is the ideal that each of us holds that allows us to identify the imperfect reflections of trees all around us.

**Poltergeist Agent (PA):** Phenomena usually surrounding a young child, which is usually a girl; the P.A. (the child) is almost always around when the poltergeist activity occurs; this usually involves objects being thrown around when there is no one around, unexplainable tapping and scratching noises and objects disappearing and reappearing hours, days or weeks later; in worst-case scenarios there can be injuries to human beings from thrown objects and scratches appearing on the flesh of the P.A.; fires are also known to occur in the worst cases - sometimes with catastrophic results.

**Potential Energy**: Energy that is stored; Energy of position or state.

**PRE (PSI Related or Paranormal Related Experience):** An experience where the subject/witness feels or believes a paranormal phenomena has occurred without judging whether or not that is objectively the case.

## Q

**Quantum Mechanics**: The well-tested theory of the behavior of matter on the microscopic scales of atoms and computer chips, where the subatomic particles that compose all matter behave simultaneously like waves and particles.

**Quarks**: Fundamental particles, incapable of independent existence, that combines to form particles such as protons and neutrons.

## R

**Radiation**: Energy that is radiated or transmitted in the form of rays or waves or particles.

**Residual Haunting**: Probably the most common type of haunting; this is best described as an imprint on the environment; a moment in time, burnt onto the surroundings of a specific location; playing out roles and situations over and over again for centuries at a time; most researchers compare this to a looped video that repeats itself forever; in these cases you might hear footsteps and other strange noises; however, if you see the event being played out, you will not be able to interfere; the "ghosts" here are not conscious of their surroundings; they may not be sentient.

## S

**The Scientific Method:** A systematic approach to observing phenomena, drawing conclusions and testing hypotheses. The scientific method follows a series of steps: (1) identify a problem you would like to solve, (2) formulate a hypothesis, (3) test the hypothesis, (4) collect and analyze the data, (5) make conclusions.

**Semiconductor**: A substance through which the flow of electricity can be controlled — its conductive properties are between those of a metal conductor and an insulator

**Simulacra**: (from Wikipedia.org): Simulacrum is a Latin word originally meaning a material object representing something (such as an idol representing a deity, or a painted still-life of a bowl of fruit). By the 1800s it developed a sense of a "mere" image, an empty form devoid of spirit, and descended to a specious or fallow representation. In other words: Something that looks like something else done deliberately. (see also: Pareidolia)

**Skeptic**: Someone who habitually doubts accepted beliefs

**Systemic**: Pertaining to or affecting a system, such that the body or system is affected as a whole.

**Systems Theory**: Systems Theory sees our world in terms of 'systems', where each system is a 'whole' that is more than the sum of its parts, but also itself a 'part' of larger systems. For example, a cell is more than just a pile of molecules and itself is a part of larger systems e.g. an organ. An organ is on one level a whole in itself, but on another, it is a part of a system at the level of an individual person. A family and a community can both be seen as 'systems' where the 'parts' are people. (Taken from "What is Deep Ecology?" by Chris Johnstone)

## T

**Thermometer**: any device used for measuring temperature

**Traditional Haunting**: see Classic Haunting.

**Triple-axis meter**: a type of EMF meter; uses three coils and three metal plates on an x, y, and z-axis; that way the user can read fields from three different directions; the metal plates detect AC or DC electric fields; each coil has a different calibration that lets you detect all angles instead of just the area in front of the device; on most models you can switch between each setting or, using a computer circuit, reads the sum of the magnetic and electric.

## V

**Voltage** - The force that pushes electricity through a wire.

## W

**Worm Hole**: A hypothetical shortcut through the space-time continuum. Also called an Einstein-Rosen bridge.

## X

**X-Ray**: High-energy radiation with waves shorter than those of visible light.

# APPENDIX VI: WEBSITES OF NOTE

The American Institute of Parapsychologist
www.parapsychologylab.com

The Barringer Crater
www.barringercrater.com/science

Bible and History
www.piney.com

The Gallop Organization
www.gallup.com

The Center for Voice
www.voice.northwestern.edu

Cole Parmer
www.coleparmer.com

Cosmic Pantheon Press
www.cosmicpantheon.com

Cyphers by Ritter
www.ciphersbyritter.com

Ghosts of Gettysburg (Mark Nesbitt)
www.ghostsofgettysburg.com

Ghost Science the Official Site of Vince Wilson
www.ghostscience.net

Electronics Club
www.kpsec.freeuk.com

Google
www.google.com

History & Hauntings/Ghosts of the Prairie (Troy Taylor)
www.prairieghosts.com

How Stuff Works
www.howstuffworks.com

Infrared, Inc.
www.infrared.com

Less EMF
www.lessemf.com

Loyd Auerbach
www.invisiblesignals.com and
www.mindreader.com

Myst and Lace
www.mystandlace.com

NASA
www.nasa.gov

News Paper Archives
www.newspaperarchives.com

Nexus Magazine
www.nexusmagazine.com

Parapsychology Foundation, Inc.
www.parapsychology.org

PBS Glossary
http://www.pbs.org/transistor/glossary.html

Rick Fisher
www.paranormalpa.com

PhysLink.com
www.physlink.com
Sacred Texts
www.sacred-texts.com

The Science Company
www.sciencecompany.com

SMS.AC
www.sms.ac

Space Weather
www.spaceweather.com

The Time Line Index
www.timelineindex.com

Troy Taylor
www.prairieghosts.com

The Trickster and the Paranormal
www.tricksterbook.com

Wikipedia
en.wikipedia.org

# SPECIAL THANKS

To BETH NORATEL – For editing this book!

To RUSS NORATEL – A good friend!

TO DR. ANDREW (ANDY) NICHOLS – For knowing so much!

TO DR. BARRY TAFF – For his advice!

TO LOYD AUERBACH – For being more than a colleague!

TO DON WINGO – For being the magical weirdo that he is.

TO TROY TAYLOR – My good friend and original mentor!

# ABOUT THE AUTHOR

**... Wilson is perhaps the foremost expert on the technology of ghost hunting in the US."**

- Wired Magazine

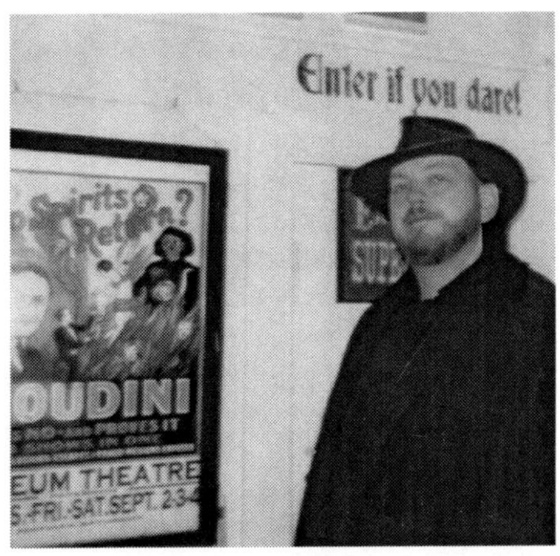


Vince Wilson has always been interested in science, history, and the unexplained since as far back as he can remember. Together with a long-time high school friend, he founded the Baltimore Society for Paranormal Research. He soon set his sights higher and joined the American Institute of Parapsychology — a collection of groups dedicated to serious paranormal research and scientific observation. Wilson is the author of Ghost Tech and Ghost Science. He has lectured on ghost hunting technology and has also appeared on all the major local TV stations in the Baltimore area and on numerous radio stations in regards to his work in paranormal research. Vince has also been featured on Creepy Canada in 2005 aboard the USS Constellation and the Discovery Channel in 2006 for an investigation he did at the Edgar Allan Poe House in Baltimore. He is also very studied on the occult and supernatural and many aspects of the unexplained. In 2011 Vince achieved a lifelong dream when he was certified by the American Institute for Parapsychology as a *parapsychologist*. He lives in The Haunted Cottage Paranormal Research Center in Harpers Ferry, WV.

Contact info: vince@ghostscience.net
Phone: 304-885-0707

CPSIA information can be obtained at www.ICGtesting.com
Printed in the USA
BVOW040155251012

303817BV00004B/4/P